Parameters carry information in and
out of subprograms.

Root - output parameter
ERR - input parameter

Codes - page 52

INTRODUCTION
TO
COMPUTER
SCIENCE
SHORT EDITION

SCIENCE RESEARCH ASSOCIATES, INC.
Chicago, Palo Alto, Toronto, Henley-on-Thames, Sydney
S R A
A Subsidiary of IBM

C. W. GEAR
University of Illinois
Urbana, Illinois

INTRODUCTION TO COMPUTER SCIENCE

SHORT EDITION

To the near Ms.

We wish to acknowledge the following: Monroe, The Calculator Company, for Figure 2.5; International Business Machines, for Figure 2.7; Control Data Corporation, for Figures 2.8 and 2.9; American Airlines, for Figure 4.5; and NCR, for Figure 4.6.

Library of Congress Catalog Card Number: 72–86105

CONTENTS

3 Flowchart Language I

4 Computing Systems

5   Flowchart Language II   173

6   Errors, or "When the Program runs, are the Answers Right?   239

Preface

This book and its companion language manuals are intended for a first course in computer science. It is basically concerned with the computer problem-solving process; it covers problem-solving methods, the nature and capabilities of computers, organization of computer programs, and the structure of data used by computers. The language manuals apply these ideas in specific programming environments.

No specific prerequisites are required of students; those not concerned with mathematics can skip the sections and examples involving numerical problems. Except for two optional short sections, the numerical problems can be handled without calculus.

The purpose of this book is not to teach a specific computer language; rather, it is to give the student a background with which he can readily learn any of the common languages such as BASIC, FORTRAN, PL/I, ALGOL, or their variants such as WATFOR/WATFIV and PL/C. The emphasis of this book is on the basic principles. When the student grasps these and gains experience with one computer language, he can rapidly become familiar with another language if the need arises.

An essential ingredient in understanding problem solving is practice, so a student should learn at least one of these languages at the time he studies this text. He should also use a computer to solve a variety of simple problems. Some colleges offer a short "programming" course before the introduction to computer science course. A student who has had such a course can go to a greater depth into the intricacies of his first language or learn a second language as he studies this book.

A flowchart language is used throughout the text to solve examples and problems. It is similar to common computer languages, so solutions can be transliterated easily into any of them.

The book is organized in the order in which I have taught it. Since there is no general agreement on the "best" way of introducing the material, it has been written so that sections can be left until later or omitted entirely, if an instructor desires. Chapters 1 to 6 cover the basic material which I consider fundamental. Chapter 8 deals with non-numerical problems. Any or all of these can be omitted if the time available or the ability of the students warrants.

The greatest disagreement among computer science instructors centers on the question of when to discuss the inner workings of the machine and how much detail to cover. Some instructors like to treat the computer as a black box and jump right into a higher-level language. This has the advantage of allowing the student to begin his practical work early. Others like to explain some aspects of machine/assembly language first, because it is then easier to give reasons for the procedural basis of a higher language. I favor the latter approach. However, Chapter 2, Computer Organization, is written so that the instructor can skip as much as he wishes. As a minimum, Sections 2.1, 2.5, and 2.5.1 to 2.5.3 on memory and number representation should be covered before Chapter 3. Some instructors may wish to skip only Sections 2.2.1, 2.3.1, 2.4.1, 2.5.4, 2.6.1 and 2.6.2, which discuss machine/assembly language, and either cover them after Chapter 3 or omit them entirely. Chapter 4, Computing Systems, may be used before Chapter 3 if desired.

The text generally assumes, without explicitly saying so, that a decimal machine is being used, but nothing is dependent on decimal representation. If the instructor wishes, Section 2.7 can be used to introduce the binary and hexadecimal systems.

This book has been used in a semester course offered by the University of Illinois at Champaign-Urbana. Two hours of lectures were devoted to the text and one hour of smaller lecture/discussion sections was used to teach the language material. The first half of the semester covered WATFIV, the second PL/1. About seven computer problems were assigned for lab work. The first of these was an exercise to acquaint the student with the system. He was given a listing of a working program and was required to punch it, prepare his own ID card for the system, and run it. Examples of the problems used in the earlier part of the semester are given in the Instructor's Guide. Later problems were taken from the problems in Chapter 7. (If a remote terminal is used, I favor giving more short problems [ten to fifteen lines of code] in the early part of the semester, but a student should have experience with one or two larger programs [fifty to one hundred lines of code].)

Exercises, *questions*, and *problems* are given at the end of most sections. *Exercises* are simple tasks that help the student learn the material, *questions* test his retention of basic ideas and vocabulary, and *problems* require some thought and application of ideas presented earlier. Many of the problems can be used as the basis for computer programs. For the instructor's and student's convenience, some of these problems are also given at appropriate points in the language manuals.

I would like to acknowledge the assistance given by the staff of SRA. Valuable criticism and much encouragement was given by the following persons who either reviewed or class-tested earlier versions of the manuscript. They include Richard Austing, University of Maryland; Ruth and Hal Hart, Purdue University; Don Kelley, Georgia Institute of Technology; Katherine Nooning, University of Kentucky; Angus Pearson, University of Texas; Doug

Seeley, University of British Columbia. A special note of thanks is due Marilyn Bohl of IBM.

I am also grateful to people at the University of Illinois, particularly the students who commented on the material, and to Barbara Armstrong who typed the manuscript rapidly and accurately.

The following are programming language texts that have been written to complement this text:

Marilyn Bohl and Arline Walter, *Introduction to PL/I Programming and PL/C*

James Parker and Marilyn Bohl, *FORTRAN Programming and WATFIV*

John Sack and Judy Meadows, *Entering BASIC*

C. W. Gear

INTRODUCTION

1. Introduction

The objective of this book is to introduce you to the basic principles of computer usage. Since a computer is used to solve various kinds of problems, we must first understand its capabilities—and then understand how problems are solved.

A computer is a device that can perform very simple operations such as the multiplication of two numbers or the comparison of two words. It can also store data such as sets of words or sets of numbers; that is, it can retain information so that at some time in the future the data will be available for processing or printing. For example, all of the text of this book could be easily stored inside any one of a wide variety of available computers. A person could cause that computer to print any specific part of it on request. The simple operations that are within the computer's capability can be performed on the data stored inside it, although the sequence of operations that it is to perform must be specified by a person. Such a sequence is called a *program*. The sequence will have to be expressed in a form that can be "understood" by the computer. Such a form is called a *computer language*, just as English is a language; that is, it is a form in which letters may be combined so that the resulting sentences can be understood. In the pages that follow we will examine the simple operations that a computer can perform and see how these sequences can be constructed to perform other more complex operations.

You are probably taking basic computer science primarily for one of two reasons. For some it is the start of a sequence of study in computer science, and their objective is to get a background necessary to begin more specialized study. For others it is a terminal course designed to provide them with another tool for use in their own field of study. However, the material both types of students study should not differ significantly. If you are to specialize in other areas, it is important that you be aware of the further possibilities of computers and the subject matter of computer science, so that when you meet problems for which the tools provided by this basic course are inadequate, you will know where to start searching for further techniques.

Computer science is a new discipline that reaches from the fields of mathematics, science, and engineering on one side to business on another and into the humanities on a third. On the periphery of computer science we find the application areas concerned with the organization and processing of data, whether it be files of management data in a business application, long sequences of sentences in a humanities application, or lists of experimental data in a science application. Nearer to the core of computer science are questions of the design and use of computers for general classes of problems. The study of a computer design to solve specific types of problems efficiently leads to *switching theory*, which is a mathematical abstraction of the way in which many of the circuits used in computers behave. It also leads to *automata theory*, which is concerned with the computing capabilities of different kinds of computer organizations. For example, switching theory allows us to analyze the circuits that control an automatic elevator, remembering at which floors it must stop, whether to continue in the direction it is going or to go the other way, not to go up to the twenty-first floor if there are only twenty floors, and so forth. Automata theory tackles such questions as, "If we are allowed to use only this set of computer parts, can we compute that set of numbers?" The study of the way in which numbers are manipulated in order to solve numerical problems leads to the field of *numerical analysis*. Numerical analysis investigates questions such as, "If we solve this set of equations but the initial data is in error by up to 1%, how accurate are the answers?" *Non-numerical processing* is the manipulation of data other than numeric data. Studies in this area lead to the theories of *artificial languages* and *artificial intelligence*. Artificial languages include those that are designed for use in writing programs for computers. Artificial intelligence is concerned with imitating, and hence understanding, aspects of intelligent behavior. For example, programs have been written so that the computer can "play" chess; that is so that it can decide on the next move when the description of the present board position is stored in its memory.

In all of these subjects the underlying component is the computer and its use. Before we can go very far into any one of them we must first understand basic principles about the computer. In this book we will discuss the general-purpose computer, which is usually electronic and capable of performing any basic computer function. In recent years computers have become useful in very specialized operations, but we will not discuss them in detail. Fortunately, the basic principles of the system are the same whether the computer is used in automatic traffic control or in keeping bank records, so we need not be overly concerned with the type of applications we study. Examples and exercises will be chosen to illustrate points of computer usage, not to instruct in the application of computers to a particular subject.

1.1 Uses of Computers

Computers are used in many seemingly different ways in modern life, to the point that they are frequently misnamed "electronic brains." However, all these different applications use the same basic principles, and all must be first analyzed as problems *by a person* before the computer can be used. For example, a computer may be used to perform routine work of a repetitive nature, such as maintaining the bank accounts of all of the customers of a bank.

Previously this job was done by manual labor. Bookkeepers were instructed about the rules to be followed for a typical account and then they applied them to each account. Now the computer can do this, but the rules must first be established by a person. This is an example of the use of a computer to save human drudgery in processing repetitive information (see Figure 1.1a).

Computers are also used to control systems in environments where it is not feasible for humans to act, as, for example, in unmanned space flight. A computer may be organized to respond in predetermined ways to measurements made by on-board instruments such as radar and to signals sent from ground stations. It may also compute the position and the velocity of the spacecraft in order to find out where the craft is heading in relation to the desired destination. Using the information available, the computer can send signals to the spacecraft control systems to keep the craft on the desired course and to perform the planned maneuvers. However, again notice that all of the operations had to be planned ahead of time by people. A person had to think out the response to each combination of circumstances and to organize the computer to produce those responses. Thus a person might have decided that the braking rockets should be fired with a thrust proportional to the velocity and the inverse of the distance to the target. When the computer is properly prepared, it can control the braking rockets, but the decision about *how* they are fired is made by a person when he writes the program. This type of computer use is shown in Figure 1.1b.

The third major area of computer application is to assist people in solving problems that are beyond human capabilities. For example, a computer can be used to perform long sequences of computations that could never be performed by people because of human proneness to error and slow speed. Such situations commonly arise in mathematics or engineering when computations can only be performed *sequentially*; that is, when the results of one calculation must be known before the next can be performed. Manual calculation of the stresses in a modern airplane wing, for example, would be out of the question. Although the designer of the plane makes the basic decisions about the style of the wing and how the stresses are to be analyzed, the computer makes it possible to perform the analysis in a practical length of time.

This type of calculation is different from that in which computations can be done in *parallel*. For example, if a bank attracts more customers, it will have to handle more transactions each day. It can make this possible either by getting more bookkeepers *or* by getting a computer. More bookkeepers can do the job because each bookkeeper can be working on a different transaction in parallel. But hiring more people would not make it possible to analyze a larger airplane wing than can be analyzed by one person, because

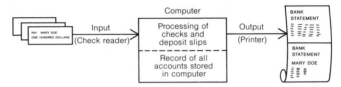

(a) Processing of a Repetitive Kind—Bank Deposits and Withdrawals

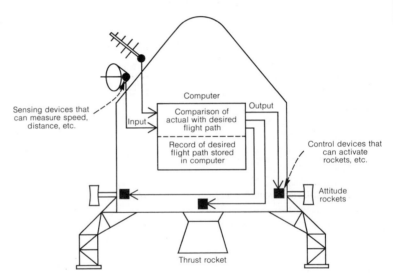

(b) Control of Complex Tasks—Guiding a Spacecraft

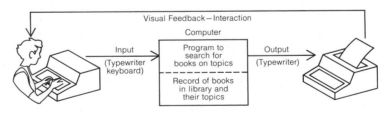

(c) Help in Problem Solving—Information Retrieval

Fig. 1.1   Three uses of a computer

a second person could not start his calculations until the first had finished his.

Another example of computer aid to human powers is in *information retrieval*. A researcher involved in searching through libraries of information may be aided by a computerized information retrieval system that can look at all of the records of the library and tell him which ones contain specific references to those topics that interest him. In these applications, the computer will have been organized to perform the appropriate set of calculations or to do the searches of the data in a certain way before the operations are actually performed.

The use of a computer to aid people in a problem-solving process such as information retrieval is shown in Figure 1.1c. Here we see that the action of a user may be influenced by the output from the computer. If the book he is searching for is not present, he may then search under other topics. This is called *interactive* use of a computer.

Although the *amount* of work performed by the computer and the man together in all these examples is much greater than could have been performed by the man alone, the *type* of work that has been done could have been performed, in principle, by the man. He has to organize it in either case.

These four examples of applications—the bank record keeping, the control of unmanned spacecraft, the execution of large-scale calculations, and the library search—all contain two common elements that must be considered in any problem we attempt to solve by computer.

The first element of a problem is the *control structure*. A problem involves taking various actions in response to various conditions. Thus in the bank application, one control action may be to initiate a nasty letter to the customer when a check is deducted from an account with insufficient funds to cover it. The spacecraft application contains mainly control actions. As new data on position, velocity, and other conditions are received, the spacecraft propulsion systems must be controlled to perform the desired maneuvers. In the calculation of wing stresses, little control is present, although certain actions may be required if the stresses exceed limits previously set by the human designer. The library search may involve a series of control actions depending on the presence or absence of certain topic titles in the records.

The second element in a problem is called the *data structure*. In the information retrieval problem in particular, the structure of the data is the primary factor that must be considered in solving the problem. The desired information is already present in the stored information; the research worker needs to have it presented to him in a different form. Thus in one sense the problem of finding the phone number of Mr. X. Smith of 2 Broadway, New York, is solved by handing the questioner a current copy of the New York phone directory. However, the questioner wants the data organized in a different way so that he can immediately read the required phone number. He would be satisfied if we handed him the phone book open to the correct page with the required number underlined clearly (unless he worked for the phone company). We would have solved the problem by reorganizing the data. When we retrieve the information requested from a library, all we have done is reorganized the data and presented it differently. In the sense that "two plus two" and "four" are different ways of saying, or presenting, the same information, all we are doing when we perform numerical computations is reorganizing the data; that is, changing its structure.

When we consider ways to solve a problem we must examine the structure of the data initially available and decide on the structure of the data to be presented as the answer. This may be completely specified in the description of the problem or some of it may be left up to the person solving the problem to decide. For example, if a table of numbers has to be presented, we may have the freedom to arrange those numbers in a column or in a row. If the table is large and has several sets of data to be placed in columns or rows, the choice may affect the organization of the computer program that is to be written to handle the problem.

We must also examine the control actions that will be required and make sure all possibilities have been considered. What, for example, should the computer do, if in searching for a given topic title in the library, it finds no references at all? Certainly it should not keep on searching forever; hence, when a person prepares the computer to perform this task, he must make specific provision for this case.

Problems

**1. Try to describe very briefly three applications of computers. The first should be a routine type that could be done by people. The second should be of the type that is impossible for people to perform because of limitations on the environment or factors of speed. The third should be the type in which the computer enhances human capabilities.

*2. Describe some aspect of the data and the control structure for each of your problems.

(**) A double asterisk in front of an exercise, question, or problem indicates that it is solved in part in the appendix.
(*) A single asterisk indicates that the complete solution is given in the appendix.

1.2 Problem Solving

It is not usually expedient to use a computer to solve only one problem; rather, if the effort of writing a program is to be made, the program should be capable of solving several similar problems. Thus writing a program for the information retrieval problem to look for only one book would not be worthwhile, but it would be valuable if many millions of books were to be referenced over a period of time by the same program. Similarly, it would not be worth writing a program to process only one bank transaction, but such a program is economically justified if almost all transactions can be processed automatically, rapidly, and reliably by it. Therefore when we write a computer program, we write it to solve a set of problems, not just one. We must determine the nature of this set of problems—for example, what types of transactions are to be permitted, the allowable size of the numbers, and so forth—and then prepare a program that will handle any of the allowed cases. We will say that we have *solved the problem* when we have written such a program. (Handling a specific case of the data—for example, processing an actual bank transaction—is solving a specific example of the problem.)

The program that is to be prepared for the computer consists of a sequence of operations. It contains only those operations that the computer can perform. Problem solving is the task of expressing the solution of complex problems in terms of the simple operations "understood" by the computer.

In order to solve a problem by computer, whether it is the problem of designing a system in which the computer can control a spacecraft or of computing a numerical approximation to the deflection of a bridge when a train crosses it, we must pass through certain stages. These stages are:

(a) Precise formulation of the problem—stating all assumptions clearly and specifying the action to be taken in the event of any possibility.

(b) Analysis of the problem—may include performing some transformations that provide alternative ways for computing the required information from the input data. In the case of numerical problems it may also include an analysis of the accuracy of the answer. The end result of this analysis is the selection of a method to be used on the computer or the determination that a computer should not be used either because the processing time is excessive or because after analysis the problem is seen to be so simple that manual methods are better.

(c) Computation — programming the computer to perform the computation. Since errors may occur at this and earlier stages, it includes checking to see if the method and its implementation on the computer are correct.

We will illustrate the stages of problem solution with some examples. These are deliberately trivial to avoid confusing us with details of particular problems at this stage. Later we will investigate more difficult examples.

Example 1.1 — Computation of Income Tax

The problem, as first stated, is to compute a person's annual income tax. He is allowed tax deductions of $650 for each dependent. Also, he can take a deduction of 10% of his salary less the dependent deductions, or a deduction of actual expenses such as interest, state taxes, and other deductible items. The remainder of his salary is taxed at 20%. (Note that the problem is actually to prepare a program to handle any size income, any number of dependents, and any amount of deductions.)

Stage (a) of problem solving should reveal that the problem is not yet precisely stated. Two alternative ways of calculating deductions are given, but no rule is given for choosing between them. If the taxpayer rather than the Internal Revenue Service is organizing this calculation, the rule is presumably to choose the computation that yields the lowest income tax liability. We should also recognize in this stage that we are not told what data is available for input. However, from the nature of the problem we can see that we will need to know the number of dependents, the annual income, and all expenses that are tax deductible. We can now restate the problem definition by saying: given this information, compute the minimum tax liability for the person.

In the second stage we analyze the problem and realize that it is not necessary to compute the tax both ways; rather, we determine which method leads to the larger deduction. This will lead to the minimum tax liability but will require less computation. Thus we multiply the number of dependents by $650 and deduct this figure from the annual salary. The tax-deductible expenses are then added and the larger of this result or 10% of the annual salary less dependent deductions is used as an additional deduction to be taken from the annual salary. Finally the tax liability is computed as 20% of what is left. In the third stage we must prepare a program to perform these computations. We notice that in the second stage we outlined a procedure for solving the problem. This procedure consisted of a series of steps that were to be performed sequentially. To write down the procedure in a more precise way we use a flowchart such as shown in Figure 1.2.

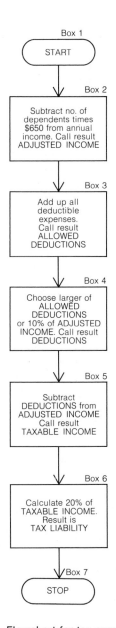

Fig. 1.2 Flowchart for tax computation

A *flowchart* consists of a set of *symbols*, whose shapes indicate the general type of functions they contain, connected by *flowlines*. Each symbol contains at least one operation that is to be performed when that symbol is obeyed. Thus the symbols serve as boxes to

9

hold these operations, so we will also call them *boxes*. We can think of the computer following flowlines and executing the operations described in the boxes. We start at the oval box marked START and follow the flowlines in the direction of the arrows. Each rectangular box contains some instructions for processing the data. If we follow these instructions we will compute the tax liability for a person and then stop.

There would have been little point in preparing a computer to perform these computations if they were to be done for only one person. It would have been much faster to do them by hand, using a pencil and paper or desk calculator. Presumably we wish to perform them for many different sets of data (many different people). Consequently, we modify the flowchart of Figure 1.2 to produce that of Figure 1.3. Two new box shapes have been introduced. The first is

which looks like a punched card and indicates that we expect the computer to read some data from punched cards. It is called the *punched card symbol*. All input will be by means of punched cards in the examples in this text, so we will think of this as an *input box*. The second is

and represents a sheet of paper torn from the printer. It is used to indicate that some information is to be printed by the computer and is called the *document symbol*. All output will be by means of a printer in this text, so we will think of this as an *output box*. (In some cases different forms of input and output may be used, such as a computer controlled typewriter, in which case the input box would refer to the user pressing the typewriter keys while the output box would refer to the computer typing.)

After one computation has been completed, the long flowline takes us back to the beginning of the flowchart to process another set of data. This is called a *loop*. It is necessary to prepare this flowchart only once. Once the computer has been programmed to execute it, the operations can be performed on many different sets of data.

We gave English-language descriptions of the operations to be performed in the flowchart boxes. In fact, we are restricted to the use of only those operations understood by the computer, and we must express them in a language acceptable to it. (This language is presented in Chapters 3 and 5.)

After we have prepared this flowchart as our solution to the problem, we must check that we have not made any errors. One way to do this would be to try it on some sample cases and then compare the answers with ones computed by hand. Since we do not have a computer that will directly accept a flowchart such as the one we have drawn, either we will have to wait until we have expressed this flowchart description of the solution procedure in a computer language, or we will have to simulate the behavior of a computer by following the flowchart ourselves.

In this simple problem we can certainly do the latter. Suppose we follow the flowchart for the two cases:

Case I

Annual income	$10,000
No. of dependents	4
Deductible expenses	$200 — taxes
	$400 — interest
	$100 — charity

Case II

Annual income	$4,000
No. of dependents	6
Deductible expenses	$750 — medical
	$50 — taxes
	$100 — interest

In the first case, we compute the following numbers:

In Box 2 we compute	ADJUSTED INCOME	as	$7400
In Box 3 we compute	ALLOWED DEDUCTIONS	as	$ 700
In Box 4 we compute	DEDUCTIONS	as	$ 740
In Box 5 we compute	TAXABLE INCOME	as	$6660
In Box 6 we compute	TAX LIABILITY	as	$1332

Note that the boxes are followed in sequence, and that one computation must be completed before the computation in the next box can be started because it uses the result from the previous box.

In the second case we compute the following numbers:

In Box 2 we compute	ADJUSTED INCOME	as	$100
In Box 3 we compute	ALLOWED DEDUCTIONS	as	$900
In Box 4 we compute	DEDUCTIONS	as	$900
In Box 5 we compute	TAXABLE INCOME	as	−$800
In Box 6 we compute	TAX LIABILITY	as	−$160

11

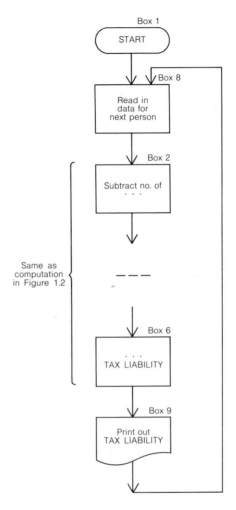

Fig. 1.3 Changes to flowchart to allow the tax
for many people to be computed

Although the person in Case 2 could use a negative tax, the Internal Revenue Service is not so generous, and the negative result from this test indicates an error. In this case the error is in the statement of the problem. Our flowchart correctly performs the computations specified, but we did not take into account another rule for tax computations: namely, that taxes cannot be negative. If the taxable income is less than zero, there is no tax. Consequently, we must modify Box 6 to read, "Calculate 20% of TAX LIABILITY. If this is positive, call the result TAX LIABILITY. Otherwise, make

TAX LIABILITY zero.'' With this change, the last case would give a TAX LIABILITY of $0, since $0 is larger than the —$160 computed by the 20% rule.

This error points out, in a trivial way, a frequent difficulty in the solution of problems by computer: the original problem is seldom properly stated. Many things that are ''obvious'' are left unsaid, but unfortunately, they are not obvious to the computer (which is, in this example, perfectly happy to produce negative answers). Frequently during the testing of a proposed solution to a problem, we will find cases that have not been covered in the problem definition. If so, we must go back to the first stage of the problem-solving process and modify the statement of the problem.

Example 1.2 — Telephone Number Search

Suppose we have a set of cards, each containing a name and a phone number. The problem is to find the phone number corresponding to any given name. To avoid confusion we will refer to the set of information on each card (name and phone number) as a record.

In the first stage of the problem solution we must be more precise about the structure of the input data. For example, are the names in the records in alphabetical order, like the names in a phone book, or are they in random order? In this example, we will assume that they are not in any particular order but that we can read through the records one at a time, from the first to the last. We must also decide what *control action* to take if the name we are looking for is not in any of the records. The problem was not precisely stated because it did not tell us what to do in this situation. Therefore we correct the problem statement by requiring that the output either be the phone number of the person or the statement that the name is not present.

In the analysis of the problem, we decide that the only reasonable method, given the structure of the input data, is to look at each record in turn and compare the name it contains with the name being sought. When we find such a record we stop and report the number in that record; otherwise we continue and look at the next record. If we reach the end of the set of records without finding the name, we output the message that the name is not present.

To prepare a flowchart of the solution we need to know what operations are to be allowed in the flowchart boxes. As was stated above, we assume that the basic allowed operations include the ability to read the records of information on the cards (this information could be in the computer's memory) and the ability to compare information in the records with the name being searched. Conceptually, it is as if we have a stack of cards, each containing a record of information. We can set the stack of cards face up in front

13

of us so that we are looking at the first one. This positions us at the first record. Then we can move to the next by turning the top one over onto another stack. The card we can see on top of the first stack contains the *current record*. Another way of visualizing this operation is by thinking of running one's finger down the entries in a phone book, one at a time. The current entry is the one at which we are pointing. Figure 1.4 gives a flowchart for this process. A new symbol has been introduced. It is

and is used for a *decision*. When the desired name is compared with the name in the current record, we wish to take actions that depend on whether they match or not. This is thus a control action. We also use a decision box to determine whether or not there are more entries in the phone list.

Whereas each process, input, or output box had only one exit line indicating the unique control path to be followed after the instructions in that box had been performed, each decision box shown in Figure 1.4 has *two* exit lines. The question inside the box will have a YES or a NO answer. The line with that label should be followed. Thus, one flowchart box will be uniquely determined as the next one to be executed, although we will not know which one it is until the question in the decision box has been answered. It is this feature that allows us to take the control actions necessary in solving a problem. At the time that we prepare the program for the above example, we do not know how many times the loop (which consists of reading the current entry, comparing it with the required name, and moving to the following entry) will be transversed; the flowchart, or rather the computer that executes it, will make that decision based on our instructions.

The method used to solve this problem was virtually the only one available because we decided that the structure of the data was random. In practice, of course, telephone numbers are in a telephone book, which has much more structure: it is usually ordered alphabetically, and that feature can be used to develop much better methods for searching. We will examine some of these methods later in the book.

When looking for a method to solve a problem, there are usually many different methods we can consider, but some of them may not be practically feasible. Thus, if the phone list were alphabetically ordered, we could still use the sequential search method given in Figure 1.4. However, such a method is not practical in a large phone list. (Consider looking at each entry in the phone book of a city such

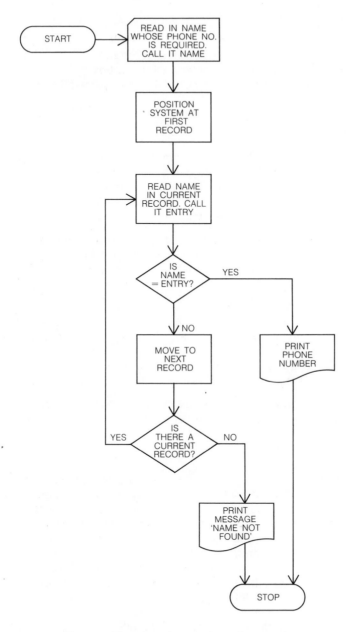

Fig. 1.4 Flowchart for telephone list search

as Chicago, only to find that the name is not in the book!) During
the analysis of the problem we must consider the different ways of
solving the problem and select from them on the basis of efficiency.

15

QUESTIONS

1. How many flowlines may leave a process box?
2. How many flowlines may enter a decision box?
3. Can we have more than one output box in a flowchart?

PROBLEMS

*1. The solution to Example 1.2 in Figure 1.4 is not completely correct. If the list of phone numbers is empty (i.e., has no members), the flowchart attempts to read from a nonexistent record. Assuming that the operation "position system at first record" is valid even if the list is empty, correct the flowchart.

2. Suppose you have a stack of cards, each containing a number. You wish to prepare a flowchart to find the largest number. In the flowchart you may use only the following operations:

   a. Copy the number that is on the top card of the stack onto a pad of paper provided.
   b. Compare the number on the top card of the stack with the last number written on the pad of paper (this goes in a decision box).
   c. Remove the top card from the stack of cards.
   d. See if there are any more cards in the stack (in a decision box).

   Prepare a flowchart that will leave the largest number on the pad.

1.3 Algorithms

In the last section we discussed two problems and described procedures for solving them by means of flowcharts. These procedures were step-by-step instructions to be followed. They are implementations of a method of solution that involves only certain basic operations that we have agreed can be used. Although we never explicitly stated what operations were allowed in the last section, we tacitly assumed that simple computations such as "take 10% of a given number" or "take the maximum of two numbers" were allowed and could be understood by the person or computer reading the flowchart. Such a method of solution is called an *algorithm*. An algorithm is a method for solving a problem using operations from a given set of basic operations, which produces the answer in a finite number of such operations. We say that the algorithm solves the problem. The use of only a finite number of operations is important, since, on a computer, each operation is going to take a finite amount of time (typically about one-millionth of a second, written 10^{-6} seconds, or 1 microsecond). If an unlimited number of steps are required it will not be possible to complete the solution in a finite amount of time. It is important that the number of operations be small. If 2,000,000,000,000,000 (2×10^{15}) operations were required, each taking about a microsecond, the total process would take about a century—which would not make it very practical for human or computer use.

If an algorithm is to be found to solve a problem, the statement of the problem must make a finite algorithm possible.

Example 1.3—Square Root

We are to compute the square root of two as a decimal number using only the operations of addition, subtraction, multiplication, and comparison.

It can be shown mathematically that no finite set of such operations will produce the square root of two, which can be represented only by an unlimited number of decimal digits. Hence it is not possible to find an algorithm for this problem. However, if we modify the problem statement to say, "Find the largest four-digit decimal number that is less than the square root of two," we have a problem that can be solved in a finite number of steps. One such algorithm is to start with the number 1.000, which we can easily see is less than the square root of two, and increase the second digit by one (an addition operation). The number is then squared (a multiplication operation), and if the result is greater than two (a comparison operation), our number is now too large, so the second digit is decreased by one (a subtraction operation). Otherwise, the second digit is increased again. This process is repeated until we know the second digit of the square root. Then we perform the same process on the third digit, and finally on the fourth digit. A flowchart for this algorithm is shown in Figure 1.5. This flowchart consists of a series of three loops to increase the second, third, and fourth digits, respectively. The basic operations that are allowed are assumed to be addition, subtraction, comparison for *greater than* (indicated by the sign $>$; "A $>$ B" means "A greater than B"), and *assignment*; that is, the operation, "Set ROOT to be 1.000," assigns the value 1.000 to ROOT. This operation will be discussed in Chapter 2.

Obviously, one of the most important facts we must consider when designing algorithms is the set of operations that are basic. If the operation, "Find the telephone number of a man named X in this list," is a basic operation, then the algorithm for the telephone number search consists of that one operation. If the basic operations are to read a name, compare names, read a phone number, check to see if there are more entries, and move to the next entry, then the algorithm proposed in Example 1.2 is needed. We can evi-

17

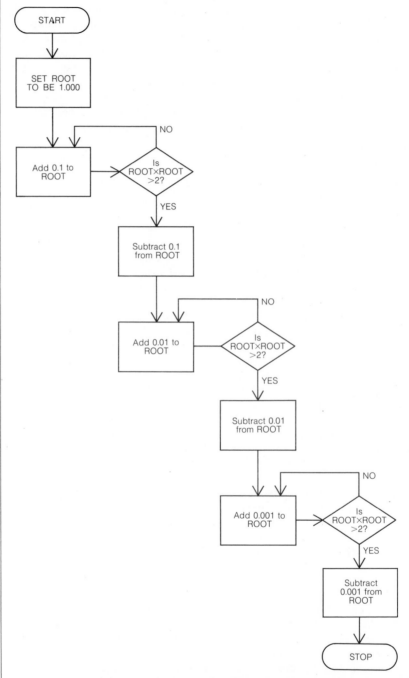

Fig. 1.5 Flowchart for square root of 2

dently define more complex operations in terms of simpler ones, just as we described the operation of searching for a phone number by a procedure using more basic functions. Thus we can think of a hierarchy of operations, each of which is more complex than earlier ones, and which can be defined in terms of earlier ones.

We could start with the operations of addition, subtraction, multiplication, and division as our basic ones, but if we consider for a moment how we do them by hand, we will see that even these can be broken down further. Most of us do addition, for example, a digit at a time, whereas a computer usually performs the addition of numbers consisting of several digits in one step. Similarly, most of us do subtraction and multiplication a digit at a time. These operations are used to construct multiple-digit arithmetic. The point to be understood from this is that we can accept almost anything for use as basic operations. If these operations are fairly general, we will be able to perform all the other operations needed by using them. Once we have decided on the basic operations, we can construct our algorithms from them. Usually we will accept the standard arithmetic operations of addition, subtraction, multiplication, and division as basic. When we have seen ways to combine them to produce more complex operations such as square root, we can express algorithms using these more complex operations, realizing that we really mean for them to be written out in terms of the simpler ones. We gave a method for finding the square root of two in Example 1.3. This could, with some changes, have been applied to any positive number, so it provides us with a method to compute the square root approximately using only additions and subtractions and a comparison control operation, which we will also take as basic. (Better ways of computing the square root will be given later—this is a very bad way!) Because we know that the square root can be obtained approximately in this way, we will allow ourselves to use the square root operation in algorithms—provided that it is needed only approximately—and say that we have given an algorithm that uses only our basic arithmetic and comparison operations. Most of the operations we commonly perform can be expressed simply in terms of the basic arithmetic operations and the comparison operations. In the remainder of this section we will give some algorithms for common operations.

Example 1.4—Prime Numbers

Given a positive integer number N, find out if it is prime.

Since a number is prime if it is exactly divisible by no number other than 1 and itself, we can answer this question by testing each number between two and $N - 1$ to see if it divides the number N. Thus, we can use the flowchart in Figure 1.6.

19

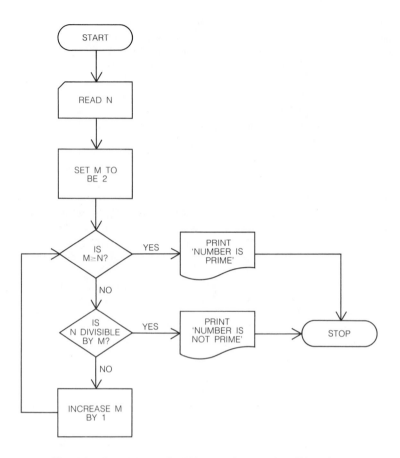

Fig. 1.6 Flowchart to find if a positive number N is prime

In this chart, we start the number M at two and increase it by one at each step until either we find a number M less than N that divides N, or we decide that the number N is prime. This flowchart has a very serious drawback that you may already have noticed. It is not expressed in terms of our basic arithmetic and comparison operations. The operation "Is N divisible by M," is not a basic operation. In order to express this properly, we must make some statements about the result of the division operation. If we divide one integer by another, what do we get? This is a question that will be taken up in Chapter 2 when we see how numbers are stored inside the computer. Until that time, we will assume that the result of such a division is also an integer, that is, $N \div M$ is an integer that is not larger than the actual numerical value, so that $5 \div 2$ would be 2, while $9 \div 3$ would be 3. That is, we do the division and discard the remainder.

20

If there is no remainder, the division is exact and $(N \div M) \times M$ is exactly N. Thus we can find out if N is divisible by M by performing the division and multiplying the answer by M again. If we get N from this step, then the integer division was exact. Thus to ask, ''Is N divisible by M,'' we can ask instead, ''Does $(N \div M) \times M = N$?'' Since this only involves our basic operations, we can now consider the flowchart in Figure 1.6 to represent an algorithm.

There are many possible algorithms, and this one in particular can be improved greatly. The first point we can note is that if N has any divisors, then one of them cannot exceed the square root of N. (If N has a divisor M, then $N \div M$ is also a divisor, and both of these cannot exceed the square root of N.) Consequently, we need only test values of M up to the square root of N. Since we have already expressed the square root of N in terms of basic operations, we may use it for this algorithm. The revised algorithm is shown in Figure 1.7.

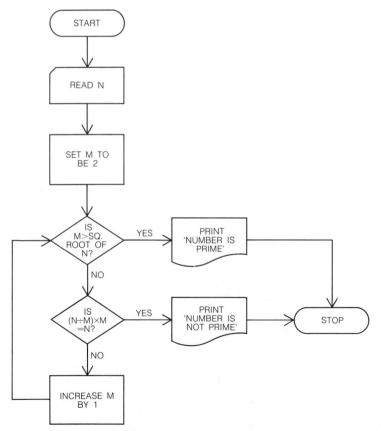

Fig. 1.7 Modified prime number flowchart

Suppose that we apply the algorithm described in Figure 1.7 to the number N = 9. The steps in their order of execution are:

> Read 9 and set N equal to 9
> Set M equal to 2
> 2 > 3? (No)
> (9 ÷ 2) × 2 = 9? (No)
> Increase M to 3
> 3 > 3 (No)
> (9 ÷ 3) × 3 = 9? (Yes)
> Print "NUMBER IS NOT PRIME"
> STOP

Example 1.5—Sine of a Number

Given a number X, find the sine of X.

Mathematically, this is a more complex operation than ones discussed earlier. It also has characteristics similar to the square root problem, in that we cannot express the sine of X, which we will write sin(X), by a finite number of basic operations. It can be shown that the value of sin(X) is given by the expression

$$\sin(X) = X - X^3/3! + X^5/5! - X^7/7! + \ldots$$

(5! means $5 \times 4 \times 3 \times 2 \times 1$.) This does not provide an algorithm for computing sin(X) since the series has an infinite number of terms, but if we are prepared to accept an approximation we can use the algorithm

$$\text{SIN}(X) = X - X^3/3! + X^5/5! - X^7/7!$$

which requires only a finite number of basic operations. Note that we are saying that our operation SIN(X) is not the same as the mathematical sin(X), but only approximately equal to it. By means of elementary numerical analysis we can show that for values of X less than one, the difference between SIN(X) and sin(X) is less than .000003. If that were not accurate enough for our use, we could modify this algorithm by using the next term in the series and have an error less than .00000003.

Problems

*1. Suppose we have two positive integer numbers A and B and we are allowed to perform the operations of increasing or decreasing either by one. Suppose also we can test either number in a decision box to see if it is zero. Write a flowchart to change the number A into a number that is the sum of the values of A and B at the start of the problem. (We really should call A and B *variables*, because we change them during the solution.)

2. The answer to problem (1) shows how addition can be implemented by use of the more basic operations of incrementing and decrementing. Use that result to show how these operations, plus the operation of changing one number to give it the value of another, can be used to multiply two positive numbers A and B and set the result into C. (Changing one number to the value of another should be written, "Set C to the value of D." If D had value 5, this would give C the value 5 and not change D.)

3. Suppose we are allowed to use the following basic operations:

   a. Set a number to one.
   b. Increase a number by one.
   c. Set a number to be equal to the value of another number.
   d. Square a number.
   e. Compare two numbers in a decision box.

   Write a program that will set a number M to be the largest integer whose square does not exceed the number N. N can be assumed to be at least one. You will need to operate on at least one other number, say L.

*4. Follow the flowchart in Figure 1.7 for the case N = 17. Write down the sequence of steps, each corresponding to the execution of a box.

1.4 Types of Algorithms

No universal rules can be given for developing algorithms that solve any given problem. All we can do is to classify some of the types of methods that can be used so that you can consider possible methods from each of these classes if they are appropriate to the particular problem. The four major classes of computational methods are:

- *Enumeration* — in which all possible "answers" are checked to find one that solves the problem.

- *Direct computation* — in which the exact answer is obtained by a sequence of elementary computations.

- *Iteration* — in which an approximate answer is available after a few operations, and such that additional sets of operations improve the accuracy. (An exact solution would require an unlimited number of operations.)

- *Trial and error*—another type of iteration in which a first approximation (which may be very inaccurate) is improved by successive manipulations based on the amount by which the current approximation fails to satisfy the problem.

Examples of these types of computations are:

- *Enumeration.* The telephone number search in Example 1.2 uses this type of method. Each entry in the list is checked to see if there is one that has the correct name. An enumeration method must allow for verifying whether any case checked satisfies the problem. This verification must be possible using basic operations, and it must be possible to check every case. We could also solve the square root problem by enumeration. If we wanted a four-digit approximation to the square root of two, we would have to check every four-digit number, starting from the smallest, until we found the first one whose square exceeded two. Enumeration methods are usually among the slowest, so they are not practical for problems in which there are many possible answers. For example, we could not use an enumeration method to find a ten-digit approximation to a square root. It might take sixteen minutes to test all ten billion cases, even on a computer that could perform a test of one case in a microsecond (one-millionth of a second).

- *Direct computation.* The tax computation in Example 1.1 was of this type.

- *Iteration.* The method for the SIN problem in Example 1.5 is of this type. The value of sin(x) is defined by an infinite series. Computationally we can evaluate any finite number of these terms and in principle get as close an approximation as we wish to the answer. (Later we will see that the accuracy of these methods is limited by something called round-off error. Because of round-off, the type of iteration in the next class of methods is often preferable.)

- *Trial and error.* The square root method in Example 1.3 is of this type. Initially an approximation of 1.000 was chosen as the first guess for the square root of 2. Then it was changed to be closer to the answer by comparing its square to the answer and incrementing it if it were still smaller. Once it passed the square root, it was reduced and incremented by smaller amounts in the same way. In trial and error methods, the trial answer is substituted into the problem (in this case we compare its square with 2), and the amount by which it fails to satisfy the problem (the error) is used to change the trial answer.

Problems

1. Suggest and flowchart an enumerative method to find the smallest integer that is a multiple of both N and M. (This is called the smallest common multiple of N and M.)

2. Trace through your solution of problem 1 with $N = 6$ and $M = 4$, showing the result of the steps in each box.

In the floating point representation given in the book the fractional part of the number (mantissa) is stored in the 5 right most digits.

2 bits is 4 codes
3 bits is 8 codes
4 bits is 16 codes
5 bits is 32 codes
6 bits is 64 codes
7 bits is 128 codes

floating pts overflow occurs when
an exponent is too large (>49)
to be stored.

underflow occurs when exponent
is too small. (<-50) to be
stored

1. ↑, ( )
2. *, /
3. +, -

Computer Organization

2. COMPUTER ORGANIZATION

To understand the capabilities of computers, we must briefly examine the way they work. We are not going to worry about the details of the electrical circuits used in their construction; rather, we will make analogies between the actual elements of the computer and more common devices that are part of our everyday experience. One such device is the mechanical desk calculator. It is not necessary for you to understand precisely how a desk calculator works to perform arithmetic. However, you must know its capabilities to use it effectively. You must know, for example, how many positions there are in the recording mechanism that accumulates numbers. In the same way, you must know some of the important characteristics of a computer before you can use it effectively. The purpose of this chapter is to provide such information.

We are going to examine some of the details of computer organization. Initially, a natural reaction to these details is that it must be almost impossible for a person to keep them all in mind while preparing programs. Fortunately, languages are available that allow a programmer to write programs without concerning himself with most of such details. However, when underlying details are understood it is easier to see why languages permit certain statements and why other actions are not allowed. It is also much easier for a programmer to track down errors in his programs if he is familiar with these details.

Recall the principal operations required by the flowchart in Figure 1.3 for the solution of the tax problem. It was necessary to input the data, to manipulate it arithmetically, to find the larger of two numbers (which means that it must be possible to compare two numbers and make a decision), and to output answers (presumably by printing). Each of these basis operations must be built into a computer in some manner. If we examine the tax problem further, we notice that numbers which were not originally input, such as ADJUSTED INCOME, were computed. Nor were these numbers to be printed; rather, they were used in the course of the problem solution. If we were performing this computation by hand, we would write these on a worksheet so we could reference them for later use. (A person who was very capable and very confident might try to remember them.) In either case, they are, in effect, being memorized for later use. We say that they have been *stored*, either on the piece of paper, or in the person's head, until they are needed again. When the tax problem is to be solved by a computer, the equivalent of the piece of paper will be needed for the storage of numbers for later use. Therefore, the basic units of a computer are *input units*, such as a *card reader*; *output units*, such as a *printer*; *storage units*, called the *memory*; and a unit for processing information, which we call the *central processing unit*, or CPU for short. These units are shown in Figure 2.1 as they are typically connected. (This figure also shows some additional details that will be the subject of the next four sections.)

29

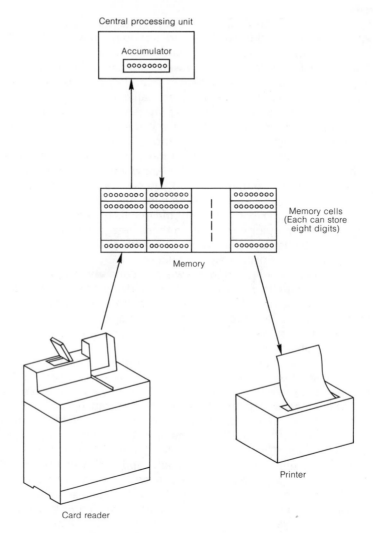

Fig. 2.1 The basic units of a computer

The process of executing a simple program for the system shown consists of the following steps:

- Prepare the program on punched cards.

- Read the program into the memory through the card reader. This reading process is done by a program that is one of the *system programs*; that is, it is a program provided for the purpose of helping a person use the computer.

- Execute the program just read. It may read data from cards in the card reader and will print answers.

- Check to see if the answers are correct.

To program effectively we must understand how the data and the program are prepared, in what form they are read and stored in the memory of the computer, and how they are processed by the CPU.

2.1 MEMORY

The analogy with a piece of paper is not a good one for thinking about a computer memory. In fact, those who have done any lengthy calculations with a desk calculator know how inconvenient paper can be as a storage mechanism for numbers generated during computation. It is difficult to change numbers once they have been written and difficult to locate those stored some time previously. Frequently, we make life a little easier for ourselves by first ruling lines on the paper to give us boxes in which to put numbers. We can divide each box into a row of squares so that each can contain one digit of the number, as shown in Figure 2.2. For a large problem we may need many such boxes.

A computer memory contains a large number of such boxes, which we will call *cells*. Each cell can store data. A memory is usually constructed of electronic devices (the *hardware* of the system) that store the information (in a way to be discussed in more detail in the optional Section 2.7). We will first talk as if memories can be used only to store numbers. Later in this chapter we will see how they can be used to store almost any type of data. In this section we will present a simple analogy for a computer memory that emphasizes some of its important characteristics. You should be aware that this description of a memory is grossly oversimplified, but it will serve as a realistic model.

When we drew boxes on a pad of paper, we divided each of them into smaller squares and wrote one digit of a number in each square.

First number | 2 | 4 | 8 | 1 | 6 |

Second number | 7 | 9 | 4 | 5 | 2 |

Fig. 2.2 Boxes containing numbers

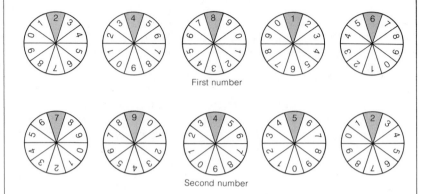

First number

Second number

Fig. 2.3 Mechanical dials storing numbers

In the same way, the cells in the memory of a computer are divided into smaller segments that we call *digital positions*. One digit of a number can be written in each digital position. The mechanical analogy we will use is that of the dials of a mechanical desk calculator, or the dials of a car odometer (the device that measures how many miles have been driven). Each digital position of a memory can be thought to contain one such dial with ten positions. These ten positions are labeled by digits 0, 1, 2, . . . , 9. A number can be written into a cell in memory by rotating the dials so that they contain the digits of the number in a position that can be read. Figure 2.3 shows two such cells, each containing a five-digit number. The digits of the numbers are positioned on the tops of the dials. Thus the first cell contains the number 24816 while the second contains 79452. The most important restriction the memory of a computer will place on the computations we can perform are that there are a limited number of cells (perhaps 100,000), and that each cell contains only a certain number of digital positions, fixed by the design of the computer.

Of course, we should make sure that the dials are turned to a position such that it is clear which digit is meant. If a dial were halfway between 3 and 4, it would not be storing any reasonable number. But why, you might ask, shouldn't that be the number 3.5? Certainly we could just use one dial for each number, and if we wanted to store the number 3.25, turn it so that it is a quarter of the way from 3 to 4.

There are computers that work in this fashion. They are called *analog* computers because an analogy is made between the size of the number and the position of a physical device. In analog computers, the size of a voltage or current is frequently used to store the size of a number. This type of computer is very useful

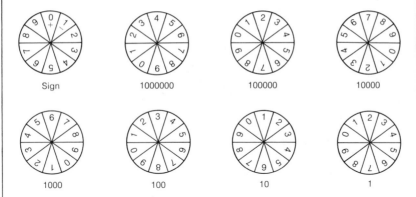

Fig. 2.4 Sign position and seven digits with weights

in certain specific applications, but it has some drawbacks. If we wanted to store the number 3.2569145, we would have to turn the dial to be .2569145 of the way between 3 and 4, a feat that is beyond present engineering capabilities. If we restrict our dials to take only positions where the digits 0 through 9 are printed, then we cannot get any errors because of inaccuracy in positioning the dials (unless there is an equipment failure). If we want to store the number 3.2569145, we will have to use a box with eight dials in it; if that were not enough accuracy we could use more dials in our computer design. Because the type of computer we are going to discuss stores numbers by storing each digit, it is called a *digital* computer.

We used several dials to store a number. Each box of dials shown can be used to store one number. We call the group of digits stored in one such box a *word*. The place where we store a word—that is, the box of dials—is called a *location*, a *cell*, or a *memory position* because it is a position in the memory in which one word can be stored.

In the remainder of this chapter we are going to discuss a simple computer that is typical of many computers. We will assume that its memory contains 100,000 cells, each of which has eight dials. Since we will be dealing with numbers that have a sign (plus or minus) we will think of the first dial as if it contained the sign rather than a regular digit. We can do this by using the zero position to mean that the number is positive and the one position to mean that the number is negative. We say that we *represent* the sign by zero or one. We could, of course, mark the dial with plus and minus as shown in Figure 2.4; however, it is the position of the dial that records the information, not the markings on it.

In Figure 2.4 we show the *sign position* and seven other positions marked with the values that they represent. Thus the last (rightmost) position is the number of ones, the next to last is the number of tens, and so forth. We say that the *weight* of the next-to-last position is ten since the value of the digit in that position is multiplied by ten to determine its contribution to the value of the number. The size of the number is obtained by multiplying each digit by its weight and adding the products together. Thus in Figure 2.4 the number represented is

$$4 \times 1000000 + 2 \times 100000 + 7 \times 10000 + 6 \times 1000$$
$$+ 3 \times 100 + 1 \times 10 + 2 \times 1 = 4276312.$$

Let us return to the flowchart in Figure 1.3. We read the input data and processed it to produce intermediate results such as AD-JUSTED INCOME. When these numbers are generated, they must be saved in some of the cells. To know which, let us assume that when we prepared the computer to handle this flowchart we marked one of the cells with the name ADJUSTED INCOME, and that some-how the computer will know this. In fact, each cell is given a unique numerical *address*, much as the houses on a street are given unique numerical addresses. If there were 100,000 cells in memory, each would have one of the numerical address between 00000 and 99999. For now we use a name such as ADJUSTED INCOME as the "ad-dress" or name of a cell. When the computer performs the compu-tation that subtracts 650 times the number of dependents from INCOME, it will store the result in the cell named ADJUSTED IN-COME. This action requires that the cell dials must be turned so that they contain the value of ADJUSTED INCOME. This operation will "destroy" the number that was there previously and replace it with the new number. The operation of storing the number is called *writing* (analogous to writing on a piece of paper). We say that writing is *destructive* because it destroys the previous informa-tion in a cell. Note that a cell will always contain some number be-cause the dials must be set to some position, but until the computer executes the write, it will not contain any number of interest to us.

Later in the flowchart we use some of the intermediate results to compute new results. Thus, in Box 5 we subtract DEDUCTIONS from ADJUSTED INCOME to get a result we will call TAXABLE INCOME. This means that there are cells named DEDUCTIONS and TAXABLE INCOME in addition to the one named ADJUSTED INCOME. The computer will *read* the numbers in ADJUSTED IN-COME and DEDUCTIONS, subtract them, and store the result into the cell named TAXABLE INCOME. The reading of a number does not have to change it; the computer only has to look at the dials, not move them, so we call such a read operation *non-destructive*.

We have a perfectly good way of expressing the operation of sub-traction more concisely using the minus sign. Therefore, we replace the contents of Box 5 by the more formal statement

TAXABLE INCOME ← ADJUSTED INCOME − DEDUCTIONS

The left-pointing arrow means that after the expression on the right-hand side has been evaluated, the result is stored (written) into the cell named TAXABLE INCOME. The expression ADJUSTED INCOME − DEDUCTIONS means that the number stored in the cell named ADJUSTED INCOME should be read and then the number stored in the cell named DEDUCTIONS should be read and subtracted from the first number to find the value of the expression. Thus the names are actually names of cells in the memory of the computer. As we become experienced in using computers, we will think of them as being the names of *variables*, which are abstract mathematical quantities whose values may change during program execution. We say that a variable is stored in a cell in the memory, meaning that its value is stored in that cell. The step of storing the value of an expression into a cell with the name Z is also called an *assignment* of the value to the variable Z.

Computer memories have a large number of cells, each of which can be used to store a variable. Computers that you may be using might be able to store from 10,000 to 1,000,000 different variables in memory; that is, a computer might have from 10,000 to 1,000,000 different locations in memory, each location with its set of eight dials or their electronic equivalent. Fortunately, these electronic devices are very small, so such a memory with all of the hardware for reading and writing in any cell that is named may occupy a box only about 2′ by 5′ by 6′. (The electronic equivalent of the dials occupies a small fraction of the total volume. The mechanism for reading and writing occupies another small fraction, while the power supplies, the need for space to blow cooling air, and the need for access room for engineers to repair it are responsible for most of the size.) These memories are very fast. Reading or writing a single word will typically take from a quarter to one microsecond, although there are memories that are faster and less expensive ones that are slower.

2.2 Central Processing Unit

The memory of the computer is used to store the intermediate results and other data. The central processing unit (CPU for short) is the part of the computer that performs the necessary manipulations on the data. Thus it is the box that does the subtraction

Fig. 2.5   Desk calculator

when we need to *execute* the statement

TAXABLE INCOME ← ADJUSTED INCOME − DEDUCTIONS

We will draw an analogy between the CPU and a desk calculator such as the one shown in Figure 2.5.

When we do the above calculation on a desk calculator, we first read the number written in the space marked ADJUSTED INCOME from our worksheet and enter it into the desk calculator. This is done by keying the number into the calculator and pushing the appropriate operation key. The desk calculator, if it is mechanical, has a row of number wheels, or dials, which store the digits of the number. We call this a *register*. It is just like a memory cell discussed earlier, but we give it this other name when it is immediately accessible to us, like the register in the desk calculator. The operation of entering a value into this register is called a LOAD operation. When we enter the value of ADJUSTED INCOME, we can say we are executing the step

LOAD   ADJUSTED INCOME

The second step is to read the number from the space on the work sheet labeled DEDUCTIONS, to key it into the desk calculator, and to press the operation key marked "Subtract." This causes the number just entered to be subtracted from the number already in the register so that the difference is now stored in that register.

The last step is to copy the number from the register of the desk calculator into the space named TAXABLE INCOME. This step does not change the register in the desk calculator—that is, it is nondestructive—although it does change the place on our worksheet where we keep TAXABLE INCOME.

We can express the subtraction step concisely as

SUBTRACT DEDUCTIONS

and the last step of copying the number back to our memory as

STORE   TAXABLE INCOME

The three steps together constitute a program for a desk calculator and the person controlling it. They can be written

LOAD   ADJUSTED INCOME
SUBTRACT DEDUCTIONS
STORE   TAXABLE INCOME

Any calculation that can be performed on a desk calculator can be expressed as a sequence of steps of this form. In this book we will use the more concise form

TAXABLE INCOME ← ADJUSTED INCOME − DEDUCTIONS

to describe the steps in such a computation. This more concise form is converted into a sequence of very basic steps such as LOADs and STOREs. The CPU in a computer functions very much like a desk calculator, executing sequences of basic steps that are stored in the computer memory.

Machine language is the basic language understood by the computing machine. Most computers have a register (many have more than one) in the CPU that is similar to the register in the desk calculator. It is called an *accumulator* because it is used to accumulate the intermediate results. The CPU can be told to load a number into its accumulator from a specific cell in the memory, to add, subtract, multiply, or divide the number in the accumulator by a number from memory, or to store a number from the accumulator into memory.

2.2.1 Machine Language

When we are directly specifying every action that the computer is to take, we are programming at the machine level. The language we use is a machine-level language, which we shall refer to as *machine language* for short.

To direct the computer at the machine level we must write sequences of basic instructions. To save writing we will use abbreviations such as ADD, SUB, MPY, and DIV. To make it clear that a name such as ADJUSTED INCOME is a single name rather than the names of two cells, we will use the underline character instead of a space. (The underline character is called the *break* character on computer keypunches.) Using this notation, the simple sequence written above for a desk calculator would be written as

```
LOAD   ADJUSTED_INCOME
SUB    DEDUCTIONS
STORE  TAXABLE_INCOME
```

for a typical CPU. This means exactly the same thing as previously, and the steps are carried out by a CPU in a manner similar to the way we would do them on a desk calculator.

If we wanted to form the value of the expression $A \times B + C$ in the accumulator, we would write

```
LOAD   A
MPY    B
ADD    C
```

Note that we first had to form the product of A and B in the accumulator, then add in the value of C. This is because the rules of arithmetic for the expression $A \times B + C$ require that multiplication be performed first, so that if the values of A, B, and C are 1, 2, and 3, respectively, the result is $(1 \times 2) + 3$, which is 5.

Example 2.1 — Machine Language for Simple Assignment Statements

The following instructions are used to perform the assignments indicated.

a) SUM $\leftarrow$ R + S + T

```
LOAD   R
ADD    S
ADD    T
STORE  SUM
```

To add three numbers, we add the first two, and then add the third to the result. In effect, we form $(R + S) + T$ where, by putting the parentheses around $R + S$, we mean that it is formed first. If R, S, and T contained 3, 7, and 4, respectively, the accumulator would contain 3 after the LOAD instruction, 10 after the first ADD instruction, and 14 after the second ADD instruction. Whereas we wrote the whole assignment statement in one line, the computer executes four separate instructions sequentially.

b) $\text{RESULT} \leftarrow \dfrac{\text{PART1} + \text{PART2}}{\text{TOTAL}}$

```
LOAD   PART1
ADD    PART2
DIV    TOTAL
STORE  RESULT
```

The DIV instruction divides the number in the accumulator by the number that is read nondestructively from the memory.

c) $\text{AVERAGE} \leftarrow \dfrac{\text{RES} + \text{P}}{\text{N1} + \text{N2}}$

Here we have a problem. In order to do the division of (RES + P) by (N1 + N2) we must have (RES + P) in the accumulator and (N1 + N2) somewhere in the memory. This means we must first compute (N1 + N2) and store it in the memory. Since we may need the numbers that are in RES, P, N1, and N2 again, we must use another cell for this other intermediate result. Let us therefore assume that another cell has been allocated for this and call it TEMP (for temporary storage, although it does not matter what the name is — we just need the cell). We use the accumulator to calculate (N1 + N2) first, then store it ready to use in the division after we have formed (RES + P).

```
LOAD   N1
ADD    N2
STORE  TEMP
LOAD   RES
ADD    P
DIV    TEMP
STORE  AVERAGE
```

d) $Q \leftarrow A \times B + C \times D$

When an expression involves additions and multiplications without parentheses, the rules of arithmetic require that the multiplications be performed first. Thus, $2 \times 3 + 4 \times 5$ is first reduced to $6 + 20$ by performing the multiplications. The addition is performed to get the answer 26. (These rules will be discussed in detail in Chapter 3.) Consequently, $A \times B + C \times D$ is evaluated in the order indicated by the parentheses in $(A \times B) + (C \times D)$. We need temporary storage for one of the products while we evaluate the other.

```
LOAD   A
MPY    B
STORE  TEMP
```

39

```
LOAD   C
MPY    D
ADD    TEMP
STORE  Q
```

e) $R \leftarrow U + V \times W + Z$

This time we do not need temporary storage because we can rearrange the expression on the right-hand side of the assignment to be $V \times W + U + Z$. The instructions are

```
LOAD   V
MPY    W
ADD    U
ADD    Z
STORE  R
```

Different types of computers take different lengths of time to execute their instructions. An ADD, SUB, LOAD, or STORE instruction typically takes about twice the time it takes to read from or write into memory, that is, from a quarter to two microseconds. Very often, the time of an instruction will be measured in *memory cycles*. A memory cycle is the time for the memory to completely execute one read or write. MPY instructions are usually slower than additions by a factor of about two; that is, they take from two to four memory cycles. Divide instructions are usually slower than multiplications by another factor of 1.5 to 2. We will assume the following speeds for our hypothetical computer for purposes of deciding on the best code when there is a choice:

Memory read or write	0.5	microseconds		
LOAD, ADD, SUB, STORE	1	"	2	memory cycles
MPY	2	"	4	"
DIV	3	"	6	"

When division is slower than multiplication, it is sometimes worthwhile to rewrite some calculations to remove divisions. Thus, instead of writing

$$A \leftarrow B/2.5$$

we could write

$$A \leftarrow B \times 0.4$$

Another case occurs when a large number of values, say one thousand, are to be divided by the same value X. Instead of performing the assignment

$$A \leftarrow B/X$$

one thousand times—which takes 5000 microseconds—we could first form T by

$$T \leftarrow 1/X$$

which takes 5 microseconds, and then perform

$$A \leftarrow B \times T$$

one thousand times. This takes another 4000 microseconds, which gives a net saving of 995 microseconds, almost 20% of the first figure.

  Because of the sequential flow of execution, it is often necessary to save the values of some variables temporarily in other locations, as their values will be needed again after the cell containing them has been changed. For example, suppose we wish to exchange the values of A and B. We might write

```
EXCHANGE
A AND B
```

Unfortunately, we do not have an instruction called *exchange* (although some computers do). Consequently, we are tempted to write

```
A ← B
B ← A
```

for that box, which would be programmed as

```
LOAD   A
STORE  B
LOAD   B
STORE  A
```

Unfortunately, once the first LOAD, STORE pair has been executed, the contents of the cells A and B are the same, both containing the original contents of cell A. To overcome this problem, we must first move the contents of one cell, say A, to a temporary location, which we will call TEMP. Then we can copy B into A, and finally copy the original contents of A, now held in TEMP, into the cell. Thus our code is:

```
LOAD   A
STORE  TEMP
```

LOAD   B
STORE   A
LOAD   TEMP
STORE   B

EXERCISES

1. Write instructions to perform the following assignments:

   *a. A ← B + (C/D) × E
   b. F ← G × H + (I/J)
   c. K ← (L + M) × (P + Q) × (R + S)
   d. T ← (U × V + W) × X × Y

**2. How long does it take our hypothetical computer to execute the set of instructions for each of the above assignments?

3. If the cells B, C, D, and E contain 2, 6, 2, and 3, give the contents of the accumulator after each of the instructions has been executed in your solution to 1a.

QUESTIONS

1. Why must instructions be performed sequentially in the order given?

PROBLEMS

1. There are usually several sequences of instructions that could be used for any assignment statement. We usually want the shortest, either in number of instructions or in execution time. Give two sequences that do not use the same instructions but contain the same number of instructions, and will perform the assignment

$$A ← (B × C + D) × (B × C)$$

   Which sequence is faster?

2. Give the sequence of operations that will evaluate the expression (A/B) × D + (2 × A × C)/B in the shortest time. (You may assume that any constants you need are in memory and that the expression can be rearranged in any way that does not change its value.)

*3. Write a sequence of instructions to exchange the contents of cells A, B, and C; that is, after execution of the program, A should contain the original contents of B, B should contain the original contents of C, and C should contain the original contents of A.

2.3 Input and Output

A computer that is to communicate with people must be able to accept information prepared by them and to return answers in a form they can accept. The actual memory of a computer is made of electronic devices and information is stored by means of the presence of current in various wires or by the way in which a piece of material is magnetized. Although it is theoretically possible for a person to attach wires to the computer and directly set the memory to contain desired input data or to connect measuring devices that display the state of the memory, these are not convenient methods of input or output. One of the primary purposes of a computer is to make routine tasks more convenient, so direct connection and measurement is left to the maintenance engineer who must see that all of the circuits are functioning correctly. The computer user must be able to prepare his input on a medium that is easy for him to handle and receive his answers in a similar form.

A number of different media are used for input and output. The most familiar are punched cards and printed pages. The most familiar form of punched card is a thin rectangular card a little larger than a dollar bill with positions for punching small holes. In most cards these positions are grouped as eighty columns. Each column has twelve positions. Different computers interpret the holes in different ways. In one common form, each column contains one character. Various combinations of punching in the twelve positions in a column are used to represent different characters. The actual characters that can be used depend on the type of machine and data representation code. Usually any of the decimal digits 0 to 9, the upper-case letters A to Z, and some of the special characters such as +, −, *, /, (, and) can be used.

The card shown in Figure 2.6 is punched with Hollerith code, which is the code most commonly used with punched cards. One of the upper corners of the card is usually cut off. It is not significant to the computer, but is of help to the user to detect when cards are upside down or back to front in a large deck of cards.

The equipment used to punch cards is like a typewriter, but instead of printing the characters on paper, it punches the appropriate hole combinations into the card. It can also print characters at the top of the card above the columns containing the punched characters. This device is called a *keypunch*. A typical model is shown in Figure 2.7. A card such as shown in Figure 2.6 can contain up to 80 characters. If we think of the space (also called a *blank*) as

43

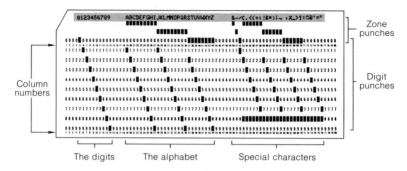

Fig. 2.6 Hollerith-punched card

if it were a character, we can say that one of these cards always contains 80 characters. (The blank character is represented by the lack of holes, so initially a card contains 80 blanks. A blank can always be changed to another character, but most other characters cannot be changed once they have been punched, unlike typewriter copy where it is possible to erase and correct. If there is an error on a card, it is usually necessary to repunch the card completely.) Punched cards are read by a *card reader*.

Other input devices include punched paper tape readers, typewriters, and more expensive devices such as optical readers that can read typewritten and printed documents. We will assume that our computer has a card reader.

Computer printers can normally print any symbol that can be input by a punched card. They are usually *line printers*; that is, devices that print whole lines at a time. They have a fixed number of positions on each line in which characters may be printed or which may be left blank. Many printers have 132 positions across the line. The paper used by these printers is in continuous sheets so that any number of lines may be printed (limited only by the user's ability to pay the computer costs). However, the paper is usually folded into pages of about 60 lines each for easy handling. A typical line printer is shown in Figure 2.8.

The card reader and the printer are connected to the memory of the computer so that information can be transferred between the memory and the input/output media. On actual computers, this connection is very elaborate to match the relatively low data transfer speed of mechanical devices such as readers and printers to the higher data transfer speed of the memory.

We refer to the set of input cards as a *sequential data set* because it is possible to read a card only after the preceding card has been read. In the same way, the set of lines that can be printed forms a sequential data set because it is necessary to print one line before

44

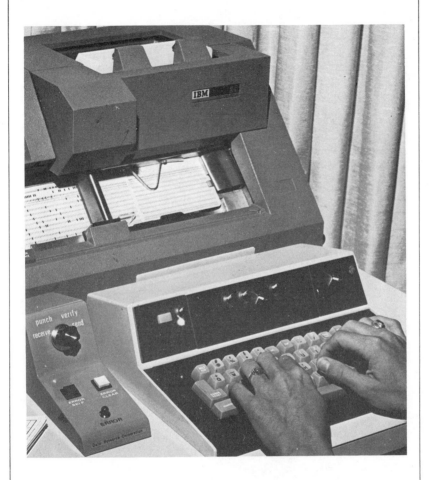

Fig. 2.7 IBM Model 029 Keypunch

the next can be printed. The data is not structured so that it is possible to get at any item immediately.

Reading cards and printing lines are relatively slow operations. About 1000 or 2000 lines or cards can be printed or read per minute. However, practical machines are not usually limited by this; there are techniques whereby reading from one card, performing calculations on the data read previously, and printing the results of other calculations can be done simultaneously. This helps to increase the overall efficiency of computer operations. In Chapter 4 we will discuss some of the ways in which the system can be organized to provide this capability.

45

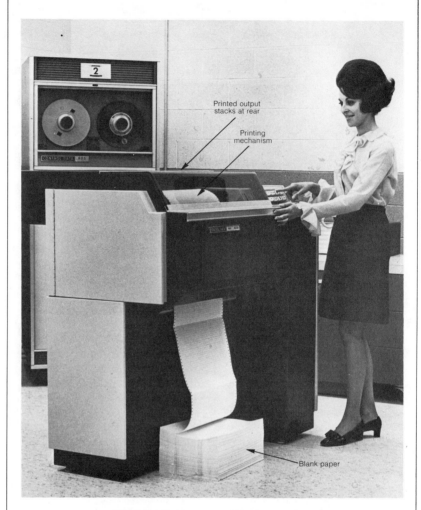

Fig. 2.8 Control Data 9350 line printer

2.3.1 Machine Language for Input/Output

We will use a very simple connection in our hypothetical computer. The card reader will execute two different types of operations. The first asks the reader to take the next card from the input hopper and place it under the reading mechanism. We call this operation SKIPC (Skip Card). There may be several numbers on a card, separated by blank characters. The second type of operation asks the card

reader to input these numbers, one at a time from left to right, from
the card to the computer memory. Each operation inputs one number. It is called READ. Thus, the instruction sequence

```
SKIPC
READ A
READ C
SKIPC
READ B
```

would read two numbers from the first card in the input hopper
into cells A and C. The second SKIPC instruction would then cause
the card reader to bring the second card under the reading mechanism (automatically ejecting the first card). The last READ instruction would copy the first number from the second card into cell B.
If the contents of the two cards were

1254   −6748   567

and
563   −567   89   78

respectively, the contents of cells A, C, and B would be

```
A   +0001254
C   −0006748
B   +0000563
```

after the sequence of instructions had been executed. Note that the
other numbers on the cards have been ignored. When a card is
read, it is taken from the *input hopper* and passed into the reader.
The previous card is put in the *output stacker*. It is no longer available to be read by the machine a second time. Thus each card in
the input deck can be read just once, and cards must be read in
the order in which they are presented to the computer. A typical
card reader is shown in Figure 2.9a; an illustration of the way it
works is shown in 2.9b.

Printed output is caused by similar instructions. The computer
can execute the operations PRINT and SKIPL (Skip Line). Each
operation takes a number from the memory and puts it into the next
position on the current printer line. The SKIPL operation causes
the paper to be moved up to the next line. For example, if memory
cells X, Y, and Z contain -0000013, $+0125167$, and -0000152, respectively, the instruction sequence

```
PRINT X
PRINT Y
SKIPL
PRINT Z
SKIPL
```

47

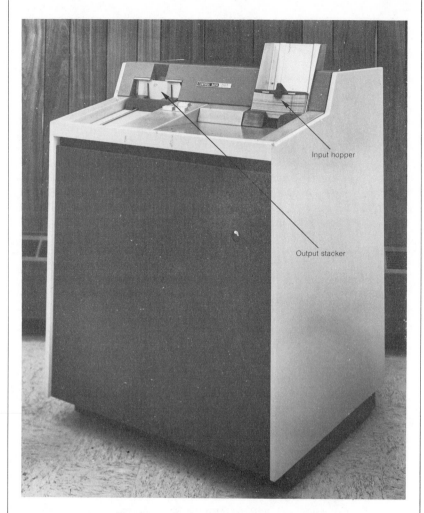

Input hopper

Output stacker

Fig. 2.9a   Control Data 224-2 card reader

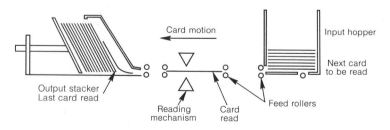

Card motion

Input hopper

Next card
to be read

Output stacker
Last card read

Reading
mechanism

Card
read

Feed rollers

Fig. 2.9b   Schematic of a card reader

48

causes two lines to be printed as follows:

$$-13 \qquad +125167$$
$$-152$$

Exercises

*1. Write an instruction sequence that will read two numbers from a card and print them in the reverse order. Thus, if the card contains 105, −21, the output line should be −21, 105.

2. Write an instruction sequence to read A, B, and C from one card, perform the assignment statements

$$X \leftarrow A \times B$$
$$Y \leftarrow C + A/B$$
$$Z \leftarrow A - B + C$$

and print two lines, the first containing A, B, and C, the second containing X, Y, and Z.

2.4 Control

We have discussed part of the organization of a simple CPU whose arithmetic instructions can be used to evaluate expressions and to perform assignments. The CPU is connected to the memory along with the input and output devices as shown in Figure 2.1. Instructions have to be given to each of the units in turn so that they perform their functions. For example, if we wish to perform $C \leftarrow A + B$ we must execute the instructions

```
LOAD   A
ADD    B
STORE  C
```

This means that the memory must first be told to read the number in the cell named A and to send it to the CPU. Simultaneously, the CPU must be told to take that number and load it into the accumulator. Then the memory must be told to read the number from the cell named B, and simultaneously the CPU must be told to add that number to the value in the accumulator. Finally, the CPU must be told to send a copy of the number in the accumulator to the memory, and simultaneously the memory must be told to write that number into the cell named C. These instructions are issued by a unit called the *control unit*. The control unit and the CPU are usually in the same box and are very intimately connected, although the control

49

unit also sends signals to other units such as the memory and input/output·units. The control unit reads the instructions and tells the individual units in the machine what to do.

From where does the control unit read its instructions? It would certainly be nice if the control unit could read our hand-drawn flowchart directly. Unfortunately, that is not currently practical, so we must convert it into a form that can be read and understood by the computer. This means that the flowchart must be converted into characters that can be put on punched cards and be read. It would be possible for the computer to read a card for each instruction, execute that instruction, then read another card for the next instruction, and so on. However, the computer would then be restricted in a number of ways. For example, it would be slowed to the speed of the card reader (which we have seen to be very slow) and would be restricted to executing each instruction once unless we took the cards from the output stacker and put them back into the input hopper.

Instead, we read all of the instructions into memory and store them there. This means that each instruction must be coded in a form that can be stored in a memory cell. An instruction, such as LOAD DEDUCTIONS, contains two parts: the name of an operation and the name of a memory cell. In Section 2.1 it was pointed out that each memory cell has a unique memory address. If there are 100,000 cells, the address can be represented in five decimal digits that can take any value between 00000 and 99999. An instruction can be stored in an eight-digit memory word by using three digits to encode the operation and·the remaining five for the address as shown in Figure 2.10. An operation, such as ADD, is assigned a three-digit internal form called the *operation code* (*op-code* for short) when the computer is designed. If the op-code ADD is 020, the instruction ADD A where A is memory location 17253 is represented internally as 02017253.

Instructions are stored in the memory in the order in which they are to be executed. So that the control unit knows from where in memory to fetch the next instruction, it contains a register called the *instruction counter*, which holds the address of the next instruction to be executed. When the execution of one instruction has been completed, the control unit sends the address in the instruction counter to the memory and requests a read of the information from that address. This information is returned to the control unit and used as an instruction. At the same time, the instruction counter contents are increased by one so that the counter contains the address of the following instruction. The sequence of steps that sends the instruction address to the memory, receives the instruction, and increments the instruction counter is called the *fetch sequence*. The act of looking at the op-code to see what operation it represents is called *decoding* the op-code.

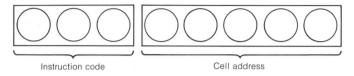

Instruction code   Cell address

Fig. 2.10 Instruction format

Straight-line flowcharts, that is, ones in which each box follows only one other box, can be converted into sequences of instructions that can be stored sequentially in memory and executed one after another. This is not possible when there is more than one way of getting to a given box. For example, in the flowchart in Figure 1.3, Box 8 is preceded by Boxes 1 and 9. It is not possible for the instructions representing Box 8 to follow immediately after both the instructions representing Box 1 and those representing Box 9. To overcome this problem we must introduce an operation that functions like the flowlines in the flowchart and tells the control unit to go to another place in the memory to continue execution. We can tell the control unit from where to fetch the next instruction by specifying its address. The operation that does this is called a *branch* (or *jump* or *transfer*) operation. The instruction

BRNCH X

causes the next instruction to be fetched from the cell labeled X. If X were understood to be the cell with address 24731, then execution of BRNCH would cause the operand address (that is, 24731, representing cell X) to be placed in the instruction counter. Since the next instruction is read from the cell addressed by the contents of the instruction counter, the next instruction will be fetched from location X. We also call the action a *transfer of control*.

The instruction BRNCH X always causes a branch to X. For this reason it is called an *unconditional branch* instruction. It was used in the example above to complete a loop. The lack of more cards stopped the loop from being executed endlessly. In the prime number example solved in Figures 1.6 and 1.7, it was necessary to test for arithmetic relationships. We needed, for example, to see if two numbers were equal to know if M divided N exactly. If the two numbers were equal, control was transferred out of the loop to a print statement. Such decision-making steps are implemented in the computer by means of *conditional branch* instructions. A conditional branch instruction acts like a branch instruction if a specified condition is met. We have, for example, a *branch if the accumulator is positive* instruction that will transfer control to the operand address if the number in the accumulator is greater than or equal to zero. A conditional branch instruction has no effect if the condition is not met.

Most general-purpose computers can execute a hundred or more different operations. Each of the operations must have a different code so that the control unit can recognize it. The instruction format shown in Figure 2.10 allows for 1000 different op-codes, although few computers have this many different operations. The operations fall into broad classes: arithmetic operations such as SUBTRACT, ADD, and so forth; branch operations; input/output operations; data movement operations such as LOAD, STORE; and logical operations to be discussed later.

2.4.1 MACHINE LANGUAGE

We have introduced a number of operations for our hypothetical computer. They have the following op-codes:

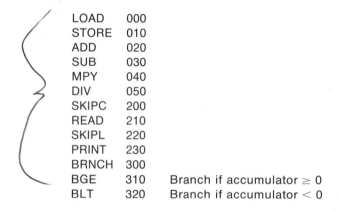

LOAD	000	
STORE	010	
ADD	020	
SUB	030	
MPY	040	
DIV	050	
SKIPC	200	
READ	210	
SKIPL	220	
PRINT	230	
BRNCH	300	
BGE	310	Branch if accumulator ≥ 0
BLT	320	Branch if accumulator < 0

The control unit reads instructions from memory. After each instruction has been read, the operation code is examined to see which operation is to be performed and then the operation is executed. Thus if the sequence of three instructions

000	05471
020	05483
010	05034

is read, the first instruction (which has op-code 000) is a LOAD. The address 05471 will be sent to the memory by the control unit with a request to read. The word in cell 05471 will be transmitted back to the CPU to be loaded into the accumulator on command from the control unit. The second instruction (op-code 020) is an ADD, so the address 05483 is sent to memory with a request to read. The word in cell 05483 is returned to the CPU, and the CPU is told to add it to the value in the accumulator. Finally, the third instruction is a STORE (op-code 010). The word in the accumulator is sent to the memory along with the address 05034 with a request to write. Thus, the sum of the contents of cells 05471 and 05483 is calculated and stored in cell 05034. If these are the cells we have decided to call A, B, and C, then we have performed the computation $C \leftarrow A + B$.

Each instruction has two addresses associated with it: the address of the cell in which it is stored, called the *instruction address*, and the address in the last five digits of the instruction, which tells where the data (called the *operand*) for the operation is to be obtained (in the case of LOAD, ADD, SUB, MPY, DIV, and PRINT) or to be returned (in the case of STORE and READ). This second address is called the *operand address*. (Some operations, such as SKIPC and SKIPL do not use an operand, so the operand address is meaningless. However, those five digits in the instruction must be set to some value. We will assume that this value is 00000.)

To start the computer when there are no instructions stored in memory, the operator presses a control button on the console of the machine. Pushing this button causes one of the input devices — most computer systems have several different input devices — to read a record of information into memory. The instruction counter is set to the address of the first of the cells assigned a value by the read operation. If the initial record — for example, the 80 columns of a card — contains a short program to read more cards into memory, this program is executed, causing the memory to be loaded as desired. Fortunately we do not have to concern ourselves with the details of getting started because a number of programs are provided in the computer system for this purpose. These programs, called *system programs*, will read in our program after it has been punched on cards in a suitable form and arrange for the instruction counter to be set to the address of the first instruction in our program.

We have seen how the operations indicated in a flowchart can be converted into a program stored in the memory and can be executed by the control unit of our computer. The steps in the conversion are to allocate memory cells to each variable name used and then to convert the expressions and assignment statements into sequences of arithmetic instructions. The input and output boxes are directly converted into READ and PRINT instructions. When a flowline is to be followed, we simply arrange for the code in a subsequent box to appear immediately after the code in a preceding

box. Thus, if our flowchart contains

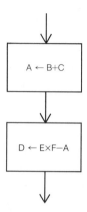

and the cells allocated to the various variables are

A	05471
B	05483
C	05034
D	16436
E	16435
F	16324

we generate the section of the program as follows:

Memory Contents		Earlier Form	
000	05483	LOAD	B
020	05034	ADD	C
010	05471	STORE	A
000	16435	LOAD	E
040	16324	MPY	F
030	05471	SUB	A
010	16436	STORE	D

We have represented the program in three ways above, the first as a section of a flowchart, the second and third as sequences of instructions—one sequence in the numeric form stored in the computer, and the other in an alphabetic form more convenient for people to read and understand. We should realize that the instructions are stored in numeric form, but, at least for our own use, we can write them in alphabetic form.

When we write a branch instruction, we want the operand address to be the address of another instruction. In order to represent the fact that X is the address of a particular instruction, we will write X in front of that instruction when we write the program in alphabetical form. Thus the beginning and the end of the program for the tax problem flowcharted in Figure 1.3 might be

```
X   READ  ANNUAL_INCOME
    READ  NUMBER_DEPENDENTS
    . . .
    PRINT TAX_LIABILITY
    BRNCH X
```

Although this program has no direct way of stopping, it is assumed that the machine will stop when there are no more cards. Most computer systems are controlled in such a way that trying to read more data when all of the data cards have been read can terminate execution of a program.

Conditional branch instructions are used to determine the sequence of instructions to be executed. For example, to put the larger of A or B into location C, we write the flowchart

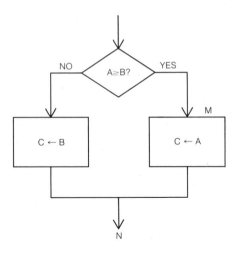

M and N refer to instruction addresses in the equivalent program below.

```
      LOAD    A
      SUB     B
      BGE     M
      LOAD    B
X     STORE   C
      BRNCH   N
M     LOAD    A
P     STORE   C
N . . .       (next instruction)
```

If control starts at the LOAD A instruction, it will execute instructions sequentially until it reaches one of the transfer instructions. It will then skip the three instructions LOAD B, STORE C, and BRNCH N if the accumulator is positive; otherwise it will execute these three and skip the pair LOAD A, STORE C. Not all of the instructions in a program have to be executed during any one execution of the program. (In this example, an alert programmer would use one less instruction than in the above program. The instruction STORE C labeled X can be omitted, and the following instruction changed to BRNCH P to make use of the STORE instruction there. The execution time is not changed, but the amount of memory space used is reduced. Both are important considerations in large programs.)

EXERCISES

Assume in each case that programs are to start in location 100. Give the internal numeric form of the following programs:

*1.
```
          SKIPC
          READ   A
          READ   B
          LOAD   A
          ADD    B
          STORE  C
          PRINT  C
          SKIPL
```

if A, B, and C are in locations 298, 1073, and 1074, respectively.

2.
```
          SKIPC
          READ   A
          READ   X
          READ   Z
          LOAD   A
          MPY    Z
          ADD    X
          STORE  T
          LOAD   A
          SUB    X
          DIV    T
          STORE  T
          PRINT  A
          PRINT  X
          PRINT  T
          SKIPL
```

if A, X, Z, and T are in locations 298, 1071, 99, and 98 respectively.

Convert the following flowcharts into sequences of instructions in machine language.

3.

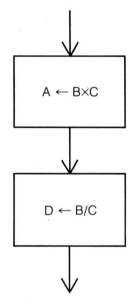

*4.

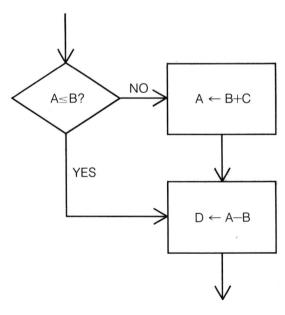

5.

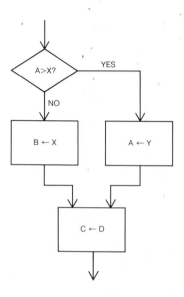

PROBLEMS

*1. Write a sequence of instructions to branch to location X if A + B > C + D. Use as few instructions as possible.

2. Write as short a sequence of instructions as possible to represent the flowchart

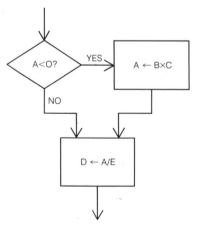

3. Write a sequence of instructions to read a number N, branch to location X if it is prime and greater than one, or to branch to

location Y otherwise. You may assume that location ONE contains the number one. (Refer to Example 1.4, page 19). You may use the instruction BZ—branch if the accumulator is zero, opcode 330.

2.5 Data Representation

We have described a memory that can store signed integers with up to seven decimal digits of accuracy. Computer programs deal with many different types of data. For example, we may wish to use a computer to handle alphabetic characters or to handle any of the other characters that can appear on the input or output medium. We may need to work with other than integers: the square root example in Chapter 1 used numbers of the form 1.414. This section will discuss ways in which other types of data can be stored in the memory and manipulated by the computer.

2.5.1 Integers

The computer memory was introduced as a device for storing integers. An integer is stored exactly, provided that it is not larger than the maximum number that can be stored (9999999 in our hypothetical computer). All integers less than this value are stored without error, and arithmetic operations—except division—can be performed exactly if the answer is also less than 9999999. The set of integers that can be represented in memory is called the *acceptable range of integers*. In our hypothetical computer, this range is the set of integers between −9999999 and +9999999. We express this more concisely by saying, "The acceptable range of integers is ±9999999." The arithmetic operations such as ADD and SUBTRACT described in Section 2.2 perform *integer arithmetic*; that is, they operate on integers, giving an integer answer. If a calculation yields a number outside of the range, the result has *overflowed*. As long as overflow does not occur, the operations of addition, subtraction, and multiplication are exact.

However, exact division is not always possible with integer arithmetic. For our hypothetical computer we assume that the result of a division operation is the largest integer not larger than the exact answer. Another way of expressing this is to say that the answer is obtained by performing the division exactly and then retaining only the integer part. The fractional part is discarded. Thus, −5 ÷ 2 is −2. We use the sign ÷ in flowcharts for integer division to indicate the property of returning an integer answer. If we wish to indicate an exact division operation, we will use the slash (/) sign. Thus, 5/2 is 2.5. Some computer languages allow both division operations.

2.5.2 Fixed–Point Numbers

Fixed-point numbers are numbers in which the decimal point is assumed to be in a fixed position. Thus, if we consider the set of numbers of the form *nnn.nnnn* where the *n* represents any of the decimal digits, we have a fixed-point number with three digits in front of the point and four digits after the point. Examples are 123.4567, 201.4000, and 001.4123. Fixed-point numbers are very similar to integers in that the results of addition and subtraction are exact provided that the range is not exceeded. In our example above the range is ±999.9999 with a precision of seven decimal digits. Integers are a special case of fixed-point numbers with the point at the extreme right. In most cases, computer multiplication of fixed-point numbers is not exact because an insufficient number of digits are available to represent the answer. The product of the two numbers 201.0001 and 001.0002 is 201.04030002. This requires eleven digits of precision for its exact representation. If the answer is to be expressed in seven digits with a range of ±999.9999, then we will have to accept an answer of 201.0403. Thus, multiplication can introduce an error due to our inability to represent all digits of an answer.

Some computer languages (for example, PL/I) allow arithmetic on fixed-point numbers. Integer arithmetic is then a special case of fixed point. Other languages, for example, FORTRAN and ALGOL, provide only for integer arithmetic and floating-point arithmetic, which is described in the next section. We will not discuss fixed-point numbers in detail since the methods by which they are handled in the computer do not give us any basic insights into computer organization.

Fixed-point arithmetic tends to be more important for business-oriented data processing; scientific work uses integer and floating-point arithmetic. However, integers can be used for many business problems. This is illustrated simply in the following example. Suppose we wish to store a set of numbers representing the balance, in dollars and cents, of the accounts at a bank. Forty-two dollars and thirteen cents is usually written in the form $42.13; that is, as a fixed-point number with two places after the decimal point. Equally well, we could write it as 4213 cents. Both forms mean the same thing. When we store the number in our computer, we will store +0004213. We can think of this either as an integer, representing the number of cents, or as a fixed-point number with two digits after the point, representing the number of dollars.

2.5.3 Floating-Point Numbers

In many scientific calculations, use of fixed-point numbers is not convenient because the range of such numbers is inadequate. In one calculation we may wish to use numbers such as the speed of light—about 30,000,000,000 centimeters per second—and distances on the order of atomic spacings—about .00000001 centimeters. If numbers in this range were to be represented in fixed point, we would need to use at least nineteen digits of precision. Since a computer's cost is partially proportional to the precision of the numbers it can store and manipulate, we do not want to pay for a computer with more precision than is necessary.

To save writing, scientists frequently express their numbers in a more compact form, giving the nonzero digits of each number and saying where the decimal point is to appear. The two numbers given above might be written as

$$.3 \times 10^{11}$$

and

$$.1 \times 10^{-7}$$

The value of the number is the product of the power of ten and the fraction part. The latter represents the number of places the point must be moved. Thus, the number 30000000000 can be written as a fraction part of .3 multiplied by ten to the power 11. This means that the decimal point must be moved eleven places to the right to get 30000000000 from .3. The number .00000001 is represented as $.1 \times 10^{-7}$, meaning that the decimal point in .1 is to be moved seven places to the left to get the actual value of the number. We call this *floating-point* or *scientific* notation for numbers. The power of ten— that is, the number of spaces the decimal point must be moved— is called the *exponent*. The fraction part is called the *mantissa*.

We can use the eight digits in a memory word of our computer to represent floating-point numbers by storing the fraction in some of the digits and the exponent in other digits. We will use two digits for the exponent and six for the fraction. Since we will want to use positive and negative numbers, one of the six must be a sign. Therefore, we use the format in Figure 2.11 for floating-point number representation. The fraction is assumed to have a decimal point before its first digit.

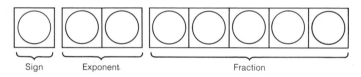

Fig. 2.11   Floating-point format

Since we use only two digit positions for the exponent, it looks as if we are restricted to values between 00 and 99. But recall that in one of the examples above we needed a negative exponent. What shall we do? If we use the first of the exponent digits as a sign we would only be able to store exponent values with a range ±9, which would not be a wide enough range for most applications. Therefore, we use a trick to avoid having to store the sign. We allow exponent values to lie between −50 and +49. These values are stored by first adding 50 to get a value between 0 and 99 that can be stored. Thus if the exponent is actually −21, we add the constant 50 to it and get 29, a number we can store. In the same way, if the exponent is 17, we get 67 by adding 50. The number we obtain by adding 50 is called the *characteristic*. On different computers, a constant other than 50 may be used. The result is still called the characteristic. To know what exponent it represents, we must know the value of the constant added.

Using this method of data representation, we can store floating-point numbers in our computer as follows:

The number	is stored as
30000000000	+ 6 1 3 0 0 0 0
.00000001	+ 4 3 1 0 0 0 0
−12.47	− 5 2 1 2 4 7 0
−.0014752	− 4 8 1 4 7 5 2

Interpretation of a Memory Word

We see that a word in the computer can be used to represent several different types of quantities. First we used the eight digits to represent seven-digit integers with a sign; then in Section 2.4 we used the eight digits to represent an instruction consisting of an operation and its operand address. Now we are using the same set of eight digits to represent floating-point numbers. How does the computer know what a word in memory, that is, a set of eight digits, represents? There is no way to know whether the eight digits 01012345 represent the integer +1012345 (using the first digit 0 to represent a plus sign), the operation STORE into address 12345 (using the first three digits 010 to represent the STORE operation), or the floating-point number $+.12345 \times 10^{-40}$ (using the two digits 10 to represent the characteristic 10, which is the same as an exponent of −40). The meaning of the contents of a memory cell is determined solely by its use.

If we execute an instruction from the cell with address 10423, we are assuming that the content of that cell represents an instruction. The control unit of the computer will interpret the content in that way by taking the first three digits as an operation code and the last five digits as an operand address for the operation. If we had made an error and stored, say, an integer in that cell, then the control unit would try to execute that integer as an instruction by using the sign and first digit as an instruction code and the last five digits as an operand address. Since not all 1000 different combinations of the first three digits are defined as operation codes, it is possible that the first three digits may not be a valid code. If they are not, the computer will stop executing our program. (It will take an action to be described in Chapter 4.)

Thus the cells of the memory can be used to store any type of information. One area of memory might be designated to store the instructions of the program, another to store the data. Some of this data may consist of integers, others may consist of floating-point numbers. In the programming languages discussed in the supplementary texts and in the flowchart language discussed in this text, we will specify the type of data involved in statements such as A ← B + C. The type of data determines the precise meaning of the operations such as addition. However, the machine language program must tell the computer which is which. This is done by providing separate operations for integer and floating-point arithmetic. The computer can execute the FLOATING POINT ADD operation as well as the ADD operation that does integer arithmetic.

Range and Precision in Floating Point

What are the range and precision of floating-point numbers? In our simple computer, the exponent can be as large as 49, since the characteristic can be as large as 99. The fraction part of the number can lie between $\pm.99999$. Therefore the number can be as large as $+.99999 \times 10^{49}$ or as small as $-.99999 \times 10^{49}$. If an arithmetic operation would give an arithmetic result with an exponent larger than 49, it would be impossible to represent that exponent in the accumulator; an *overflow* would have occurred. (This usually stops the process of the calculation. More will be said of this in Chapter 4.) If we tried to multiply the numbers $.500000 \times 10^{34}$ and $.25000 \times 10^{27}$ (to obtain an answer of $.12500 \times 10^{61}$), the computer would give an overflow indication because it would be unable to store the result. Similarly, trying to divide $-.75000 \times 10^{32}$ by $.25000 \times 10^{-17}$ (which yields an answer of $-.30000 \times 10^{50}$) would cause an overflow.

Floating-point numbers in our computer contain five digits in the fraction, so we say that the precision is five *significant digits*. The result of arithmetic operations may require more than five significant digits. For example, if we add $.12345 \times 10^2$ and $.31246 \times 10^1$, we can put them in a fixed-point form to get

$$12.345$$
$$+3.1246$$

which gives the answer 15.4696. This requires six significant digits for exact representation. Since our computer has only five digits, one must be discarded. The simplest rule is simply to chop off the last digit. This is called *truncation*. To store any number in floating point by truncation, we ignore all except the first five digits of the number. Thus:

The number	is truncated to	which is stored as
$+123.456789$	$+.12345 \times 10^3$	05312345
$-.0023415673$	$-.23415 \times 10^{-2}$	14823415
23.0	$+.23000 \times 10^2$	05223000
$+.02 \times 10^{-2}$	$+.20000 \times 10^{-3}$	04720000
26.546×10^{49}	is too large to be stored	

When we use floating-point numbers, we are attempting to represent all possible numbers between minus infinity and plus infinity (mathematically these are called the *real numbers*). Because there are only a finite number of combinations of the eight digits in a computer word, we can only represent some of this infinite set of real numbers. We have seen that numbers whose *magnitude* (that is, the value of the number when its sign is set to be positive) is greater than 10^{49} cannot be represented, and that if the decimal form of the number has more than five digits it cannot be represented exactly in floating point. The numbers that can be represented exactly can be thought of as a set of marks on the real number line. Some of these numbers are shown in Figure 2.12. If we wish to store the number $X = 2.3417689$, we have seen that we can truncate it to get 2.3417. This corresponds to moving to the first mark closer to zero than the position of X in Figure 2.12. However, the mark at 2.3418 is closer to X than is the mark at 2.3417. We would usually be happier to use the closest approximation for X. The step of choosing the closest representable number as an approximation to the number to be stored is called *rounding*. The rule we can use is to first chop off (truncate) all but the first five digits, and then, if what is discarded starts with the digit 5 or larger, add one to the rightmost digit of the first five digits. Thus, 34.56891 becomes $34.568 + .001$, which is 34.569 or $.34569 \times 10^2$ in floating-point representation.

Fig. 2.12 Representable numbers

Some examples of rounding are:

The number	is rounded to	which is stored as
−123.456789	$-.12346 \times 10^3$	15312346
+456742.13	$+.45674 \times 10^6$	05645674
−.000645785	$-.64579 \times 10^{-3}$	14764579
+.99999721	$+.10000 \times 10^1$	05110000
−.999991	$-.99999 \times 10^0$	15099999
$+.0000000001 \times 10^{-50}$	$+.00000 \times 10^{-50}$	00000000

The last case is a special one, because the *magnitude* of the number is too small to be represented in our memory. Its exponent would be −59 if the fraction were to be stored as .10000. Since the smallest exponent that can be handled is −50, we cannot represent the number in our computer. It is possible to represent a number as small as $.00001 \times 10^{-50}$ by the word 00000001; anything smaller than that is too small to represent, so we must store zero.

The result of an arithmetic operation may be too small to represent in the computer, in which case the computer should give the result of zero. Thus, if we multiply $.50000 \times 10^{-26}$ by $.40000 \times 10^{-25}$ we should get $.20000 \times 10^{-6}$. This is too small, so the computed answer should be zero. The term *underflow* refers to this loss of significant digits because the exponent cannot be made small enough.

In general, the result of floating-point operations is not exact because the result is rounded or truncated. (Which is used depends on the particular computer being used. More will be said about the importance of rounding versus truncation in Chapter 6.) We will assume that our computer rounds the result of its floating-point instructions.

A number such as .00022 can be represented several ways in five-digit floating point. It could be stored as $.00022 \times 10^0$, $.00220 \times 10^{-1}$, $.02200 \times 10^{-2}$ or $.22000 \times 10^{-3}$. The latter form with the smallest possible exponent is called the *normalized form*. Floating-point arithmetic produces normalized results in most computers.

2.5.4 Machine Language for Floating Point

Previously we introduced the integer operations ADD, SUB, MPY, and DIV. These assumed that any data in the accumulator represented an integer, and that any data in a cell addressed by an instruction also contained an integer. We also have floating-point numbers. Therefore we assign the following operation codes:

Instruction abbreviation	Code	Meaning
FADD	420	Add the number in memory to the number in the accumulator in floating-point representation.
FSUB	430	Subtract the number in memory from the number in the accumulator in floating-point representation.
FMPY	440	Multiply the number in the accumulator by the number from the memory in floating-point representation.
FDIV	450	Divide the number in the accumulator by the number from the memory in floating-point representation.

The instruction LOAD can work equally well with integers or floating-point numbers, since it causes the contents of the accumulator to be set to the contents of the memory cell addressed without changing the eight digits brought from memory in any way. Thus, if location A contains the set of digits 14235519, the instruction LOAD A sets the accumulator to hold 14235519, regardless of what this set of eight digits is being used to represent. We call this a *copy* operation as it simply copies without change. The instruction STORE is also a copy operation and can be used for integer or floating-point arithmetic.

The floating-point instructions are obeyed by the control unit in a manner different from that in which it obeys integer instructions. Suppose that location A contains 04922300 and location B contains 15110251. The instruction LOAD A would set the accumulator to contain 04922300. The instruction ADD B would interpret the accumulator as +4922300 and add −5110251 to it, resulting in

$$
\begin{array}{r}
+4922300 \\
-5110251 \\
\hline
-0187951
\end{array}
$$

which would be left in the accumulator as 10187951. If, on the other hand, we executed LOAD A followed by FADD B, the second instruction would interpret the contents of the accumulator as $+.22300 \times 10^{49-50}$ or as $+.0223$. It would also interpret the contents of location B as $-.10251 \times 10^{51-50}$ or as -1.0251. The floating add would then get the answer

$$
\begin{array}{r}
-1.0251 \\
+ .0223 \\
\hline
-1.0028
\end{array}
$$

This would be represented in the accumulator by 15110028, meaning $-.10028 \times 10^{51-50}$.

Some simple examples of computations using floating-point numbers are given below. You should note that they are similar to the corresponding programs for integer computations, but floating-point instructions are substituted for the integer instructions given earlier.

(a) $\qquad$ $C \leftarrow A + B$

```
LOAD   A
FADD   B
STORE  C
```

(b) $\qquad$ $Z \leftarrow \dfrac{U + V}{D - E}$

```
LOAD   D
FSUB   E
STORE  TEMP
LOAD   U
FADD   V
FDIV   TEMP
STORE  Z
```

(c) $\qquad$ $H \leftarrow E \times (F + G)$

```
LOAD   F
FADD   G
FMPY   E
STORE  H
```

The rules for the basic floating-point instructions are as follows:

FADD and FSUB

Put the numbers into fixed-point form and align them so the decimal points are under each other. Perform the addition or subtraction and retain the leftmost five digits of the result. Check the first ignored digit. If it is five or greater, then add one to the fifth digit of the answer. Store the five digits that result from this step into the accumulator with the appropriate sign, and form a characteristic from the position of the point in the answer.‡

Examples

(a)   15514638 + 05253416

represents

$$-.14638 \times 10^5 + .53416 \times 10^2$$

We write these as

$$
\begin{array}{r}
-14638 \\
+ \quad 53.416 \\
\hline
-14584.584
\end{array}
$$

which rounds to −14585 and is stored as 15514585.

(b)   09957643 − 19976453

represents

$$+.57643 + 10^{49} - (-.76453 \times 10^{49})$$

We write this as

$$
\begin{array}{rl}
+57643 & \text{followed by 44 zeros} \\
- \;\; -76453 & \text{followed by 44 zeros} \\
\hline
+134096 & \text{followed by 44 zeros}
\end{array}
$$

This is rounded to 13410 followed by 45 zeros, or $.13410 \times 10^{50}$; since this is too large to store in the computer, overflow occurs.

(c)   04623451 + 14623473

represents

$$+.23451 \times 10^{-4} + (-.23473 \times 10^{-4})$$

We write this as

$$
\begin{array}{r}
.000023451 \\
+ \; -.000023473 \\
\hline
-.000000022
\end{array}
$$

This is normalized to $-.22 \times 10^{-7}$ and stored as 14322000.

---

‡The actual technique used for rounding is to add .000005 with the appropriate exponent to the magnitude of the result of the addition, and then to truncate. Thus the rounded form of 14584.584 is found by the step

$$
\begin{array}{ll}
.14584584 \times 10^5 & \\
+ .000005 \quad\; \times 10^5 & \\
\hline
.14585084 \times 10^5 & \text{Rounded result: } .14585 \times 10^5
\end{array}
$$

FMPY and FDIV

To perform these operations, we first remove the exponents and perform the operations on the fractional parts. The exponent of the answer is found by adding the exponents of the two operands (the numbers in the accumulator and the memory cell addressed) in the case of multiplication, or by subtracting the exponent of the number in memory from that of the number in the accumulator in the case of division. The fractional part is then rounded to five significant digits—which may require that the exponent of the answer be changed. The result is then stored into the accumulator.

Examples

(a) 04912345×14810001

represents

$$(+.12345 \times 10^{-1}) \times (-.10001 \times 10^{-2})$$

We write this as

$$-(.12345 \times .10001) \times 10^{(-1) + (-2)}$$
$$= -.0123462345 \times 10^{-3}$$

If we did not normalize, we would have the result $-.01234 \times 10^{-3}$, but by normalizing we can get $-.12346 \times 10^{-4}$, which has one more digit of significance and accuracy.

(b) $05122444 / 04911000$

represents

$$(.22444 \times 10^{1})/(.11000 \times 10^{-1})$$

We write this as

$$(.22444 / .11000) \times 10^{1-(-1)}$$
$$= 2.04036 \ldots \times 10^{2}$$

which is normalized, rounded, and stored as 05320404.

2.5.5 CHARACTER DATA

In some of the examples discussed in Chapter 1 we talked about data such as the names in a telephone list. This type of data consists of sequences of letters, spaces, and other special characters. So far we have seen how to represent integers, instructions, and floating-point numbers. We also need to be able to store *character strings* in memory. A character string is a sequence of any of the characters that can be handled by the computer. Each cell of eight digits, each digit of which can be set to one of ten positions, can take on 10×10

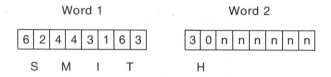

Fig. 2.13 A character string

$\times$ 10 $\times$ 10 $\times$ 10 $\times$ 10 $\times$ 10 $\times$ 10 $\times$ 10 different combinations, or 100,000,000 different settings. Since we can use memory cells to store anything we wish, we can assign a character to each combination. In this way, we could handle up to 100,000,000 different characters and use one computer word for each character. Thus, the name SMITH could be represented using five words in memory—one for each character.

Fortunately, we do not wish to use 100,000,000 different characters; most computers handle 48 or 63. See, for example, the card pictured in Figure 2.6. It shows 62 printing characters plus the blank character. Therefore it is wasteful to use so many digits to represent each character. Instead we could use just two digits, with 100 different combinations, to represent a character. If we do this, we can store four characters in one word, using the first two digits for the first character, the next two for the second, and so on. The name SMITH could be stored in one and one-quarter words. If the digit combinations for the letters S, M, I, T, and H are 62, 44, 31, 63, and 30, respectively, then the name SMITH could be stored in two words as 62443163 and 30*nnnnnn* (the digits *nnnnnn* are not required for a five-character string).

If the numbers representing the characters are arranged so that the later characters in the alphabet are represented by larger numbers than those representing the earlier characters, we can test for alphabetical order by testing for numerical order. Thus, SMIT is represented by 62443163 while SMIH is represented by 62443130. Since the latter number is less than the former, SMIH precedes SMIT alphabetically.

Most computers have a special set of operations for dealing with character strings. These instructions include tests for equality and alphabetic order, and other operations to be discussed later. Two major points to be emphasized at this stage are that character strings can be represented in memory using the same digits used to represent numbers and instructions, and that simple operations can be performed on characters. The most important operations are concerned with alphabetical ordering and testing for equality.

There is general agreement on what is meant by alphabetical order for the letters A through Z. To be able to make a test on all characters that can be represented in the computer, we must agree on an order of the nonalphabetic characters. The ordering of all characters allowed in the computer is called the *collating sequence*. It varies from one computer to another. A typical collating sequence is: blank (lowest), alphabetic characters A to Z, numerals 0 to 9, and special characters.

2.5.6 Logical Data

The idea of the control structure of a problem was mentioned in the introduction, and Section 2.4 discussed the control unit of a computer. The control unit executes an instruction by sending commands to other units, such as the CPU, and then decides which instruction to execute next. Some operations, such as BGE (branch if greater than or equal to zero) are concerned only with the control of the program. The control structure of the problem is handled by such instructions. For example, suppose the problem statement says, in part, "If the account balance is negative, send a nasty letter, otherwise update the account," we may expect to find a test of the form

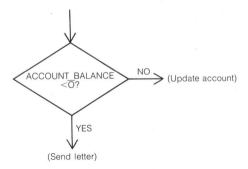

In this example, the value of the account balance is being used to control the program flow, although it is undoubtedly also being used in many arithmetic calculations. In some problems we find variables that are being used primarily to control the problem or program flow. For example, a spacecraft control computer might use a variable that is set to zero while the spacecraft is descending to the moon (and the computer is slowing it down), but set to one while it is ascending from the moon back to earth. Such a variable is a *control variable*. Since the control unit of the computer can make a two-way test (to branch or not to branch), the easiest type of control variable to use is one that takes on just two values, say zero or one. Such a variable is called a *logical variable*, and its two values are called *false* and *true*. (Frequently, the control structure of a program is called the *program logic*.)

Logical variables take on only two values, so only two states of a

71

computer word are used in their representation. *False* is usually represented by a zero and *true* by a one. Any of the eight digits in our computer word could be used to store a logical variable (or several could be packed into one word, just as we could pack four characters into one word). In our computer, the easiest digit to test is the sign; we can use the BGE operation. If the sign is zero (false), the transfer is executed, so BGE can also be used as a "branch if false." If the identical condition has to be tested frequently, it is usually worth forming a logical variable whose value is the value of the condition. For example, if the test A > B has to be made many times for unchanged values of A and B, we could find the logical value of "A > B" and test that value. In machine language this means that we can form L = B − A, which has a minus sign (true) if A > B and a positive sign (false) otherwise, and then test the sign of L with the BGE operation each time we wish to know if A > B is true. In Section 3.4 we will see how the logical variable can be specified by

$$L \leftarrow A > B$$

and we will discuss other logical operations that can be performed on logical data.

EXERCISES

1. Put the following numbers into the floating-point representation used in our computer:

   *a. −12.521
   b. .00037245
   c. 253.24×10^6

2. Give the internal floating-point representation in our computer of the following numbers (remember to round):

   *a. 45.46571
   b. −375.625
   c. -2.654315×10^{-2}

   Which of these would be stored differently if truncation were used instead?

3. Give the internal normalized form of the following numbers:

   *a. 25.3
   b. −0.005
   c. $+24.5 \times 10^5$

4. The following are internal forms of floating-point numbers that are not normalized. Give their internal forms after normalization.

   *a. 14600273
   b. 05402801
   c. 03900001
   What is their value in scientific notation?

5. Suppose locations A and B contain 15212301 and 05211012, respectively. Give the internal form of A + B, A − B, A × B, and A/B if these operations are performed in floating point, assuming that A and B contain floating-point data, and give the internal form of A + B if the addition is done in integer arithmetic, assuming that A and B contain integer data.

Questions

1. Give examples of pairs of numbers A and B in internal form such that

   a. A × B overflows in integer arithmetic
   *b. A × B overflows in floating-point arithmetic
   c. A/B   overflows in floating-point arithmetic
   *d. A + B overflows in integer arithmetic
   e. A + B overflows in floating-point arithmetic
   f. A × B underflows in floating-point arithmetic
   g. A/B   underflows in floating-point arithmetic

Problems

*1. If floating-point zero is always stored in a normalized form, do we need a special floating-point test for zero in the accumulator, or can we use an integer zero test in our hypothetical computer?

2. Does your answer to problem 1 remain true if numbers are not always normalized?

3. Show that

$$
\begin{array}{ll}
\text{LOAD} & \text{A} \\
\text{SUB} & \text{B} \\
\text{BGE} & \text{X}
\end{array}
$$

will transfer to X if A ≥ B if A and B are either both integers or both normalized floating-point numbers provided that the answer to A − B is in range as an integer.

2.6 SYSTEM PROGRAMS

In this text we will represent computer programs by means of flow-charts. In practice, programs are written in one of a number of languages, such as FORTRAN, PL/I, ALGOL, BASIC, or COBOL, which are very similar to our flowchart language. You will be learning one or more of these languages from course supplements. However, we have seen that the computer actually executes a numerically-coded language called *machine language*. Because a computer can manipulate character strings, a program can be written to read statements in a language such as FORTRAN and translate them into machine-language sequences. This is called *compilation*; a program that does this is called a *compiler*. A compiler is an important system program that will be studied in more detail in Chapter 4.

We have been writing instructions at the machine level in a symbolic form. This form is an example of another language called *assembly language*. Assembly language can also be translated into machine language by a system program. This program is called an *assembler*.

We do not normally program directly in machine language because it is too tedious. Consequently, all program input is under the control of system programs such as compilers and assemblers. The overall process of translation and execution of a program is shown in Figure 2.14.

First we will give precise rules for writing assembly language and punching it on cards; then we will discuss very briefly how the assembler works.

2.6.1 ASSEMBLY LANGUAGE

An instruction written in assembly language consists of three parts: a *location address*, an *operation code*, and an *operand address*. These are written on one line in the order given. So that the assembler can tell where one part stops and the next starts, the parts must be separated by one or more blanks, and no blanks may be used inside a part. Thus, if we want the instruction LOAD Q to appear in location Z, we will write

    Z LOAD Q

The address Z can then be used in a conditional or unconditional branch instruction. If we are not going to want to reference an instruction, we do not need to give a location address. Instead we can leave the first part blank, for example,

    Z LOAD Q
       ADD   R

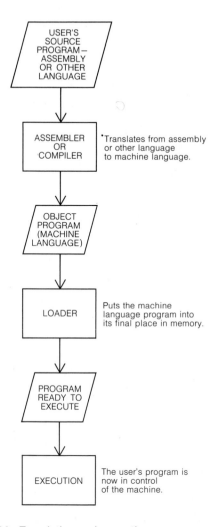

Fig. 2.14 Translation and execution

We have left some blanks in front of the ADD instruction to indicate that there is no location address. Since we do not mind how many blanks are left between the parts of an instruction in assembly language, it is conventional to use fixed columns on the card to start punching each part. We might, for example, use columns 1 through 6 for the location address if there is one, columns 10 through 14 for the operation code, and columns 16 on as far as necessary for the operand address. The program is read into the computer from punched cards, but the programmer usually writes on a coding

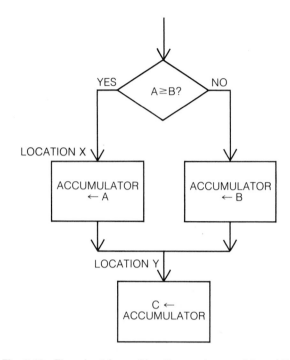

Fig. 2.15 Flowchart for putting the maximum of A and B into C

form marked in columns. A keypunch operator can then punch the cards from this form. The program given in Figure 2.15, which puts the maximum of the integers A and B into location C, is written on a typical coding form in Figure 2.16. The operation code punched in columns 10 through 15 is an abbreviation for the operation decided by the people who designed the assembler. It consists of from one to five upper-case letters. The location and operand addresses are chosen by the programmer. He usually selects names that have some significance. Thus he might use TEMP for a location used for temporary storage and LARGE for a location that holds the largest of a set of numbers.

What restrictions are put on the characters that may be used in names? In some cases we may wish to use a numeric address such as 76, so it is unreasonable to use character strings that can be interpreted as numbers. For this reason the names of locations must start with a letter. For reasons that will be more apparent later, they may contain only upper-case letters and digits. To make the job of the assembler easier, names are restricted to contain not more than six characters. Thus, some valid names are X, A2ER, CYCLES, A12345. Invalid names include:

| Program | SAMPLE ASSEMBLY LANGUAGE STATEMENTS | Page | of |
| Programmer | C ⟵ MAX (A, B) | Date | |

Name		Operation					Operand			
1	8	10	14	16	20	25		30	35	40
		LOAD		A						
		SUB		B						
		BGE		X						
		LOAD		B						
		BRNCH		Y						
X		LOAD		A						
Y		STORE		C						

Fig. 2.16 Assembly language statements for Fig. 2.15

A123456	(Too many characters)
1ABC	(Does not start with a letter)
abcd	(Does not use upper-case letters)
A + B	(Uses other than letters and digits)

Each name used as an address must be defined to be equivalent to a numerical address in some way. Since the computer executes instructions in sequence from the memory until a branch instruction is encountered, the successive lines of our program must be put into successive locations in memory. Since it does not matter to us where the program is placed, we will assume that the assembler starts assembling the program into location 0 and places successive instructions into successive locations. Consider a program to read the two numbers A and B, form A + B if B is positive or A − B if B is negative, assign the result to C, and print C. A flowchart for this is shown in Figure 2.17 and the equivalent program is shown below.

	Program		Comments	Actual Location Address
	READ	A	READ DATA	0
	READ	B		1
	LOAD	B		2
	BGE	X		3
	LOAD	A		4
	SUB	B	FORM A − B	5
	BRNCH	Y		6
X	LOAD	A		7
	ADD	B	FORM A + B	8
Y	STORE	C	STORE RESULT IN C	9
	PRINT	C	PRINT ANSWER	10
	STOP			11

(The STOP operation shown above stops execution of our program.) Each line of the program will be placed in a location with an address one larger than that of the previous line. Thus the location address for X is 7; the location address for Y is 9. Therefore the instruction BRNCH Y will be assembled as 300 00009 since the operation code for BRNCH is 300 and the address Y is 9. The assembler can find the numerical equivalent of each name used as an address by finding in which location address it appears. This enables the assembler to find equivalents for X and Y in the above example. How can it decide which locations to use for A, B, and C? We will assume that our assembler will look at the program we write and assign locations immediately after our program to all otherwise undefined names. Thus in this case it would assign the names A, B, and C to be equivalent to locations 12, 13, and 14, respectively.

Our assembler has other useful features. One is a way to define constants. For example, we might want to use the constant 2 in our program in a location to be called TWO. We will write this as

TWO   DC   2

The DC that appears where an operation code is expected tells the assembler that it is to Define a Constant. The constant appears in the operand address columns. Thus if we wanted to read the number A, double it, and print it, we would write the program

READ   A
LOAD   A
MPY   TWO

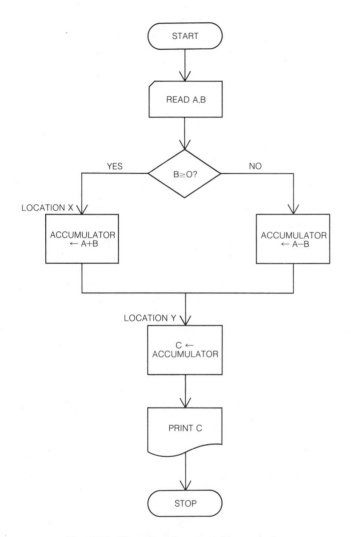

Fig. 2.17 Flowchart for assembly example

```
          STORE   TEMP
          PRINT   TEMP
          STOP
  TWO     DC      2
          END
```

(We could perfectly well have used the name THREE for the constant 2; this would not have changed the program—just made it more difficult for a person to understand.)

79

A second assembler feature is in the last line of the program above, the name END appearing in the operation columns. It is a special operation to tell the assembler that this is the end of the program. Without this, the assembler would continue reading cards.

2.6.2 ASSEMBLING A PROGRAM

An assembler reads an assembly-language program from an input device and translates it, a line at a time, into machine language. To do this, the assembler must have a table containing the symbolic forms of the operations and their numerical equivalents. Thus when it reads a line, it can look up the operation (just as we looked up a person's name in the telephone number search example in Chapter 1) and put the numerical equivalent of the operation into a word. It must also have a table of all names used by the programmer as location addresses and their equivalent numerical addresses. It can then add the numerical address to the instruction word. To get this table of names it must read the program once and construct such a table. Thus the assembly process requires that the program be read twice: a first time to build a table of all names used and store the numerical address equivalent to each name and a second time to translate the instructions into machine language. The two passes through the program could be made possible by requiring the computer operator to put the same deck of cards through twice. However, the assembler usually reads the deck the first time, stores it in memory (since the memory can be used to store character strings), and then reads the copy in memory on the second pass. The machine-language instructions created by the assembler are stored somewhere in the machine so that the loader program can place them in their proper place after the assembly process has finished. Most assemblers also make it possible for the user to get a copy of the machine-language form of the assembled program punched out on cards. This copy can be used for later computer runs by reading it back to memory from the card reader.

EXERCISES

1. Which of the following are valid names of locations?

   *a. ABC
   *b. 1B
   c. ABCDEFG
   d. X12345
   e. AB+

Questions

1. What does an assembler do for a programmer?

*2. Why is ''assembler'' an appropriate choice for the name of the system program we have been discussing?

Problems

1. How many passes does our assembler need and why?

2. Why should we not use the same location name for more than one instruction?

2.7 Binary and Hexadecimal Data Representation

We have described the memory of our computer in terms of dials, each of which holds one decimal digit. In practice, electronic and magnetic devices are used to store information. Usually each of these very small devices has only two states. For example, a transistor can be conducting electricity or not conducting electricity; a magnetic device can be magnetized in one direction or in the opposite direction. (It is possible to have partial currents or partial magnetization, but this would lead to the accuracy problem we had when we tried to use in-between positions of a dial to represent numbers in an analog fashion.) Thus basic memory elements are like dials that can only be set in two positions, or like OFF-ON switches. We can label the states 0 for OFF and 1 for ON. Unfortunately, with one such switch we can only count from 0 to 1. How do we represent a decimal digit that can take on ten different states?

Consider all the positions of two switches as shown in Figure 2.18. Four combinations are shown. It is evident that if we added a third switch we could have each of these four combinations with the third switch OFF and then each of these combinations with it ON to get a total of double the number of combinations, namely eight. Similarly a fourth switch would bring us to sixteen combinations. Thus with four switches we have more than enough combinations to store one decimal digit.

We need to assign settings of the four switches to represent the ten decimal digits. The usual method is *binary representation*. Since the state of one switch can be zero or one, we can think of it as representing a digit with this value. Since this digit can only take on two values, we call it a binary digit (abbreviated to *bit*).

In decimal representation, each digit can take ten different values,

State of AB   00   01   10   11

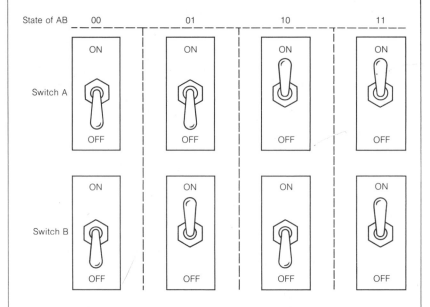

Fig. 2.18   States of two switches

labeled 0, 1, 2, . . . , 9. When we use decimal "dials," we form the value of the digits DCBA (where each of D, C, B, and A are single decimal digits) by computing $D \times 1000 + C \times 1000 + B \times 10 + A$. Consider how we get to the number DCBA by starting at 0000 and counting by ones. When the rightmost dial A has been rotated through its ten positions, it can no longer represent any more different numbers because it has no further states. Therefore it is set back to zero and the dial B on its left is rotated through one position. Hence B is used to count the number of times that A has rotated through its ten positions. Therefore B records tens. Similarly the next dial C records the number of times that the tens dial B has rotated through its ten positions, so C records hundreds. By analogy we consider a four-digit binary number ZYXW (that is, a four-bit number). We start at 0000 and count by ones. First we get to 0001. We cannot increase the rightmost digit W any more because it has already used its two states. Therefore, we set it back to zero and advance the bit X on its left by one to get 0010. Thus X records the number of times that the last bit W has been rotated through its two positions. Therefore X records the number of twos. Similarly, after W has been advanced twice more, X must be advanced once, but it cannot be increased beyond one, so it is set back to zero and Y is advanced by one. Thus Y records the number of fours. Similarly, Z records the number of eights.

Thus the number 5 can be converted into binary as follows:

There are no eights in 5, so the first digit is 0.
There is one four in 5, so the next digit is 1.
There are no twos in $5 - 4 = 1$, so the next digit is 0.
There is one one in 1, so the last digit is 1.

Thus 5 is represented by 0101 in binary. The representation of the decimal digits 0 to 9 is shown in Table 2.1.

This representation is called *binary coded decimal*. Note that we could continue counting to fifteen using four bits. The remaining six combinations are shown in Table 2.2.

Since we can represent one decimal digit in four bits, we can represent one of our computer words of eight decimal digits with 32 bits. Each bit could be stored in a single device consisting of one or more transistors. This is how many computers are constructed. The IBM 370, for example, has words that contain 32 bits. In this computer each group of four bits can be used to represent one decimal digit.

TABLE 2.1

BINARY CODED DECIMAL

Decimal	Binary	Representation
0	0000	$= 0 + 0 + 0 + 0$
1	0001	$= 0 + 0 + 0 + 1$
2	0010	$= 0 + 0 + 2 + 0$
3	0011	$= 0 + 0 + 2 + 1$
4	0100	$= 0 + 4 + 0 + 0$
5	0101	$= 0 + 4 + 0 + 1$
6	0110	$= 0 + 4 + 2 + 0$
7	0111	$= 0 + 4 + 2 + 1$
8	1000	$= 8 + 0 + 0 + 0$
9	1001	$= 8 + 0 + 0 + 1$

TABLE 2.2

FURTHER BINARY CODED DECIMAL

10	1010	$= 8 + 0 + 2 + 0$
11	1011	$= 8 + 0 + 2 + 1$
12	1100	$= 8 + 4 + 0 + 0$
13	1101	$= 8 + 4 + 0 + 1$
14	1110	$= 8 + 4 + 2 + 0$
15	1111	$= 8 + 4 + 2 + 1$

We can find the value of a digit in binary representation by simple arithmetic. Since the first bit represents the number of eights in the word, the second the number of fours, and so on, we can say that the value of the four-bit binary number DCBA is 8D + 4C + 2B + A where each of the A, B, C, and D represent one binary digit with value zero or one.

We have noted that there are six more combinations of the four bits that are not used. They are shown in Table 2.2 and take us up to value 15. Apparently we could represent more possibilities if we could make use of these combinations. Using our analogy with dials to represent numbers, it is as if each digital position was represented by a dial that had 16 rather than ten different positions or states. Suppose we wished to store integers in a device consisting of a number of sixteen-position dials. How can we store them so as to use each of the different combinations to represent a different integer? Let us start with four such dials as shown in Figure 2.19. (Remember that in a computer each such "dial" would actually be stored in four binary devices.) We proceed by analogy, with the decimal and binary representations, and consider counting from 0. The rightmost dial records a number between zero and fifteen. Its neighbor on the left records the number of times the rightmost dial has rotated through its sixteen positions, so it records sixteens; the next dial records the number of 16 × 16's, and so forth. Thus, the value of the number shown in Figure 2.22 is $14 \times 16^3 + 10 \times 16^2 + 3 \times 16 + 13$ since the digits reading from left to right are "14," "10," "3," and "13." The smallest integer that can be represented this way is 0000, which is the integer zero. The largest number is "15," "15," "15," "15," ($15 \times 16^3 + 15 \times 16^2 + 15 \times 16 + 15$), which is equal to the integer 65535. Thus by allowing our four dials to take on all possibilities, we can store integers that are about six and a half times larger than the largest integer (9999) we can store when the four dials are restricted to ten decimal positions. This is the reason that many computers use binary representation for numbers. (Although we have grouped the binary digits into fours, it can be shown to be equivalent to letting each binary digit represent the number of ones, twos, fours, eights, sixteens, and so forth, in the number.)

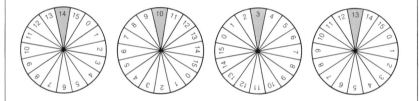

Fig. 2.19 Number '14' '10' '3' '13'

TABLE 2.3

DECIMAL, HEXADECIMAL, AND BINARY

Binary	Decimal	Hexadecimal (Base Sixteen)
1010	10	A
1011	11	B
1100	12	C
1101	13	D
1110	14	E
1111	15	F

When the binary digits are grouped into fours so that each group represents a number between zero and fifteen, we say that we have a *hexadecimal* digit or *base-sixteen* digit. The Arabic numerals we use have representations for the decimal digits zero through nine, so we must either write the hexadecimal digits ten through fifteen using two decimal digits or use other symbols. The latter makes it easier to print the numbers, so we often use the letters A through F for the hexadecimal digits ten through fifteen. The correspondence is shown in Table 2.3. Using this notation, the number in Figure 2.19 is EA3D in base sixteen.

We can convert integers from base sixteen to base ten by using the formula

$$ZYXW \text{ base } 16 = Z \times 16^3 + Y \times 16^2 + X \times 16 + W$$
$$= Z \times 4096 + Y \times 256 + X \times 16 + W$$

Base ten numbers (our usual form) can be converted to base sixteen by division by 16. Consider the decimal number 14943. Suppose it is represented by ZYXW base 16. Then we have the identity

$$14943 = Z \times 4096 + Y \times 256 + X \times 16 + W$$

If we divide by 16 in integer arithmetic we get

$$\frac{14943}{16} = \frac{Z \times 4096 + Y \times 256 + X \times 16 + W}{16}$$

or   933, remainder 15 = $Z \times 256 + Y \times 16 + X$, remainder W.

Hence W = 15, and

$$933 = Z \times 256 + Y \times 16 + X$$

Dividing by 16 again we get

$$58, \text{ remainder } 5 = Z \times 16 + Y, \text{ remainder } X$$

85

or $\qquad$ X = 5 and 58 = Z × 16 + Y

Dividing by 16 again, we get

$\qquad$ 3, remainder 10 = Z, remainder Y

or $\qquad$ Y = 10 and Z = 3

Hence the hexadecimal equivalent of 14943 is 3A5F.

Fortunately, most of us do not need to work with binary or hexadecimal numbers. The conversion rules are simple and are performed by the computer. Most languages we use allow us to write our numbers in a decimal form, even if the computer uses hexadecimal internally. Effects we need to be concerned about are:

- The increased range of numbers possible with hexadecimal integers,

- The increased precision possible in hexadecimal floating point (to be mentioned below),

- The fact that conversion takes computer time and so we should avoid situations in which more time is spent converting than in performing useful arithmetic (particularly applicable to a computer that can perform both decimal and hexadecimal arithmetic.)

Integer Representation

We have already seen how to represent positive integers. We also need to indicate a sign. In our eight-digit hypothetical computer we used one digit for a sign for decimal numbers. Since this one digital position can take on one of sixteen different values, it is wasteful to use only two of them. Therefore, when we store hexadecimal integers we will use one bit of the first hexadecimal position to represent the sign, 0 for + and 1 for −, and the other three bits to represent a number between zero and seven. Then with thirty-two bits we can represent a number in the range ±7FFFFFFF hexadecimal. This is the range

$$\pm(7 \times 16^7 + 15 \times 16^6 + 15 \times 16^5 + 15 \times 16^4 + 15 \times 16^3 + 15 \times 16^2 + 15 \times 16 + 15)$$

or ±2,147,483,647. (This is the same thing as saying we are using a sign and thirty-one bits. The range is precisely $\pm(2^{31} - 1)$.)

Examples

1. The decimal integer 391 can be converted to hexadecimal by division as follows:

16)391(24 Quotient
 32
 71
 64

Remainder ⑦

16)24(1 Quotient
 16

Remainder ⑧

16)1(0 Quotient
 0

Remainder ①

Hence 391 decimal is 187 hexadecimal. This is represented in our computer as 00000187.

2. The decimal integer −631 can be converted to hexadecimal to get −277. This will be represented in our computer as 80000277. The first digit of this representation is 8, which is 1000 in binary. The leftmost bit is one, which indicates a negative number.

3. The decimal integer $-1,073,741,824 = -2^{30} = -4 \times 16^7$ 1s -40000000 in hexadecimal. This is represented in our computer as C0000000. The first digit of this representation is C, which is 1100 in binary. The leftmost bit represents the negative sign; the remaining three bits represent the digit 4.

Floating Point

In decimal arithmetic we used a part of a word to represent the decimal exponent. Similarly, in a hexadecimal machine, we will use part of the word to represent a *hexadecimal exponent*. A hexadecimal exponent is the number of powers of sixteen by which the fractional part must be multiplied. Just as in decimal floating point, in which we represented a decimal as a fractional part times a power of ten, we will use a hexadecimal fractional part times a power of sixteen. In our hypothetical computer, we will use the last six hexadecimal digits for the fraction. If these are the digits $H_1H_2H_3H_4H_5H_6$, the value of the fraction will be

$$\frac{H_1}{16} + \frac{H_2}{16^2} + \frac{H_3}{16^3} + \frac{H_4}{16^4} + \frac{H_5}{16^5} + \frac{H_6}{16^6}$$

Another way of looking at this value is that it is the hexadecimal integer $H_1H_2H_3H_4H_5H_6$ divided by 16^6, that is, with the hexadecimal point moved left six places. We have used six of the eight digits for the fraction. That leaves two hexadecimal digits or eight bits for the

87

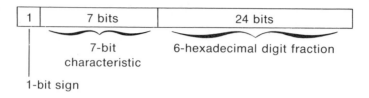

Fig. 2.20   Hexadecimal floating-point format

exponent and the sign of the number. As before, we will use the first bit of the first digit for the sign, leaving seven bits for the exponent. In hexadecimal, these seven bits range from 00 to 7F, which is 0 to 127 in decimal. As in decimal, we store a characteristic rather than an exponent by adding 64 to the actual exponent. Thus, an exponent of -2 is stored as decimal 62, which is hexadecimal 3E. The format of our hexadecimal floating point is shown in Figure 2.20. The exponent range is 16^{-64} to 16^{+63}. The number $+1/2$ could be stored with a characteristic of 64 and a fraction of 1/2, which is 40800000. It could also be stored with a characteristic of 65 and a fraction of 1/32, which is 41080000, although the latter form is not normalized. (In hexadecimal, the normalized form will have a nonzero first digit in the fractional part, unless it is zero, in which case the characteristic and the fractional part will be zero.)

Examples

1. The decimal number $10.25 = 10\ 4/16$ is equivalent to the hexadecimal number A.4. In floating point this is stored as $.A4 \times 16$ and represented by 41A40000. The last six digits of this representation are the fraction .A40000, while the first two are the characteristic 41 hexadecimal $= 65$ decimal. This is 64 plus the exponent.

2. The decimal number $-17.125 = -17\ 2/16$ is equivalent to the hexadecimal number -11.2. In floating point this is stored as $-.112 \times 16^2$ and represented by C2112000. The first digit C is 1100 in binary. The leftmost bit represents the negative sign, while the remaining three represent the first digit (4) of the characteristic 42 hexadecimal $= 66$ decimal.

3. The decimal fraction 1/5 can be converted to hexadecimal as follows. Suppose the hexadecimal form is .ABCD . . . . Then

$$\frac{1}{5} = \frac{A}{16} + \frac{B}{16^2} + \frac{C}{16^3} + \ldots$$

Multiplying by 16 we get

$$\frac{16}{5} = 3\,1/5 = A + \frac{B}{16} + \frac{D}{16^2} + \ldots$$

Since the integer parts are equal, A is 3 and we have

$$\frac{1}{5} = \frac{B}{16} + \frac{C}{16^2} + \frac{D}{16^3} + \cdots$$

Multiplying by 16 again we get B = 3 and

$$\frac{1}{5} = \frac{C}{16} + \frac{D}{16^2} + \frac{E}{16^3} + \cdots$$

Hence

$$\frac{1}{5} \text{ decimal} = .333 \ldots \text{ hexadecimal.}$$

Rounding this to six digits, we represent 1/5 as 40333333.

With hexadecimal representation we have a range of 16^{-64} to 16^{+63}, which is about 10^{-77} to 10^{+76}. Furthermore, the precision is better than one part in 16^5 rather than the one part in 10^4 available in decimal. Thus the range and precision of hexadecimal floating-point numbers are greater. (We should realize, however, that some numbers that can be represented exactly in decimal will not be exact in hexadecimal. Thus, 1/10 in decimal floating point is 05010000 exactly, but in hexadecimal it is approximately 4019999A, because $1/10 = 1/16 + 9/16^2 + 9/16^3 + 9/16^4 + \ldots$.)

Character Representation

In Section 2.5 we suggested that characters could be stored in two digits, allowing for one hundred possibilities. Using the same two digits in hexadecimal, we now have 256 (=16^2) possibilities. Each word of eight hexadecimal digits can represent four such characters. A commonly used name for a group of two hexadecimal digits or eight bits is *byte*. We frequently see memory sizes quoted in bytes. Thus a computer may have 32K bytes. The K is an abbreviation for Kilo. In scientific usage, Kilo means 1,000, but in most computer usage it means $2^{10} = 1,024$. A memory size of 32K means 32,768 = 2^{15}, since binary or hexadecimal machines will usually have a memory size that is a power of 2, for engineering reasons.

A computer may be designed to operate on hexadecimal numbers internally. In that case, the integer arithmetic instructions, such as ADD, will perform arithmetic on integers represented in hexadecimal, while floating-point instructions, such as FADD, will operate on hexadecimal floating-point numbers and character comparison operations will compare characters with 256 possibilities. However, we can, for the most part, ignore these differences. An integer is an integer regardless of the way in which it is represented, and the results of arithmetic operations are the same—except for some minor questions of range and precision in floating-point arithmetic.

89

EXERCISES

1. Convert the following decimal integers into hexadecimal integers:

   *a. 1023
   b. 3627
   c. 769
   d. −2715

2. Convert the following hexadecimal integers to decimal integers:

   *a. 3F2
   b. −18A
   c. FF
   d. 127

3. Convert the following decimal integers into our computer's internal hexadecimal form, first as an integer, then as a normalized floating-point number:

   *a. 127
   b. −91
   c. 571
   d. −85

4. What is the largest integer that can be stored in three hexadecimal digits?

5. Convert the following decimal fractions into our computer form of hexadecimal normalized floating point (round where necessary).

   *a. 3/8
   b. 71/64
   *c. 1/3
   d. 4/5

QUESTIONS

1. Give a reason why computers often use hexadecimal rather than decimal.

PROBLEMS

1. At a fishhook factory, the foreman was instructed to place 1000 hooks in 10 boxes. The boss wanted the hooks stored in a way so that, if a certain number of hooks were requested, the fore-

man could quickly bring out one or more boxes and deliver that exact amount without opening the boxes. How many hooks were in each of the 10 boxes?

*2. What is the maximum number of hooks that can be placed in 10 boxes so that it is still possible to get any amount up to that number without opening boxes?

Flowchart Language I

3. Flowchart Language I

When we solve a problem with the definition of an algorithm, we must communicate that algorithm using a language. So far we have seen the use of three different languages for the expression of algorithms. In Chapter I we used the English language and flowcharts. Neither of these were very precisely defined. In Chapter 2 we saw that the algorithm is communicated to the hardware in machine language. This *is* very precisely defined.

Computer language is used to communicate; we may be communicating an algorithm to other people or we may be communicating it to a computer. The type of language used for this process depends on the purpose of the communication. In the final instance we wish that a computer should execute the algorithm. Since the only language understood by a computer is its machine language, an algorithm must ultimately be expressed in that language. However, we have seen that a translator can convert an algorithm written in other languages into one written in machine language. These languages are more comprehensible to a person than machine language so that it is easier to understand a program when it is being written and when it is being corrected or changed.

If a programmer encodes algorithms in a machine-level language he has to be very cognizant of the organization of the computer. Instead of writing "$A \leftarrow B + C \times D$," he has to be concerned with the computer's accumulator, and whether the arithmetic has to be performed on integers or floating-point numbers. These computer details tend to obscure the procedure used in the algorithm; therefore, we often prefer to use languages that omit these details and concentrate mainly on the solution procedure. Such languages are called *high-level languages*. They are also called *procedure oriented languages* (POLs for short). If a system program is available to translate an algorithm written in a POL into the same algorithm written in machine language, we can use that POL to communicate the algorithm to the computer.

If we are going to communicate an algorithm to the computer, it must be input via a machine-readable medium. The usual input is via punched cards or typewritten lines, so most POLs are designed around these. This means that the language may use only a restricted number of characters—usually the decimal digits 0–9, the upper-case letters A–Z, and about twelve to twenty-seven other special characters (see Figure 2.6). Furthermore, the algorithm in a POL must be a sequence of cards or lines. We can view the cards as a sequence of lines—just as assembly-language programs were a sequence of lines—or a long string of characters. Either way, the input appears as one long block of characters.

Even though we may break up the string of characters by judicious use of cards with blanks or comments on them (much as we use paragraphs in this book to break up the text into self-contained

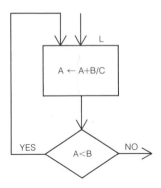

Fig. 3.1 A loop

sub-blocks), a long string of characters does not display the flow structure of the algorithm very clearly. For example, the loop in Figure 3.1 is fairly obvious because it is written in a flowchart language. However, in a language that is written as one sequence of characters or lines (a *linear* language), a loop will have to be encoded by the use of a *transfer* instruction equivalent to the machine language BRNCH. "GO TO" is the PL/I equivalent of a branch instruction. In PL/I the loop would be written as either L:A=A+B/C;IF A<B THEN GO TO L;

or   L: A = A + B/C;

                   IF   A<B   THEN   GO   TO   L;

The latter form has been made a little clearer by the use of spaces and indentation, but it is still necessary for a person to search for the label L to determine that this is a program loop.

We will use flowcharts for stating algorithms in this book. It is relatively easy for a person to follow and to change a procedure expressed as a flowchart. The conversion of flowchart programs to programs written in linear languages is straightforward and is covered in the supplementary texts on specific languages.

Common POL linear languages include FORTRAN, ALGOL, PL/I, and BASIC. Each has slightly different rules for expressing common operations such as assignments and branches. (You will have to refer to a manual for a particular language to find the specific rules for that language.) In this chapter we are going to introduce some precise rules for writing programs in a flowchart language. Since there is no flowchart language that is universally accepted, our rules may differ from rules found in other books. What is important is that you be consistent in whatever rules you adopt. Then your programs will be unambiguous and it will be easy for you to convert your flowchart programs into programs in the POL that you are using.

Flowcharts consist of symbols connected by flowlines. We will call the symbols "boxes" because we will be using the word "symbol" in other contexts. The shape of each box indicates the type of statement that appears inside. In this chapter we will discuss the boxes for assignment, input, output, connection, and decision. These have already been used informally; here we will give rules for their use. The purpose of these rules is to allow us to write algorithms unambiguously. In Chapter 5 we will introduce additional types of statements (i.e., shapes of boxes) that make programming easier.

Two elementary boxes that do not need to be discussed further are $\left(\text{START}\right)$ and $\left(\text{STOP}\right)$. START must appear just once in any complete program, while STOP may appear any number of times.

3.1 Assignment Statements

Assignment is the operation of calculating the value of an expression and storing that value in a designated cell in memory. An assignment statement should be written in the form

$$\text{"lefthand side"} \leftarrow \text{"righthand side"}$$

where "lefthand side" is the name of a variable—that is, the identification of a cell in memory—and "righthand side" is an expression that can be evaluated. Valid assignment statements include, for example,

$$A \leftarrow 17.5$$
$$B \leftarrow A \times 5.3 - 21.43$$
and $\qquad Z \leftarrow (X + Y) \times Z$

The following are *not* valid assignment statements:

$5.1 \leftarrow A \qquad$ (5.1 is a constant, not a cell in memory)
$B + C \leftarrow X$ (B + C is not a cell in memory)
$X \leftarrow \qquad$ (Righthand side is missing)
$X \leftarrow Y \times Z$ (Arrow assignment operator is missing)

An assignment box is a rectangular box that can contain one or more assignment statements, as shown in Figure 3.2. This box contains statements that exchange the values of A and B. The statements inside the box are executed sequentially in the order given. Note that only one box is executed at a time. This leads to an important restriction on assignment boxes; namely, only one flowline

97

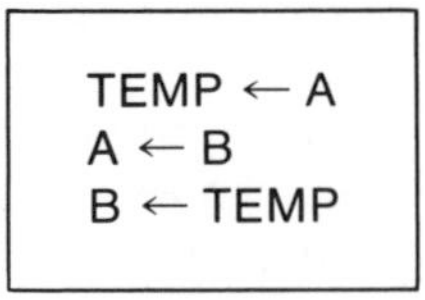

TEMP ← A
A ← B
B ← TEMP

Fig. 3.2 Assignment box

Box 1
Box 2
Box 3
Box 4

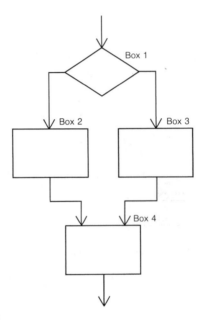

Fig. 3.3 Two flowlines to an assignment box

may *leave* the box. This path indicates the unique path to be followed after each assignment statement inside the box has been executed. Several flowlines may enter an assignment box, as shown in Figure 3.3. Box 4 is executed immediately after either Box 2 or Box 3 has been executed.

Each assignment statement has an expression on the right-hand side. In science we are accustomed to writing expressions in a variety of ways, for example

$$\text{(i)}\quad \frac{A + 5B}{16.4 + C}$$

$$\text{(ii)}\quad (x^2 + y^2)^{1/2}$$

$$(iii) \quad \frac{-B + \sqrt{B^2 - 4AC}}{2A}$$

Typical computer input devices do not provide for superscripts such as B^2 or built-up fractions such as $\frac{B}{A}$. Therefore POLs do not include them. To make our flowchart language reasonably close to POLs, we will similarly restrict our expressions. For this reason, we must introduce special symbols for superscripting and division. These symbols are $\uparrow$ and $/$, respectively. Thus we write B^2 as $B \uparrow 2$ and $\frac{A}{B}$ as A/B.‡

In the expression given in example (i) above, we also used one other common mathematical abbreviation: we wrote "5B" for "5 times B." In mathematics we can also write "AB" for "A times B." Unfortunately, we will be using variable names with more than one character. For example, we have already used "TEMP" as a name for a temporary location in many earlier examples. If we allow a person to indicate multiplication by writing two variable names next to each other, how do we know whether TEMP is

> the variable TEMP?
> the variable T times the variable EMP?
> the variable TE times the variable MP?
> and so forth.

To avoid this confusion, we insist that the multiplication operation be explicitly given by use of the "$\times$" sign. Thus the three possibilities above would be written as

> TEMP
> T $\times$ EMP

and
> TE $\times$ MP, respectively.

When we write a division operation such as

$$\frac{A}{B + C}$$

we must use parentheses to indicate that B and C are to be added before we divide the result into A. Thus we write A/(B + C). If we wanted to say

$$\frac{A}{B} + C$$

we could write (A/B) + C.

---

‡We introduced ÷ for the division operation. We will delay further discussion of the differences between ÷ and / until Section 3.2.

When we first learn arithmetic, we learn that $4 - 3 + 2$ means $(4 - 3) + 2$, which is 3. That is, we learn that we do the left-hand operation first. If we had done the right-hand operation first, we would have $4 - (3 + 2) = 4 - 5 = -1$. If we want to override the left-hand-first rule, we use parentheses. Thus, $A - (B - C)$ means "take C from B, and then take the result from A."

For multiplication, the rules of arithmetic differ slightly. $A \times B + C$ is the same as $(A \times B) + C$, but $A + B \times C$ is the same as $A + (B \times C)$. That is, multiplication is "more important" than addition and subtraction, so multiplications are done before additions and subtractions. Thus $A \times B - C \times D$ is the same as $(A \times B) - (C \times D)$. The two multiplications are done first, then the subtraction. The rule "multiplication is more important than addition and subtraction" saves us having to use parentheses in many cases. Although $(A \times B) - (C \times D)$ is correct, it is faster and simpler to write $A \times B - C \times D$. Formally we say that "multiplication takes *precedence* over addition and subtraction." We will think of division as being related to multiplication much as subtraction is related to addition. Subtraction and addition have the same *precedence level*; that is, neither takes precedence over the other, so if no parentheses are present, the operations are done from left to right. The same is true for consecutive multiplications and divisions.

Examples

The following pairs are equivalent:

$$A + B - C + D = ((A + B) - C) + D$$
$$A - (B + X) - Y = (A - (B + X)) - Y$$
$$A \times B / C \times D = ((A \times B)/C) \times D$$
$$\left(= \frac{A \times B}{C} \times D \text{ in conventional form}\right)$$
$$A \times B / (C \times D) = (A \times B) / (C \times D)$$
$$\left(= \frac{A \times B}{C \times D} \text{ in conventional form}\right)$$

Both multiplication and division have a higher precedence than addition and subtraction, so multiplications and divisions are done before additions and subtractions.

Examples

The following pairs are equivalent:

$$A \times B - C / D = (A \times B) - (C / D)$$
$$X - Y / (U - V) = X - (Y / (U - V))$$
$$\left(= X - \frac{Y}{U - V} \text{ in conventional form}\right)$$
$$A \times B - C \times D + F = ((A \times B) - (C \times D)) + F$$

$$A \times (B + C) \: / \: D - (E - F) \: / \: G$$

$$A \times \quad T1 \quad / \: D - (E - F) \: / \: G$$

Fig. 3.4 First reduction

Note that after the multiplications have been done in the last example, the additions and subtractions are done from left to right.

We can visualize the evaluation of an arithmetic expression as a series of reductions, each consisting of the execution of one of the arithmetic operations to form an intermediate result. If we start with the expression $A \times (B + C)/D - (E - F)/G$, the first reduction is to evaluate $B + C$ to get an intermediate result, say T1. This is shown in Figure 3.4. Thus the single assignment statement

$$T \leftarrow A \times (B + C)/D - (E - F)/G$$

is equivalent to the pair

$$T1 \leftarrow B + C$$
$$T \leftarrow A \times T1/D - (E - F)/G$$

The next reduction consists of the evaluation of $E - F$ to get another intermediate result, say T2. This is shown in Figure 3.5. Thus the assignment statement above is equivalent to

$$T1 \leftarrow B + C$$
$$T2 \leftarrow E - F$$
$$T \leftarrow A \times T1/D - T2/G$$

These reductions continue until there is only one operation left to perform. At this time, the original assignment statement has been replaced by a sequence of single-operator assignment statements. For the above example, we get

$$T1 \leftarrow B + C$$
$$T2 \leftarrow E - F$$
$$T3 \leftarrow A \times T1$$
$$T4 \leftarrow T3/D$$
$$T5 \leftarrow T2/G$$
$$T \leftarrow T4 - T5$$

$$A \times T1 \: / \: D - (E - F) \: / \: G$$

$$A \times T1 \: / \: D - \quad T2 \quad / \: G$$

Fig. 3.5 Next reduction

101

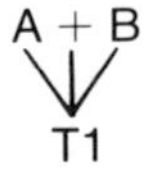

A + B
\V/
T1

Fig. 3.6 Representation of a single reduction

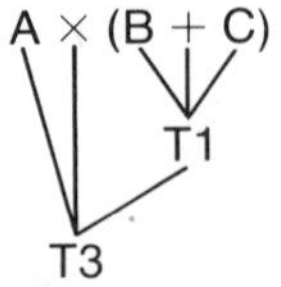

A × (B + C)

T1

T3

Fig. 3.7 Representation of two reductions

The process can be represented pictorially as follows. A single reduction is diagrammed as a triplet with three lines joining it to its reduced form. This is shown for the reduction T1 ← A + B in Figure 3.6. In this figure, A and B are the *operands* for the operation +. T1 is the operand that results from this operation. A similar figure can be drawn for T2 ← E − F. The next operation is T3 ← A × T1. The first operand for the multiplication operation is A; the second is T1, which is represented by the diagram in Figure 3.6. Consequently we represent the steps T1 ← B + C and T3 ← A × T1 by the diagram in Figure 3.7.

Continuing in this way, we finally represent the evaluation of the expression by Figure 3.8. This diagram displays the sequence of execution of the operations. In fact, it shows that there are several possible sequences. T1 must be evaluated before T3 and T4 can be formed; T2 must be evaluated before T5 can be formed. However, we could evaluate T1, T3, and T4 before or after T2 and T5 are formed. Thus we could do the evaluation in the order T1, T3, T4, T2, T5, T, or in the order T2, T5, T1, T3, T4, T. Other sequences are also possible in this example. The choice of sequence does not affect the value of the expression as long as restrictions implied by Figure 3.8 (and hence by the original expression) are obeyed. The compiler will usually choose an order that has a short machine-language equivalent.‡

We introduced the "up-arrow" symbol, ↑, for exponentiation.

---

‡Note that the compiler could choose whether to evaluate A + B + C as (A + B) + C or as A + (B + C). In Chapter 6 it will be seen that these may give different results because of numerical errors. Therefore, compilers should use the left-to-right rule and evaluate (A + B) + C. Most do.

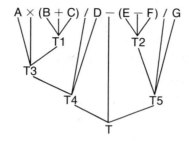

$$A \times (B + C) / D - (E - F) / G$$

Fig. 3.8 Representation of the evaluation of the expression

Thus $B \uparrow 2$ is our way of writing B^2. $X \uparrow 0.5$ is our way of writing $X^{1/2}$. This is mathematically the same as $\sqrt{X}$. The exponentiation operation must be assigned rules so that it fits in with the scheme for the other arithmetic operations. What does $A \uparrow 2 \times C$ mean? If we write this in the conventional mathematical way as $A^2 \times C$, we know that it is $(A^2) \times C$; that is, we square A and multiply it by C. Similarly, $P + Q \uparrow 2$ is our way of writing $P + Q^2$, in which we square Q and add the result to P. We use the rule that $\uparrow$ has a higher precedence than multiplication and addition. Similarly, it has a higher precedence than division and subtraction. Thus we amend our rules to require that in the absence of parentheses, exponentiations are done first, then multiplications and divisions, and finally additions and subtractions. Operations at the same level of precedence are done from left to right.

Examples

$$A \uparrow B + C \times D \quad = (A \uparrow B) + (C \times D)$$
$$X - Y / Z \uparrow P \times Q = X - ((Y / (Z \uparrow P)) \times Q)$$
$$A \uparrow B \uparrow C \quad\quad\quad = (A \uparrow B) \uparrow C$$

(Some POLs obey exponentiation operations from right to left; that is, $A \uparrow B \uparrow C$ is the same as $A \uparrow (B \uparrow C)$, which is equivalent to the mathematical expression A^{B^C}. We have adopted the left-to-right rule for consistency with the other operations.)

Binary and Unary Operators

Usually the operators $+$, $-$, $\times$, $/$, and $\uparrow$ are used with two *operands* — that is, two variables or constants that provide the data for the operation. Therefore, they are called *binary operators*. The two operators $+$ and $-$ can be used in a special way with only one operand. For example, we might write $Z \leftarrow -X$ or $A \leftarrow +B$. We call

103

the operators $+$ and $-$ *unary operators* when they are used in this way. (Binary is also called *diadic* and unary is also called *monadic*.) The unary arithmetic operators take precedence over all of the binary operators and must be performed first. Thus,

$$-A + B = (-A) + B = B - A$$
$$A \uparrow - B = A \uparrow (-B) = A^{-B}$$
$$C / + D = C / (+D) = C / D$$

Variable Names

Variable names are the names of cells in memory. When a variable name is used in an expression, the contents of the cell with that name is used. Many POLs restrict the length of variable names. Some FORTRAN compilers, for example, allow six or less characters starting with a letter and containing only letters or digits. Because space inside boxes is usually an important consideration in flowcharts, we will follow the same restrictions in the rest of this book.

Constants

We have been writing expressions using variable names and numbers but have never given any definite rules for valid ways to write numbers. We will allow ourselves to write numbers in the natural way. For example,

523	-1.25
10.74	$-3_{10}11$
-27.1	$0.2517_{10}-12$
$+3$	-4

They can be signed (that is, have a plus or minus sign). They may or may not have a decimal point and can have a decimal exponent written after a subscript "10." (We assume that this character is available, as it is in ALGOL. Many languages—for example, PL/I and FORTRAN—use the character "E" instead.)

Exercises

1. Which of the following names are valid?

    a. GOOD
    b. BAD
    c. A $+$ B
    d. 6J6
    e. A123

2. Write the following expressions in the form allowed in our flowcharts:

   a. $\dfrac{A+B}{C+D}$

   *b. X^{2Y}

   *c. $(A+B)C$

   d. $\dfrac{P^3+G}{4.5-\dfrac{A}{B}}$

3. Rewrite the following assignment statements using sequences of single arithmetic operation assignment statements such as $A \leftarrow B \times C$. You can use as many storage cells T1, T2, . . . , as you need.

   *a. $P \leftarrow Q + R \times S$

   b. $D \leftarrow (G+H) \uparrow (I/J)$

   c. $U \leftarrow V \uparrow W \times (X+Y)/(Z-U)$

4. What are the possible sequences of execution of the operations in these assignment statements?

   *a. $A \leftarrow B \times C + D/E$

   b. $P \leftarrow Q \uparrow (R+S) - T/U$

Questions

1. Which pairs of operators have the same precedence level?

2. Is there an operator that has a higher precedence than at least one other operator and a lower precedence than a third?

3. Give an expression that uses both unary and binary minus operators.

4. Mathematically it does not matter if we evaluate $A + B + C$ as $(A + B) + C$ or as $A + (B + C)$. Is this true for every operator?

3.2 Data Types

In the statement of an algorithm we use names to refer to data. When the algorithm is encoded as a machine-language program, these names refer to memory cells. Data referred to in the algorithm usually has an implied type. For example, if we talk about "names in the phone book," we are talking about character strings; if we

105

talk about "a telephone number in New York City," we are talking
about a seven-digit decimal number; if we talk about "the population of France," we are talking about an integer; or if we talk about
"the distance between the spacecraft and earth in miles," we are
talking about a real number, one we would want to represent as a
floating-point number in the computer.

When we define an algorithm, we specify operations that must
be performed on the data. In most cases, the type of the result
will also be implied. For example, if we indicate the step, "Find the
population of North America by adding together the populations of
the USA and Canada," we also know that the result is an integer.
If we used the names PNA, PUSA, and PCAN for populations of
North America, the USA, and Canada we could formally write this
step as

$$PNA \leftarrow PUSA + PCAN$$

A person reading this step would know that the addition operations
are to be performed with integers if he knows that the names PNA,
PCAN, and so forth, refer to integer variables. There is an important
difference in the use of the names in machine-language programs:
they refer to cells in the memory, not to variables. The computer
does not know that they represent populations. As the names of
cells in memory, they do not have an associated data type. The cell
PUSA can be used to store an integer, a real number in floating-
point representation, a logical variable, or some other data type.
The type of data is "known" to the machine only by the instructions
that use it.

If the variable PCAN is used in an integer addition operation, the
computer knows that PCAN contains an integer. The same is true
of PUSA and PNA. Let us look again at the problem and the three
ways we have stated the solution.

Solution in English language	Add the populations of the USA and Canada. The result is the population of North America.	Integer data type is implied by name "population."
Solution in flowchart language	PNA ← PUSA + PCAN	Data type?
Solution in machine language	LOAD PUSA ADD PCAN . . .	Data type implied by instructions.

To complete a statement of the solution in flowchart language we
must also indicate the type of data involved. This information is

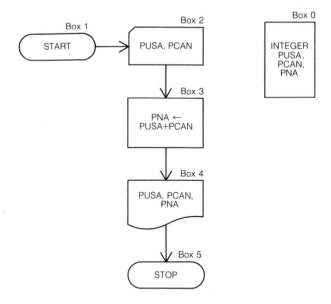

Fig. 3.9 Flowchart showing declaration statements

needed so that a translator knows which operations to use in the machine-language version of the flowchart language. Therefore, we must declare the type of variables being used in a flowchart. This is done in *declaration statements*. We place them inside rectangular boxes with *no* connecting flowlines. They will be put at the top right-hand corner of our flowcharts. An example is given in Figure 3.9.

Here we declare the three variables PUSA, PCAN, and PNA to be integers. With this information we can interpret the statements in the flowchart. Thus Box 2, the READ statement, tells us that the first step is to input the next two numbers from the card reader and to store them as integers in the cells PUSA and PCAN. The assignment statement in Box 3 is to be carried out with integer arithmetic, while Box 4 is to print integers.

A declaration box is never executed, since no flowlines enter it. Declaration statements are called *non-executable* statements. They tell the reader facts that apply to the whole flowchart.

Formally, our declaration box is a rectangle "on its side"—that is, taller than it is wide. It can contain statements such as

INTEGER variable 1, variable 2, . . . , variable *n*

where variable 1, variable 2, etc., are the names of variables that are to be integers. Similarly we will allow real numbers (which will be represented in floating point) to be declared by a statement such as

REAL variable rl, variable r2, . . . , variable rn

This says that the variables named are to be stored in floating-point representation.

Logical variables were introduced in Chapter 2. They can take on values "True" or "False". If a set of names is to be used for a logical variable, they must be declared by the statement

LOGICAL variable l1, variable l2, . . . , variable ln

Many POLs allow character string variables. You will become familiar with them if the language you are using has this capability. A typical declaration statement for character string variables is

CHARACTER variable c1, variable c2, . . . , variable cn

Most POLs allow variables to be declared in statements similar to these. Some POLs—FORTRAN in particular—also allow the programmer to omit some specific declarations of types. Many scientists use the letters i, j, k, l, m, and n to stand for integers in equations as a matter of habit. This practice has been taken over into these languages by adopting the following rule for variable names: "Unless a declaration is made otherwise, variables whose names start with I, J, K, L, M, or N are integers; all others are real." This convention saves a lot of writing in many cases, so we will adopt it in our flowcharts. We will assume that all variables used in the text follow this rule unless we state otherwise.

When an assignment statement such as

$$N \leftarrow I + J \times K$$

is used, it is fairly obvious that we expect the arithmetic to be done with integers, since all of the variables are integers, but what does

$$A \leftarrow I + J \times K$$

mean? Since the expression involves integers only, it can be evaluated to get an integer result. However, the left-hand side is a floating-point variable, so the value of the expression must be converted into the equivalent floating-point representation before it can be stored. We did not give any instructions in the description of our computer's machine language for converting from fixed to floating point, but we assume that such exist. Hence, the machine-language version of the assignment above will use integer arithmetic to evaluate the expression and then convert the result into floating-point representation.

Example

If I $= 3$, J $= 2$, and K $= 5$, the value of the expression I $+$ J $\times$ K is 13.

This must be converted into $.13 \times 10^2$ to be stored as a floating-point number in cell A. This is a case of

Rule 1

If in the assignment statement

$$\text{"variable"} \leftarrow \text{"expression"}$$

"expression" is an integer quantity and "variable" is a real number, the integer is converted into floating-point representation before the assignment. This rule can result in loss of accuracy. For example, if $I = 3$, $J = 1000$, and $K = 1123$, $I + J \times K$ is 1123003. Since our floating-point numbers have only five digits of precision, this integer would be converted into

$$.11230 \times 10^7$$

If, in the example, I had been 573, the expression $I + J \times K$ would have been 1123573. This time we would convert it to the floating-point number $.11236 \times 10^7$ because, **whenever a number has to be shortened to store it in floating point, we want the closest approximation, so we round it.**

Now let us consider the following: We are given the average annual water consumption per person in the U.S. in gallons (a real number), say AGAL. We wish to estimate the number of people (say NPEOP) served by a given water company by taking the number of gallons that the company delivers in a year (say GAL) and dividing it by the average consumption per person, that is

$$\text{Number of people} = \frac{\text{annual water used}}{\text{average annual water used per person}}$$

or

$$\text{NPEOP} \leftarrow \text{GAL/AGAL}$$

The right-hand side is the quotient of two floating-point numbers; the left-hand side is naturally an integer (number of people). What rule shall we use?

Rule 2

If in

$$\text{"variable"} \leftarrow \text{"expression"}$$

"expression" is a real number and "variable" is an integer, the floating-point value of "expression" is truncated to an integer.

109

Example

$$\text{NPEOP} \leftarrow \text{GAL/AGAL}$$

If GAL = .10752 × 10^{11} and AGAL = .10000 × 10^6, then GAL/AGAL = .10752 × 10^6 so NPEOP would become 107520.

The rule above tells us what to do with an expression on the right-hand side after it has been evaluated. We still need rules for evaluating it. If all variables in a given expression are of the same type (integer or floating), the arithmetic must be performed using that type. For example, the number of tires an automobile manufacturer must order is five times the number of cars (NCAR) — assuming five tires per car. We naturally expect 5 × NCAR to be evaluated as an integer.

A special case was mentioned in Chapter 1 when we wanted to divide two integers. In this case it is not apparent which answer is natural. For example, if we divide the number of cars in the U.S. (NCARS) by the number of people (NPEOP) in the U.S., we get the average number of cars per person. The latter is not an integer, so we want this division to be done in floating point. We will write this as

$$\text{NCARS/NPEOP}$$

and say that the division operation represented by "/" always uses floating-point arithmetic.

Example

If NCARS = 632657 and NPEOP = 2000000 NCARS/NPEOP is .3163285, which will be represented as .31633 × 10^0.

If we specifically want an integer result, we will use the "÷" sign for the division. The rule for I ÷ J is to form the correct fixed-point value and truncate by discarding all digits after the decimal point. For example, we can find the remainder after dividing I by J from the expression

$$\text{I} - (\text{I} \div \text{J}) \times \text{J}$$

We are thus led to

Rule 3

If the operands for the arithmetic operators +, −, ×, and ↑ are both integers, the result is an integer. If the operands for the arithmetic operators +, −, ×, and ↑ are both real numbers, the result is a real number. The operator ÷ always gives an integer result; the operator / always gives a real result.

When an operator is to be applied to operands of different types, one operand must be converted to be the same type as the other before the arithmetic is performed. Since it is possible to convert integers (if they are small enough) into floating-point representation without loss of accuracy, whereas most numbers in floating-point representation will either be rounded or overflow if they are converted to integers, we chose to convert integers into floating-point numbers before the arithmetic operation. This leads us to

Rule 4

If one operand for the arithmetic operators +, −, ×, and ↑ is an integer and the other is a real number, the result is a real number.

Example

$$L \leftarrow I \times J \times (K + B)$$

The order of operation execution is:

1 — Multiplication of I and J. Result is an integer.

2 — Addition of K and B. K is converted to a real number since B is a real number. Result $K + B$ is a real number.

3 — Multiplication of $(I \times J)$ and $(K + B)$. Since $(K + B)$ is a real number, $(I \times J)$ is converted to a real number. The result is a real number.

4 — Assignment. The value computed in step 3 is truncated to an integer and stored in cell L.

The above example illustrates the importance of the order of evaluation of an expression. The left-to-right rule for multiplication indicates that $I \times J$ is formed and then multiplied by $(K + B)$. If, instead, the expression were to be evaluated as $I \times (J \times (K + B))$, the result might be different because of rounding or overflow. For example, if I and J were both 10^6 and K and B were both 1, the evaluation of $I \times J \times (K + B)$ would give an overflow when $I \times J (= 10^{12})$ is formed, whereas $I \times (J \times (K + B))$ gives 2×10^{13} correctly. Alternatively, if we started with $I = 123453$, $J = 2$, $K = 1$, $B = .1 \times 10^1$, then

$$
\begin{aligned}
I \times J \times (K + B) \quad &= 123453 \times 2 \times (1 + .1 \times 10^1) \\
&= 246906 \times (.2 \times 10^1) \\
(\text{Convert } I \times J \quad &= (.24691 \times 10^6) \times (.2 \times 10^1) \\
\text{to floating point}) \quad & \\
&= .49382 \times 10^6
\end{aligned}
$$

whereas

$$
\begin{aligned}
I \times (J \times (K + B)) \quad &= 123453 \times (2 \times (1 + .1 \times 10^1)) \\
&= 123453 \times (2 \times .2 \times 10^1)
\end{aligned}
$$

111

$$\text{(Convert J to floating point and multiply)} \quad = 123453 \times (.4 \times 10^1)$$

$$\text{(Convert I to floating point)} \quad = (.12345 \times 10^6) \times (.4 \times 10^1)$$

$$= .49380 \times 10^6$$

Usually we do not have to be concerned with these small details, but we should be aware of potential hazards in unusual situations.

Constants

An expression uses operands that can be variable names or constants. Constants are stored in the computer memory by the compiler so that they can be used in the evaluation of an expression. Therefore the compiler must know in what form to store them—as integers, floating-point numbers, logical values, or character strings.

Numerical constants will be stored either as integers or floating-point numbers. A numerical constant will be stored as an integer if it contains no decimal point and no exponent. Otherwise it will be stored as a floating-point number.

Examples

Integers	Floating-point numbers
15	1.5
−173	$-25_{10}3$
1	$2.7_{10}-4$

Character string constants are written by surrounding the string by quotes. For example, 'THIS IS A CHARACTER STRING'. We sidestep the problem of how these constants are stored in memory (we have seen that characters can be stored). We will see one use for character strings in the next section on output.

The logical constants are written "TRUE" and "FALSE". Here we use the double quotes sign to indicate that the four characters TRUE and five characters FALSE are neither a name nor a character string.

The evaluation of an arithmetic expression is affected by the type of a constant in exactly the same way as it is affected by a variable.

Examples

The result of	is the type
$2 + I$	Integer
$2.0 \uparrow I$	Real
$2 - A$	Real
$2.0 \times A$	Real

EXERCISES

1. Give the type of the following constants, if valid:

   *a. -1.7
   *b. 25
   c. $-2.5_{10}3$
   d. 'TRUE'
   e. "FALSE"
   *f. "STRING"
   *g. '$1.7_{10}3$'
   h. $2.5-_{10}3$
   i. -17
   j. $25_{10}0$

2. Which of the following expressions are type integer and which are type real, assuming that no specific declarations have been made?

   a. $A + Z \times I$
   b. $I \uparrow J - 2$
   c. $X \uparrow 2 - 3$
   d. $I / J + K$

3. What value is assigned to the variable on the left of the assignment in the following statements if the variables A, B, C, I, and J contains the values 3.5, 1.7, -10.5, 10, and -3 respectively?

   *a. $D \leftarrow I \times 3 - J$
   *b. $K \leftarrow C / A + 3.4$
   *c. $E \leftarrow I / J + 4$
   d. $K \leftarrow J \uparrow 2 + A / B$
   e. $D \leftarrow (I + J) \times B$
   f. $E \leftarrow A \div B + I - 7$
   g. $L \leftarrow C \div (-B) \times I$

3.3 INPUT/OUTPUT STATEMENTS

In Chapter 1 we introduced boxes shaped like cards and torn printer paper for input and output. These boxes may have one or more paths leading to them, indicating different reasons for which they may be executed. However, they must have exactly one path *from* them to the unique box whose execution must immediately follow.

   The input box is drawn as in Figure 3.10. It contains a list of variable names. When the box is executed, values are read from the cards in the card reader and assigned to the variables in the list. Execution of this box will cause four numbers to be read and stored

113

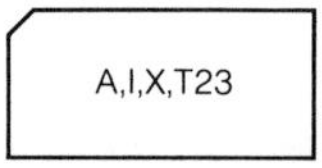

Fig. 3.10 Input box

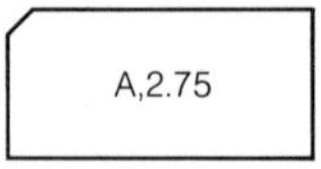

Fig. 3.11 Invalid input box with constant

in A, I, X, and T23. Only variable names may appear in the list, as its purpose is to provide a set of cells in memory where input data can be stored. It would not make sense, for example, to write a constant in an input box as shown in Figure 3.11. '2.75' is not the name of a cell in memory, so no data can be read from a card and stored in '2.75'. A READ statement functions like an assignment statement in that values are assigned to the variables. Thus any memory cell specification valid for the left-hand side of an assignment is valid in a READ statement.

The statement in Figure 3.10 reads four numbers from a card. How are these numbers punched? We will use what is called *list-directed input/output*. The numbers are assumed to be punched in a form such that there is a clear demarcation between consecutive data items — either a group of spaces, a comma, or both. Thus if the data on the next two cards in the card reader is

$$17.52,375 \quad 82$$
$$921.25_{10}+7 \quad 29.5,19,3,1$$

execution of Figure 3.10 would be equivalent to

$$A \quad \leftarrow 17.52$$
$$I \quad \leftarrow 375$$
$$X \quad \leftarrow 82$$
$$T23 \leftarrow 921.25_{10}+7$$

As many cards as necessary are read to get the required data. Reading can stop in the middle of a card (we read cards from left to right). In the example in Figure 3.10, the remaining four numbers on the second card would not be read because reading would stop on the space between $921.25_{10}+7$ and 29.5. If the program looped back and executed Figure 3.10 again, it would start reading from there, and assign the values 29.5, 19, 3, and 1 to the variables A, I, X, and T23, respectively.

The names of the variables in the READ statement determine the representation used when the data is stored in memory. If the data on the input cards has a different form, a conversion is necessary. This follows the rules for assignment statements given in the last section. In the example in Figure 3.10, X is a floating-point variable. If 82 is read for the value of X, it will be stored as $.82 \times 10^2$.

A simple form of output is shown in Figure 3.12. A list of variable names appears in an output box. This causes values of the variables to be printed on the output printer when the box is executed. They are printed in a list-directed fashion; that is, each is printed in a suitable form and spaces are left between it and the next. The actual page layout depends on the language used and the type of output equipment. (You can find this information in local manuals, or by observing your output and experimenting.)

In addition to variable names, we can put constants in output lists. These constants are printed directly. For an example, see Figure 3.13. The output list contains four values: the character string FOR I =, the variable name I, the character string A =, and the variable name A. If Box I in Figure 3.13 is executed with I = 3, A is set to $.27000 \times 10^1$. Box 2 causes the output

$$\text{FOR I} = \quad 3 \quad \text{A} = \quad .27000_{10}{+}01$$

Fig. 3.12 Output box

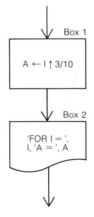

Fig. 3.13 Output list

115

The character string has been printed directly. The quotes have been removed because the constant is the string inside the quotes. The quotes are used to distinguish string constants from names and other parts of the language.

The members of an output list are just like the right-hand sides of assignment statements; they provide values to be printed just as the right-hand sides provide values to be assigned. Therefore, anything that is valid for the right-hand side of an assignment statement is valid in an output list. Hence expressions can be used in output lists. The example shown in Figure 3.14 is a valid output statement. Alternatively, it can be replaced by Figure 3.15.

A,B,A+B

Fig. 3.14   Output statement including expression

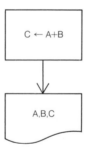

C ← A+B

A,B,C

Fig. 3.15   Alternative output statement

Exercises

1. Draw a flowchart to read required data values, to perform the assignments required, and to print both the input and the result for:

   *a. $P \leftarrow \dfrac{X^2 - Y}{Z}$

   b. $Z5AB \leftarrow [A \times B]^{C/D}$

   c. $TEMP \leftarrow \dfrac{P}{Q + R}$

   $OUT \leftarrow \dfrac{TEMP + 3.5}{TEMP - 3.5}$

3.4 Program Logic

The power of a computer derives from two sources: its ability to process information rapidly and accurately, and its ability to test data and take action dependent on the outcome of the test. In a flowchart representation of a procedure, the diamond-shaped decision box is used to select between alternative flowpaths. The step, "If A is less than B, take action X; otherwise take action Y," translates into the flowchart shown in Figure 3.16.

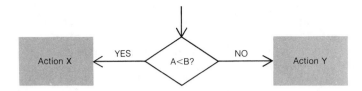

Fig. 3.16   Program decision

So far we have used questions that can be answered YES or NO inside decision boxes. These are frequently phrased as true/false statements. In the future we will use these statements. Thus "A < B" is a statement that is either TRUE or FALSE. The flowlines leaving the box will be labeled TRUE and FALSE. When a decision box is executed, the expression inside is examined. If it is TRUE, the flowline labeled TRUE is followed to find the next box that must be executed. Otherwise, the flowline labeled FALSE is followed.

The expression in a decision box frequently uses one of the *relational operators* shown in Table 3.1. Relational operators are similar to binary arithmetic operators in that they use two numerical

TABLE 3.1

RELATIONAL OPERATORS

Operator	Meaning
$<$	Less than
$>$	Greater than
$\leq$	Less than or equal to
$\geq$	Greater than or equal to
$=$	Equal to
$\neq$	Not equal to

or character operands.‡ They differ in that the value of such an expression is logical; that is, it has the value "TRUE" or "FALSE". Any expression that has a logical value can appear in a decision box. In particular, a logical variable, say L, could appear by itself. The TRUE branch from the box is followed if the value of L is "TRUE"; otherwise, the FALSE branch is followed. A logical variable can be assigned a value by assignment statements such as

$$L \leftarrow \text{"TRUE"}$$

and $$L1 \leftarrow P \geq Q$$

In the first example the right-hand side is a logical constant; in the second it is a logical expression. Later in the section we will introduce other logical expressions. Any of these can appear in a decision box or on the right-hand side of an assignment statement if the left-hand side is a logical variable.

Examples

If $A = 17.3$, $B = 21.3$, $I = 7$, $J = 4$, $K = 3$

the expression	has the value
$A > B$	FALSE
$I \neq A$	TRUE
$(A - B) \geq 0$	FALSE
$(J + K) = I$	TRUE

In the last example we compare the value of a variable with the value of an expression. In fact we can write this as $J + K = I$ by using additional precedence information. The precedence of each of the arithmetic operators ($+$, $-$, $\times$, $/$, $\div$, and $\uparrow$) is higher than the precedence of each of the relational operators. Thus the order of execution of the operations is to do the arithmetic operators first, then the relational operators. The precedence of each of the relational operators is the same, so they are done from left to right.

Examples

1. The precedence of the operators in $A \times B \neq I + J$ is shown in Figure 3.17.

   The value of the expression is the value of the logical variable T3 where T3 is constructed by

   $$T1 \leftarrow A \times B$$

   ---

   ‡The relational operators $=$ and $\neq$ can be used to compare any two operands of the same type—for example, both logical. Some languages allow all relational operators to be used on all types of data.

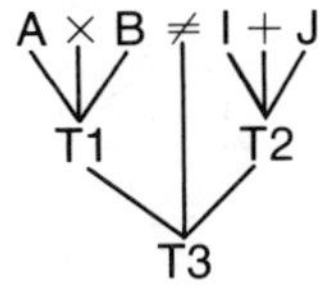

$$A \times B \neq I + J$$

Fig. 3.17   Precedence in $A \times B \neq I + J$

$$T2 \leftarrow I + J$$
$$T3 \leftarrow T1 \neq T2$$

2. The precedence of operators in $A - B = C \times D \neq (A < B)$ is shown in Figure 3.18.

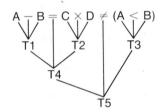

Fig. 3.18   Precedence in $A - B = C \times D \neq (A < B)$

The precedence levels of $=$ and $\neq$ are the same, so the leftmost operator, the $=$, is performed first.

We use decision boxes to implement control actions required in the problem statement as in Figure 3.18; we also use them to test for conditions that are introduced in the algorithm.

Example 3.1 — Average

Problem: Read in a deck of cards, each of which contains two numbers. The first is a seven-digit student ID number, the other that student's score on an exam. Compute the average exam score of all the students and print it.

Since the average score is the total of all the scores divided by the number of students, we must find the number of students. This can be done by setting an integer variable N to zero and then, as each card is read, adding one to N. Thus after the last student card has been read, N will contain the number of students. We must also find the total score. This can be formed by *accumulating* the sum

119

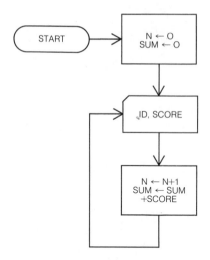

Fig. 3.19 Accumulating SUM

of all student scores read in another variable, say SUM. This part of the algorithm is shown in Figure 3.19.

The process must be stopped after the last student card has been read, so we need a way of testing to determine whether we have come to the last card. To do this we use the common technique of adding another card after the deck of student cards. This card is distinguished from the others because it contains "impossible" information. In this example, all student ID's are positive numbers, so we put a negative number on the card as a fake ID; the exam score can be anything since it is not processed. After reading a card, we test to see whether the ID is negative. If it is, then we have already read and processed the last student card. The flowchart of the complete algorithm is given in Figure 3.20.

Logical Expressions

In some problems a compound decision must be made. An example of a compound decision is "Go to Box P if both A > B and C = D, otherwise go to Box Q." One way of writing this is shown in Figure 3.21. Compound decisions of this form are common, so languages provide shorthand ways of writing single, logical expressions that are true in the desired cases. In the above example, we wished to know if the expressions "A > B" and "C = D" both had "TRUE" values. For this we use the logical operator "AND". This is a binary operator, both of whose operands must have logical values. The result of the "AND" operator is "TRUE" only if the value of both operands is "TRUE". Otherwise, the result if "FALSE". Thus, if

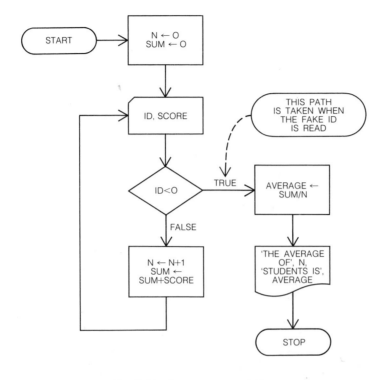

Fig. 3.20 Average computation

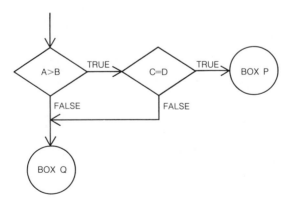

Fig. 3.21 Flowchart of a compound decision

A = 3.1, B = 2.4, C = 17.5, D = 17.5, then (A > B) "AND" (C = D) has
the value "TRUE".

121

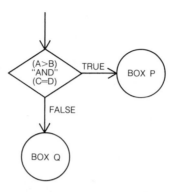

Fig. 3.22 Short form of Figure 3.21

If P and Q are logical variables or expressions, P "AND" Q is a valid logical expression. Its value is shown in Table 3.2.

The logical operators "OR" and "NOT" can also be used. "OR" is a binary operator, and P "OR" Q is "TRUE" if either P or Q or both have the value "TRUE". If both P and Q are "FALSE", the expression is "FALSE". If either P or Q is not a logical variable, then P "OR" Q is meaningless. "NOT" Q is "TRUE" if Q is "FALSE" and vice versa. "NOT" is a unary operator. The values of "OR" and "NOT" are shown in Tables 3.3 and 3.4. Thus, we can shorten Figure 3.21 to Figure 3.22.

When a logical expression involves more than one operator, we must know the precedence rules that determine the order of execution of the operators. The logical operators have lower precedence than arithmetic and relational operators. Within the logical operators, "NOT" has the highest precedence and "OR" the lowest. A complete list of precedence levels is shown in Table 3.5. Thus A "AND" B "OR" "NOT" C is equivalent to (A "AND" B) "OR" ("NOT" C). Other examples are

$$A \text{ "OR" } B \text{ "AND" } C \quad \text{is} \quad A \text{ "OR" } (B \text{ "AND" } C)$$
$$A \text{ "AND" "NOT" } B \quad \text{is} \quad A \text{ "AND" } (\text{"NOT" } B)$$
$$X > P + Q \text{ "AND" } I = J \text{ is} \quad (X > (P + Q)) \text{ "AND" } (I = J)$$

The decision boxes we have introduced have exactly two paths leaving them. (They can have one or more paths entering.) The exit paths are labeled TRUE and FALSE. From now on we will abbreviate these to T and F although you should be careful not to confuse handwritten forms of the two. Sometimes we wish to test for several cases; for example, we may wish to go to Box P if A < 0, Box Q if A = 0, or Box R if A > 0. This is shown in Figure 3.23.

Figure 3.24 shows a shorter way of writing this using more than two exits labeled with the conditions under which they are to be

TABLE 3.2

VALUE OF "AND"

P	Q	P "AND" Q
"FALSE"	"FALSE"	"FALSE"
"FALSE"	"TRUE"	"FALSE"
"TRUE"	"FALSE"	"FALSE"
"TRUE"	"TRUE"	"TRUE"

TABLE 3.3

VALUE OF "OR"

P	Q	P "OR" Q
"FALSE"	"FALSE"	"FALSE"
"FALSE"	"TRUE"	"TRUE"
"TRUE"	"FALSE"	"TRUE"
"TRUE"	"TRUE"	"TRUE"

TABLE 3.4

VALUE OF "NOT"

Q	"NOT" Q
"FALSE"	"TRUE"
"TRUE"	"FALSE"

TABLE 3.5

PRECEDENCE LEVELS

Unary + and − ↑ $\times$ / ÷ + − > < ≥ ≤ = ≠ "NOT" "AND" "OR"	Highest precedence
	Lowest precedence

taken. If many exits are possible, we will draw a decision box as in Figure 3.25. This would go to Box U if B < 1, Box V if B = 1, Box W if B = 2, and Box X if B > 2.

123

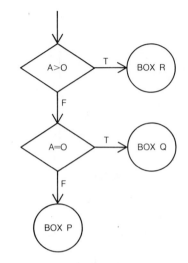

Fig. 3.23   Testing for several cases

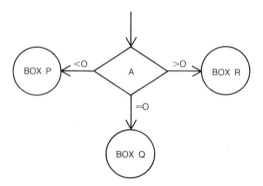

Fig. 3.24   Short form of Figure 3.23

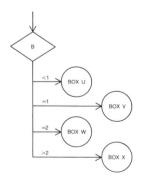

Fig. 3.25   Decision box with many exits

Connector Boxes

We have been using the circular boxes to indicate connections to other parts of the flowchart. We use these when a flowchart gets too large for one sheet of paper and we need a path going from one sheet to another.

Example

Effectively both circles labeled ''A'' are at one point. In the example below, it is as if the TRUE exit of Box X were directly connected to Box Y. The connector box does not cause any operations to be performed.

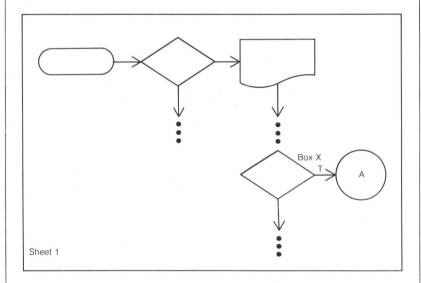

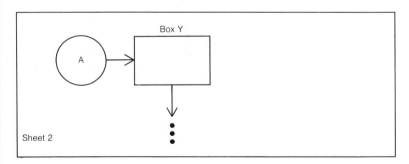

Fig. 3.26   Connector boxes

Exercises

1. Draw flowcharts whose decision boxes use single relational operators to implement a transfer of control to connector H if the following logical conditions are TRUE, and to connector G otherwise.

   *a. (A > B) "OR" (C = D)
   b. (P < Q) "OR" "NOT" (R = P)
   *c. (X > 2) "AND" (P = 3) "OR" (Q < R)
   d. (X < 0) "AND" (Y = 3) "OR" (X > 0) "AND" (Z < 0)

2. Give a logical expression that is true if the following flowcharts transfer control to connector Z:

(a)

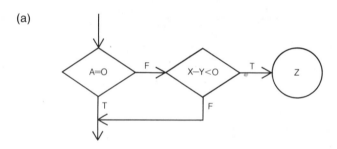

*(b)

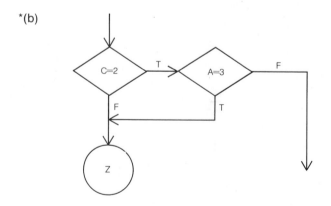

(c)

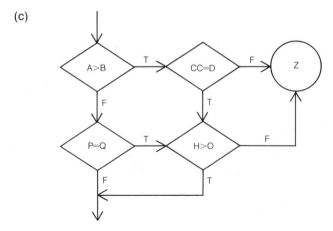

3.5 Program Loops

One of the ways in which computers are able to out-perform people is in the repetitive execution of identical tasks on different data. An example of this is the income tax problem discussed in Chapter 1. A procedure was written to compute the tax for an individual. It functioned by reading in data, processing it, and printing the answers. By transferring back to the start of the procedure, data for a second individual can be read and processed similarly. Thus the one program can be used to perform any number of tax calculations. This program loop was formed as shown in Figure 3.27.

The loop terminates when the data is exhausted. Each execution is independent of all previous executions and provides the numerical answer of another specific case.

Another example of a loop was given in the previous section. In that problem, the average of a set of scores was calculated and a loop was formed to sum the numbers on a deck of cards. Each execution was dependent on previous executions. A sum of a number of items was formed by adding to a running total. If we ignore the problem of reading the input, the basic form of the loop is as shown in Figure 3.28.

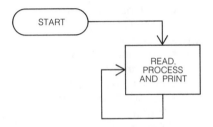

Fig. 3.27 Program loop

127

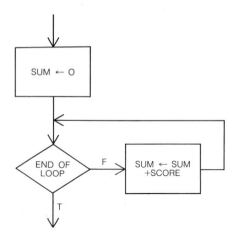

Fig. 3.28 Basic loop

The three boxes in Figure 3.28 display the three important procedures associated with this kind of program loop—the initialization (setting SUM to zero), the end test (checking for the last card), and the processing inside the loop (forming the running sum).

This kind of loop, which we will call a *cumulative loop*, processes data left from a previous execution (in this case the value in SUM). Before the first execution, the variables that are to be processed must be initialized. In this case, SUM must initially be zero.

Example 3.2—
Finding the Difference Between Largest and Smallest

Write a procedure that will read a set of cards, each containing one positive integer, and find the difference between the largest and smallest of these integers.

Again we do not know how many cards have to be read, so we will add one more card with a negative integer on it as an *end-of-file* indicator.

The largest and smallest numbers of a set of numbers is best found using the method we would use by hand. We would look at the first number and say, "If I do not find anything larger or smaller, then this is the largest and smallest." If we did find something larger or smaller as we read through the numbers, we would choose that one as the largest or smallest. The basic form of the loop is shown in Figure 3.29. (In terms of our flowchart language, this can be written as in Figure 3.30.) If there are no cards containing positive integers, the program in Figure 3.29 will set LARGE and SMALL to a negative number and DIFF to be zero.

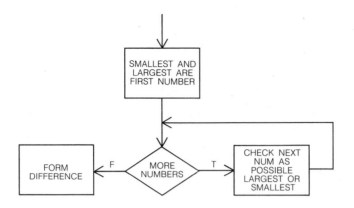

Fig. 3.29 Form of program to find largest difference

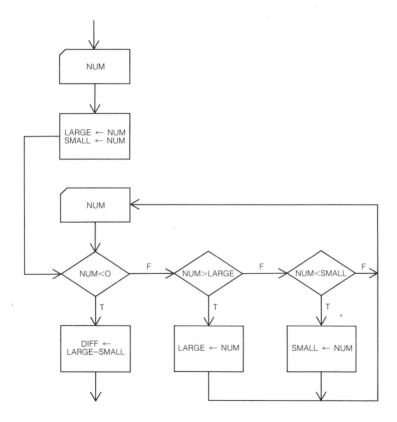

Fig. 3.30 Flowchart of the procedure

The problem statement did not say what was to happen if there were no integers in the set, so we have, in effect, corrected the problem statement by setting LARGE and SMALL to be negative as an indicator for this special case.

Example 3.3 — The Method of Bisection

A common problem in numerical processing is to find a value of x that satisfies an equation such as

$$x^3 + 3x - 5 = 0$$

The graph in Figure 3.31 shows the function $x^3 + 3x - 5$. As can be seen, the function is below the x-axis at $x = 0$ and above it at $x = 2$. Since the function is a continuous line, it must cross the x-axis somewhere between $x = 0$ and $x = 2$. Hence, for some value of x between zero and two, $x^3 + 3x - 5 = 0$.

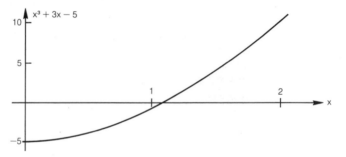

Fig. 3.31 $x^2 + 3x - 5$

If we set the value of LOW to be zero and HIGH to be two, then there is a solution of the problem between LOW and HIGH, as shown in Figure 3.32. The important characteristic of the two points LOW and HIGH is that the value of the function is negative at LOW and positive at HIGH. Now let us find the point MID midway between LOW and HIGH as shown in Figure 3.32. If we look at the sign of the function at MID we have two cases:

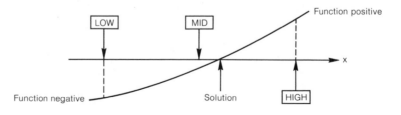

Fig. 3.32   Relation of computed points to solution

Case 1. Function is negative at MID (as shown). Since the function is positive at HIGH, a solution lies between MID and HIGH. Consequently, we can move LOW over to the point MID to get Figure 3.33. (Note that the solution still lies between LOW and HIGH.)

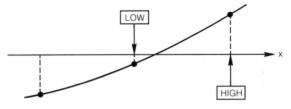

Fig. 3.33   Halving the interval: negative at MID

Case 2. Function is positive at MID. In this case a solution lies between LOW and MID. Consequently, we can move HIGH over to the point MID as shown in Figure 3.34.

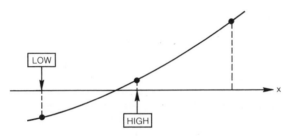

Fig. 3.34   Halving the interval: positive at MID

In either case, we finish up with the points LOW and HIGH such that the function is still negative at LOW and positive at HIGH. Furthermore, the distance between LOW and HIGH is now half of what it was initially.

This process can be repeated by setting MID to the midpoint between the new LOW and HIGH and repeating the analysis. This is shown in Figure 3.35.

It can be seen that the points LOW and HIGH are getting closer at each step. Since the solution of the original problem lies between LOW and HIGH after each step, we are getting a better and better idea of the position of the solution x. The process is shown as a cumulative loop in Figure 3.36. (If you have not yet covered data types, ignore the box in the top right-hand corner that contains REAL. . . .) This loop has no end test, so it never stops.

In the computer, we can represent only a finite number of values exactly. In general, the solution x will not be one of the values we can represent exactly, so we can only hope to compute an approxi-

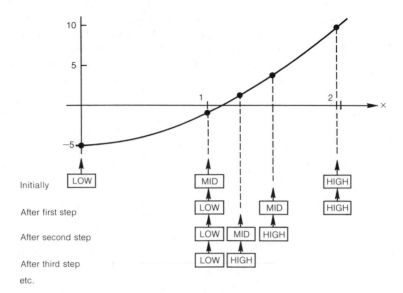

Initially

After first step

After second step

After third step

etc.

Fig. 3.35 Successive approximations

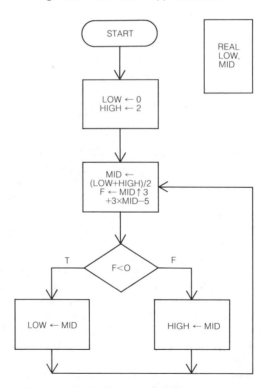

Fig. 3.36 Basic flow for bisection procedure

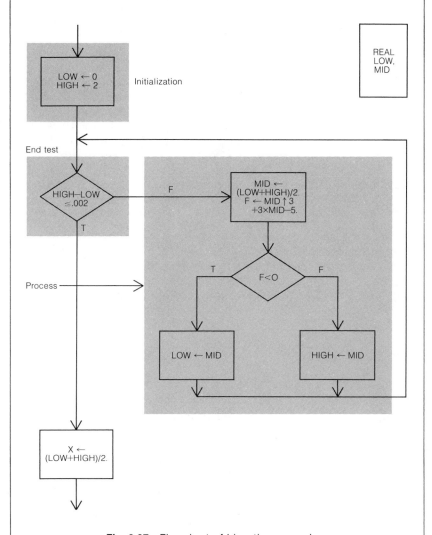

Fig. 3.37 Flowchart of bisection procedure

mation to it. Therefore we can stop when LOW and HIGH are within the accuracy we want. For example, if we want an answer accurate to .001, we can stop when HIGH-LOW ≤ .002. The solution can be taken to be the midpoint of LOW and HIGH. Since this is within .001 of both LOW and HIGH, it must be within .001 of the solution.‡ This is shown in Figure 3.37.

---

‡Considerations of rounding errors can make this statement false, but we will delay a discussion of those problems until Chapter 6.

Example 3.4—Population Growth

The following is an example of what is called simulation. *We want to estimate the population of the world at future times. To do this we set up a mathematical model of the processes we believe control the population and compute its behavior. We assume that the model has a constant population throughout the year, that on January 1 of each year a number of people are born, and that this number is a fixed given fraction of the population on December 31 of the previous year. This fraction is the annual birthrate. Further, we assume that on January 1 of each year a number of people die. This number is a fraction of the number of people alive on the day before, but this fraction (called the deathrate) is assumed to be proportional to the number of people alive on that December 31.*

We compute the behavior of this model by keeping track of the population and by calculating the change in the population from one year to another. Let us suppose that the birthrate is a real number to be input into BRATE, and the initial integer population is to be input into POP. Suppose also that the deathrate (DRATE) is a given fraction (DEATH) of the population, and that DEATH is to be input.

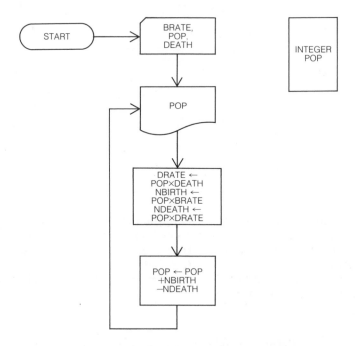

Fig. 3.38 First solution for population problem

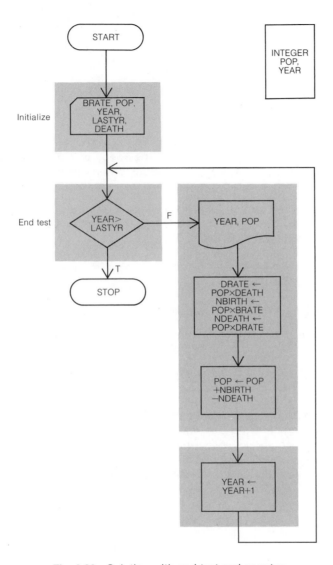

Fig. 3.39 Solution with end test and counter

We first propose the solution shown in Figure 3.38. The output from this program is a series of population sizes with no indication of the year for which the population has that size. The loop does not stop because we forgot to put in an end test—in fact, the problem specification failed to say for how long we should simulate. We must, therefore, add a *counter* that says how many years have elapsed and an end test that stops the loop. To do this we also require as input the integer date (YEAR) on which the first population is specified and the year up to which we must simulate (LASTYR). The solution is shown in Figure 3.39. The loop is stopped when the value of YEAR exceeds the last year to be simulated.

We have seen three examples of loops, each with a different stopping criterion. They were

- End of input in Examples 3.1 and 3.2.

- Accuracy. Each pass through the loop, called an *iteration*, improved the answer in Example 3.3. When the answer reached the desired accuracy, the iteration was stopped.

- A count. A counter (YEAR) was used to record passes through the loop. When it reached a terminal value, the simulation was stopped in Example 3.4.

Many loops are controlled by counters. The important steps in the counting process are

- Initialization: Setting the counter to its first value.

- Incrementation: Incrementing the counter, in this case by one, at the end of the processing in the loop.

- Testing: Seeing if the counter has exceeded its final value.

The use of one as an increment is not fundamental. If our model had specified that the population changed only on February 29, the counter could have been increased by 4. Or we could have two days a year when births and deaths are permitted, in which case the counter would have to be increased by 0.5.

Questions

1. What are the three important procedures associated with a program loop?

2. When a counter is used to control the termination of a loop, what are the three numbers that determine its action?

Problems

*1. A deck of cards, each containing a pair of numbers A and B, is to be read. Write a program to do this and to find the sum S1 of those numbers B for which $A < B$, the sum S2 of those numbers B for which $A = B$, and the sum S3 of those numbers B for which $A > B$. Print S1, S2, and S3. You may assume that the numbers A and B are both positive.

2. Suppose that in Example 3.3 (page 130) we knew only that the signs of the values of $x^3 + 3x - 5$ initially differed at $x = $ LOW and $x = $ HIGH, but did not know which was negative and which was positive when the program was to be written. The solution in Figure 3.36 works only for the case that the sign at $x = $ LOW is negative. Modify it so that it checks the sign at $x = $ LOW for the initial value of LOW, setting the logical variable ZNEG to be "TRUE" if that sign is negative, "FALSE" otherwise. Then modify the rest of the flowchart so that it works in either case.

3.6 Arrays

In one of the earlier examples we input a set of student exam scores and calculated their average. Let us amend that problem and ask also that the computer print out the difference between each student's score and the average score. All the scores must be processed and the average score must be calculated before we can compute the difference between each student's score and the average. Consequently we must pass over the list of student scores twice, the first time computing the average, the second time computing the difference. There are two methods of doing this. The first method is to require that the deck of student scores be returned to the input hopper of the card reader after the first reading—a slow and inconvenient process. The second method is to store the scores in memory after the first reading. In this section we will look at techniques that are helpful to the second method.

Each student card contains a score that will require one cell for storage. A different cell will have to be used for each score. We could try to allocate a set of cells by using the names SCOREA, SCOREB, . . ., etc., for cells for the first student, the second student, . . ., etc. Then the input section of the flowchart would look something like:

This approach would work fine if there were exactly six students. What if there were more or less? Since we do not know how many students there are, we cannot give individual names to the unknown number of different cells. What we need is a set of cells for the scores. This set should be arranged so that we can read into any one of them and get the results back from any one of them. In other words, we want to arrange the set of scores in a *data structure* such that we can access each.

There are various types of data structures. Many will be discussed in Chapters 7 and 8; one of them is called an *array*. An array is a set of cells in memory such that we can access any one of them directly. By "accessing an element directly" we mean that we can refer to a particular one, such as the tenth. The mathematical notation for vectors is a useful one for arrays. In mathematics, a vector **B** is a set of N numbers, called B_1, B_2, B_3, . . . , B_N. We refer to the Ith as B_I. Because our input devices cannot handle subscripting, we will write B_I as B[I]. The set of N elements B[1], B[2], . . . , B[N] is an array of elements that we can access directly. We will allow arrays in our flowchart language. The student scores can then be stored in SCORE[1], SCORE[2], . . . , etc. The score of the Ith student will be stored in SCORE[I]. The input section of the solution now takes the form of a loop that reads first to SCORE[1], then to SCORE[2], etc. A counter I is initialized to one and incremented by one. This is shown in Figure 3.40. Note that we can use SCORE[I] wherever we can use a simple name like SCORE, because it represents a cell in memory. The second part of the problem uses a similar loop to form the difference between each score and the average; however, this loop is controlled by a counter.

You can understand data structures better if you know the way they are stored and accessed in memory. An array such as we used is stored in a *contiguous* block of cells, that is, a set of cells with addresses M, M + 1, M + 2, . . . , and so on. The first cell of the block contains the first element of the array. Thus, SCORE[1] is stored in the first cell of the block used for the array SCORE. If we think of the address of the first cell of the array SCORE as having the name SCORE, then SCORE[1] is in location SCORE, SCORE[2] is in location SCORE+1, . . . , SCORE[I] is in location SCORE+I−1, and so on. Section 3.6.2 discusses how arrays are handled in machine language.

Example 3.5 — Printing the Student ID

In the student problem above, we wish to print the student ID along with the difference between his score and the average.

This can be handled by using an array ID such that the ID of the Ith student is stored in ID[I], while his score is in SCORE[I] as shown in Figure 3.41. The flowchart in Figure 3.40 is modified by changing Boxes 2, 3, and 9 to that shown in Figure 3.42.

Example 3.6 — Putting the Largest of B[I] and C[I] into A[I]

Suppose we have three arrays, A, B, and C, each with N elements, and we wish to put the largest of B[I] and C[I] into A[I] for I = 1, 2, . . . , N.

The solution is shown in Figure 3.43.

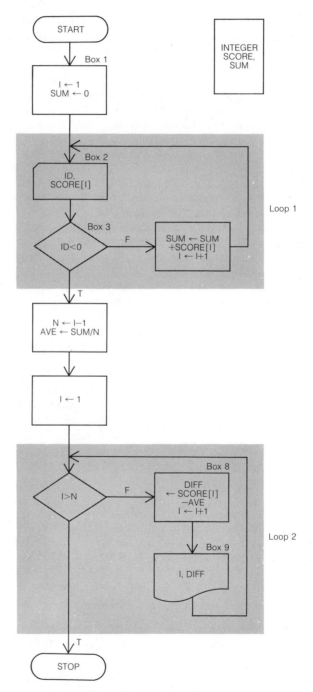

Fig. 3.40 Using two loops

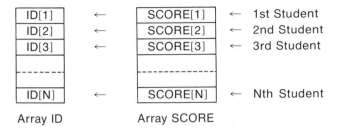

Fig. 3.41   Two arrays with related data

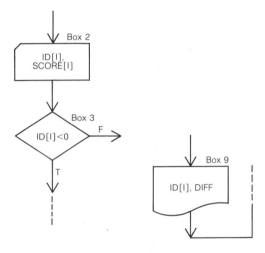

Fig. 3.42   Modification to Fig. 3.40

3.6.1 Higher Dimensional Arrays

Arrays were introduced as a means of storing lists of items that were
to be directly read or written. The data was assumed to be of the
form where it was naturally a *linear array* or *one-dimensional array—*
a list of student scores, for example. Often we encounter data that
has a more complex structure. In Example 3.5 the information con-
sisted of lists of ID numbers and student scores. Two separate arrays were used to store these lists. Suppose we have a list of bank
account identification numbers and a corresponding list of bank
balances. We could think of this as a structure consisting of a list
of pairs of numbers—the first member of a pair being the account
number, the second being the account balance. A natural way to

141

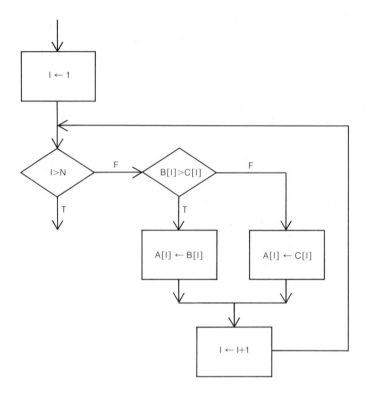

Fig. 3.43   Solution for Example 3.6

	Column 1	Column 2
Row 1	ACCOUNT ID 1	BALANCE 1
	ACCOUNT ID 2	BALANCE 2
Row N	ACCOUNT ID N	BALANCE N

Fig. 3.44   Two-dimensional array

store this information is in a *two-dimensional array* as shown in Figure 3.44.

A two-dimensional array is one that has both rows and columns. Suppose the name of this array is BANK. We would access the items by writing BANK[I, J] where I, the first index, refers to the account number (the row number in Figure 3.44), and J, the second index, tells us whether we are talking about the ID (J = 1) or the balance (J = 2). Thus J is the column number in Figure 3.44.

The notation for two-dimensional arrays is a natural translitera-
tion of the mathematical notation for matrices. A matrix is a rectangular array of numbers written in the form

$$A_{11} \ A_{12} \ A_{13} \ . \ . \ . \ A_{1N}$$
$$A_{21} \ A_{22} \ A_{23} \ . \ . \ . \ A_{2N}$$
$$. \ . \ . \qquad\qquad . \ . \ .$$
$$A_{M1} \ A_{M2} \ A_{M3} \ . \ . \ . \ A_{MN}$$

The general element is A_{IJ}, which we must write as A[I,J].

A two-dimensional array could be stored in contiguous memory
locations in any of several ways. If it were *stored by row*, we would
start at location A, say, and store the first row in A and the next
N − 1 locations; the second row would be stored in the following
N locations; and so forth. This would be in the form shown in
Figure 3.45. The address of the element A[I,J] could be found by
noting that for each increase in I we must move down by N locations
(the range of the J subscript). Thus, A[I,J] is in location A + (I − 1)
× N + J − 1.

Location	Element stored
A	A[1,1]
A+1	A[1,2]
. . .	
A+N−1	A[1,N]
A+N	A[2,1]
A+N+1	A[2,2]
. . .	
A+(I−1)×N+J−1	A[I,J]
. . .	
A+N×M−1	A[M,N]

Fig. 3.45 Storing an array by rows

If the two-dimensional array were *stored by columns*, the first
column would be stored in the first M cells starting at A, the second
column in the next M, and so on. This time the address of A[I,J]
would be A + (J − 1) × M + I − 1. Some POLs store matrices by
column (FORTRAN, for example) and some by row (PL/I, for example). We will avoid the issue by never making major use of the
way in which arrays are stored.

Example 3.7 — Weighted Sum of Array

*An example of the use of a two-dimensional array is the set of stu-
dent scores in a course. Each student takes several exams and does*

143

Location	Element stored
A	A⎮1,1⎮
A+1	A⎮2,1⎮
. . .	
A+M−1	A⎮M,1⎮
A+M	A⎮1,2⎮
A+M+1	A⎮2,2⎮
. . .	
A+(J−1)×M+I−1	A⎮I,J⎮
. . .	
A+N×M−1	A⎮M,N⎮

Fig. 3.46 Storing an array by columns

homework assignments. He receives a score for each of these. Therefore there is a one-dimensional array of scores for each student. This could be called SCORE[J], $J = 1, \ldots, N$, assuming that there are N different exams or homework assignments. However, there are many students, say M, in the class, so we will need many arrays. The best way to handle these is to group them into a two-dimensional array. Thus A[I,J] can contain the score of the Ith student on the Jth exam. It contains $N \times M$ scores.

Suppose that the instructor wishes to compute a total score for the Ith student. He does this by forming the expression[‡]

$$A[I,1] + A[I,2] + \ldots + A[I,N]$$

A more common way of arriving at the score for the whole course is to form a *weighted* sum. The instructor may have announced that each of six homework assignments counts 10% towards the grade, the mid-term counts 15%, and that the final counts 25%. In that case he would want to form

$$A[I,1] \times 0.1 + \ldots + A[I,6] \times 0.1 + A[I,7] \times 0.15 + A[I,8] \times 0.25$$

This is a weighted sum. In general we want to form

$$C[I] = \sum_{J=1}^{N} A[I,J] \times B[J]$$

where B[J] are the weights. (This calculation occurs frequently in

---

[‡]This is written more concisely with the mathematical operator, Σ, meaning sum. Thus, $\sum_{J=1}^{N} A[I,J]$ means sum A[I,J] for all values of J from 1 to N.

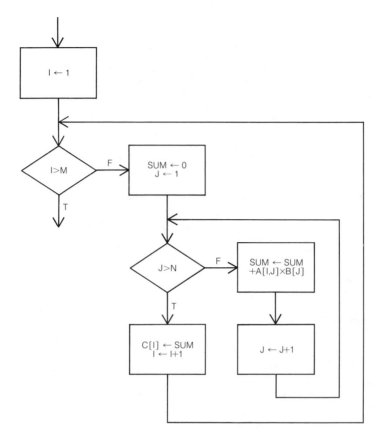

Fig. 3.47 Solution for Example 3.7

scientific work and is called the product of a matrix and a vector.)
It can be done using a double loop. The inner one computes the sum
of the N products. The outer one changes I over the range 1 to M.
A solution is shown in Figure 3.47.

In some problems we encounter even higher dimensional arrays.
A *three-dimensional array*, for example, is an array of two-dimensional arrays. It is accessed by specifying three subscripts. Thus,
if the array is B, we can refer to B[I,J,K]. A "picture" of a three-
dimensional array is given in Figure 3.48. One frequent use of three-
dimensional arrays is to store approximations to a physical variable
—for example, temperature or the flow of air around an airplane
wing. Assume that approximations to temperature are stored as a
set of points on a *rectangular grid* in ordinary three-dimensional
space. Looking at Figure 3.48 we can see that we can fill up a region
of space with these points so that there is always a point within

145

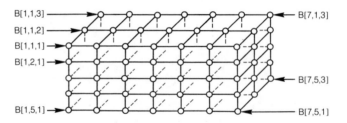

Fig. 3.48 Three-dimensional array

a small distance. If the temperature does not change too rapidly as one moves from one place to another, the temperature at an arbitrary point is reasonably approximated by the temperature at the nearest point in the matrix.

Questions

1. If array element A[13] is in location 1451, in what location is element A[29]?

*2. If A[2,3] is in location 1756 and A[3,3] is in location 1760, where is A[4,4]?

3. If A[1,1] is in location 245, A[3,4] is in location 262, and A[2,2] is in location 253, where is A[5,3]?

4. If A[2,2] is in location 127 and A[7,5] is in location 144, where is A[6,6]?

Problems

*1. The array A[I] contains N elements, I = 1, . . . , N. Write a program to find the largest difference between two consecutive elements; that is, the largest value of A[I] − A[I + 1] for I = 1, 2, . . . , N − 1.

2. Modify the program you write for problem 1 to also find the *index* of the largest difference; that is, to find a J such that A[J] − A[J + 1] is maximum.

3. The array VALUE[I] contains M elements. Write a program to find the number of elements less than the average value of all elements and the number of elements greater than that average.

4. Assume that A[I,J], I = 1, . . . , M, J = 1, . . . , N contains the Jth score of the Ith student. Assume that W[J] contains the weight of the Jth problem.

146

Write a program to *rank order* the students by storing into
K[I] the position of the Ith student in the class.

3.6.2 Handling Arrays in Machine Language

The machine language form of the program has to be able to access
the elements of SCORE. How does it do this? Recall from Chapter 2
that instructions are stored in memory cells just like data. Therefore we can do arithmetic on them. Suppose we wish to LOAD the
I[th] element of SCORE, where I is stored in a cell with that name.
The program

```
        LOAD  B
        ADD   I
        SUB   ONE
        STORE A
     A  LOAD  SCORE
          . . .
   ONE DC    1
     B  LOAD  SCORE
```

will do this. Location B contains a constant that is equivalent to
"LOAD SCORE" as an instruction. If the address SCORE is 3127,
this constant is 000 03127. If I contains the number 11, then LOAD B,
ADD I puts 000 03138 into the accumulator. The SUB ONE reduces
this to 000 03137, which is then stored in location A. Consequently,
when the contents of cell A are executed as an instruction, they
represent "LOAD SCORE+10". Modern computers provide other
faster techniques, called *indexing*, for doing this type of operation;
we will not discuss them here.

3.7 Built-In Functions

In Chapter I we pointed out that although the computer has only a
few basic capabilities such as addition and testing, many other
common operations can be formed from or approximated by combinations of these. Because such other operations are common,
we adopt a special notation for them and allow them to be used
directly. An example we have met already is the square root process.
If we have a number stored in cell X, we know that it is possible to
get an approximation to $\sqrt{X}$ by use of the basic arithmetic operators.
We will denote this by SQRT(X). SQRT is called a *function*. Because
it is one provided by our language, it is called a *built-in function*.
(It is built-in to the language, not to the hardware of the machine.)

147

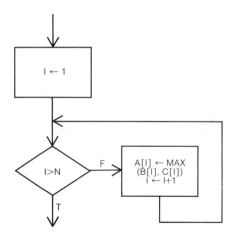

Fig. 3.49 Use of built-in functions for Example 3.6

We can use the expression SQRT(X) whenever the value of an expression approximately equal to $\sqrt{X}$ is needed. Thus

$$B \leftarrow A + SQRT(X)$$

is valid, as is

$$Q \leftarrow B + SQRT(X + Y)$$

The latter example first forms the value of $X + Y$, then finds its square root, and finally adds B to it before storing it in Q.

Other built-in functions that we will use include:

ABS(X)	Value is the magnitude (absolute value) of X
TRUNC(X)	Gives the integer part of X by truncation
ROUND(X)	Gives the integer part of X by rounding
SIN(X)	Gives an approximation to sin X
COS(X)	Gives an approximation to cos X

The above functions have a single *argument*; that is, the variable X whose value determines the value of the function. The following have two or more arguments:

MAX(A, B)	Gives a number that is the maximum of A and B. MAX(A, B, C) gives the maximum of A, B, and C, and so forth
MIN(A, B)	Gives the minimum of A and B

These functions do not add to the power of the language; they do abbreviate the writing. Thus, Example 3.6 in the previous section can be written as in Figure 3.49.

148

Computing Systems

4. Computing Systems

In Chapter 2 we discussed the way in which the physical components of a computer are organized so that it can perform useful computations. The collection of components that make up the computer is called the *hardware*. Most computer systems allow users to write procedures in one of several languages with the features of our flowchart language. Procedures written in these languages can be translated into the machine language of the system by other computer programs. They can then be executed by the hardware. These translation programs and other programs that we will discuss in this chapter form the *software* of the computer system. The software makes it possible for a user to prepare procedures and have them executed by the computer with a minimum of effort. The combination of the hardware and the software is the computer system.

The user writes his procedure in one of the available languages. Different languages have been designed to meet different needs. Among the most common languages are

FORTRAN   standing for FORmula TRANslation. This was one of the first POLs, developed by IBM in the 1950s for the IBM 704. It is mainly oriented towards scientific/engineering computing, as most of its statements provide for numerical calculations. There are a number of different versions of FORTRAN available, the differences depending partly on the computer manufacturer. Some versions of FORTRAN, for example, provide character string variables. Two special versions of FORTRAN are:

WATFOR and   WATerloo FORtran is a version of FORTRAN de-
WATFIV   veloped at the University of Waterloo, Canada. It is particularly useful for student use since it provides much better diagnostics than most compilers. (*Diagnostics* consist of comments by the system on the user program that help the user to detect errors. We will be discussing diagnostics later in this chapter.) WATFIV is a more recent version of WATFOR. It has additional data and and statement types.

ALGOL   standing for ALGOrithmic Language, was designed by an international committee. It is a language intended both as a computer language and as a publication language. It is a very precisely defined language so that different implementations of ALGOL behave identically (apart from

151

round-off error problems, which are machine dependent). It is more commonly used in Europe than in North America, where the preponderance of IBM machines makes FORTRAN and PL/I more common.

BASIC was designed as an easy-to-learn language for student use at Dartmouth. It was originally implemented for a timesharing system (see later in this chapter) on General Electric computers. It has since been implemented on many other computers.

COBOL standing for COmmon Business Oriented Language, was designed by a committee of users interested in the type of data processing common in business applications. It provides extensive facilities for handling large volumes of data and pays particular attention to input and output, since large sets of data on disk and tape and the generation of elaborate reports are an important part of business data processing.

PL/I Programming Language One was defined by a group of IBM users. It is intended to provide facilities for both business and scientific users. As such, it includes many of the facilities of FORTRAN, ALGOL, and COBOL, and is a very complex language. However, it is designed so that a user need only be aware of those features that he needs.

PL/C Is a version of PL/I developed at Cornell University. It bears the same relation to PL/I as WATFOR does to FORTRAN, so it is better for student use.

A computer system usually relies heavily on the fact that there is a large amount of storage space available that is not directly used by the user program. Because fast storage of the type discussed in Chapter 2 (called the main memory) is usually expensive, much of the storage is of a different type, such as a *disk file*. A disk file is a magnetic device that can be likened to a file drawer of paper records. Any time the computer needs to examine a record, a copy must be fetched from the file and placed in the main memory. If the computer wishes to change a record, it will have to move a copy from the main memory back into the file to replace the information currently there. Secondary memories—such as disk files—are usually much slower than the regular memory, so if programs are stored on disk, a copy is first put into the regular memory and is executed from there. (Reading from a disk file is nondestructive, while writing is destructive.) Most system programs are stored on disk files, so that copies of the required programs can be put into the main memory when they are needed.

Disk files can also be used for input and output in a restricted sense. If a user wishes to save a large amount of data or lines of program, they can be stored on a disk semipermanently and read back to the main memory days or weeks later. As will be seen in Section 4.4, the *disk pack*, which is the part of the disk file with the magnetic storage medium, can be removed for long-term storage or taken to another machine.

In Section 4.4 we will also discuss other types of input/output devices, such as typewriters. (You may be using these to input your programs.) Whether the input is transmitted to the computer system from a card reader or a typewriter, or a disk file used as an input device, the system sees the input as a series of statements in one or more languages — possibly followed by lines of data.

A simple input for a card input system using FORTRAN is shown in Figure 4.1. A similar input for a typewriter system using BASIC is shown in Figure 4.2. The input to the card system is in what we call the *batch processing mode*. The complete program and data are fed to the computer in one batch. The input to the typewriter system is in the *interactive mode*. The characters underlined in Figure 4.2 were output by the computer onto the typewriter. They are requests to the user to provide information about the job. In this case, the user interacts with the computer as he writes his program. In either

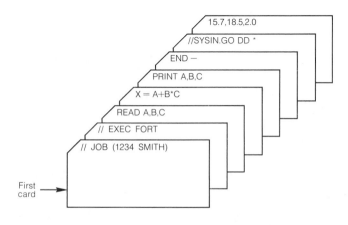

Fig. 4.1 Typical card input for FORTRAN

```
LOGIN:        1234SMITH
LANGUAGE:     BASIC
OLD OR NEW:   NEW:TEST
READY
10   INPUT A,B,C
20   LET X = A+B*C
30   PRINT A,B,C,X
40   END
RUN
?    15.7, 18.5, 2.0
     52.7
```

Fig. 4.2   Typewriter system input using BASIC

case, the information provided is essentially the same. To begin, the user gives his identification code and name. This allows the system to check that he has permission to use the computer resources and allows an appropriate account to be charged for the costs incurred. Then an indication of the language to be used is given. At some point an interactive system allows him to refer to programs previously input and stored on a disk file; this is the purpose of the OLD OR NEW request in Figure 4.2. These *commands* to the system are followed by the program and then by a command that serves to indicate the end of the program. Usually this command is RUN. It also indicates compilation and execution. When the program reaches an input statement, execution pauses for the user to type data. When it executes a PRINT statement the output appears on the typewriter immediately. In a batch processing system a command is put on a *control card*. In the IBM System 360/370 control cards are distinguished by // in columns one and two. The seventh card shown in Figure 4.1 indicates that the data for the preceding program follows immediately.

Processing a complete job involves several system programs. The flow of information and control from one program to another is shown in Figure 4.3. A brief description of each of the system programs is given below for the card example in Figure 4.1.

Processing Program	Actions
1 Accounting Program	Reads in the job card and checks that the user is allowed use of the system resources. (Tables of valid user names are usually kept on a disk file.)
2 Job Control Interpreter	Reads in the job control cards that tell the system what is to happen. In our

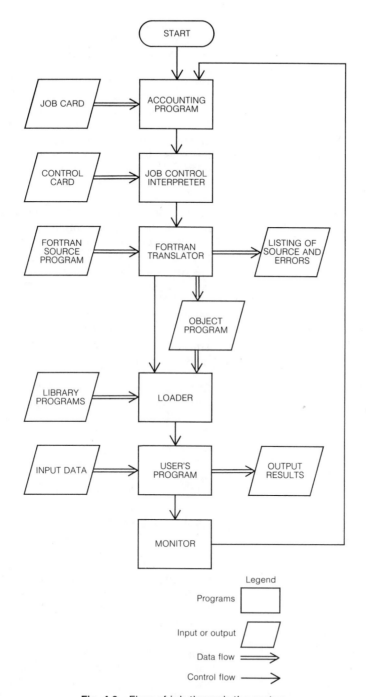

Fig. 4.3 Flow of job through the system

case, they will say that the FORTRAN compiler is to be brought into main memory from the disk file.

3 FORTRAN Compiler   Reads in the FORTRAN user program —called the source program—as input data, and translates it into machine language. The output, called the object program, is usually saved on the disk file. If the FORTRAN compilation was without error, control will be passed to the loader.

4 Loader   Loads the object program saved on the disk file by the compiler into the main memory. Any built-in subroutines and functions required by the program are loaded with it. (These built-in subroutines are programs such as SIN, SQRT, and programs for converting between cards or paper and memory formats during input/output. They form part of what is called the *system library*.)

5 User's Program   Executes the user procedure, possibly reading data cards. Input and output is done when the user requests it by library routines automatically provided by the loader. This step will often fail during program checking. The failure may be caused by an attempt to use a region of memory not available, by trying to execute a word set to a digit combination that does not represent an instruction, or any of several other reasons. If a failure occurs, execution of the program cannot continue, so control branches to an area of memory that contains part of the system software called the *monitor*.

6 Monitor   Monitors the progress of the user's job. One of its functions is to control system operations when something not allowed has been attempted. In

some cases it may allow the user to continue after corrective action has been taken by the monitor. For example, *underflow* may cause control to be transferred to the monitor, which could then set the result of the operation creating the underflow condition to floating point zero and transfer control back to the user program. If nothing can be done to save the user program, the job is terminated. (Note that there is no stop box in Figure 4.3. As soon as one job is terminated we wish to start processing the next.)

The above is only a sketch of what is happening in a simple system for a simple job. We will discuss these steps in more detail in the following sections.

4.1 Job Control Interpreter

The Job Control Interpreter is the key system program in deciding what is to be done with a user's job. Whereas there is some amount of commonality between versions of standard procedural language compilers at different computer installations and between different makes of computers, there is, unfortunately, almost no agreement between job control languages on different makes of computer systems. In many cases, installations will modify their system so that differences occur even between systems that have identical machines. Therefore we cannot talk about details of job control languages in this book. We will mention general principles, but you must find out the all-important details from your instructor or from locally available information.

A complete job may consist of a number of programs, some of which may be on cards, others of which may be already on devices such as disk files that are part of the system. Similarly, the data for the program may be available from a number of different sources such as cards or disk. The job control language provides the user a language in which he can tell the system what is to be done with his job. Statements in the language will specify such information as

- Which system program to load and execute
- Where the input data for the program is located
- Where the output from the program is to be placed

For example, a series of statements may say that the FORTRAN compiler is to be executed, that the FORTRAN source program is on the deck of cards following, and that the output is to be placed on the disk. After these job control cards would come the FORTRAN source program. These could be followed by a set of job control cards that specify that the program just stored on disk by the FORTRAN compiler is to be loaded and executed. Another control card could say that the input data is to be found on a certain disk pack. The system, at the request of the job control interpreter, would ask the operator to mount the requested disk pack on a disk unit so that the data could be read. Messages to the operator are usually printed on a *console typewriter* or displayed on a cathode ray tube for the operator to read.

The system is often designed so that the simplest usages are so-called *default* conditions; that is, if the user's program and data are on cards, it is not necessary for him to make a specific statement to that effect—the system assumes that they are on cards unless it is told otherwise.

4.2 Language Translators

A language compiler accepts as input a set of statements called a *source program*, and produces as output a set of instructions called an *object program* and a listing of the source program and any errors detected by the translator. Generally the object program is a machine language program that can be executed on the computer.

The source program language we have been using in Chapter 3 is a flowchart language. Although there is no reason that a compiler could not be written to accept this language, none exists because there are currently no convenient ways of inputting flowcharts. Instead, most systems accept a number of source languages that provide facilities similar to those of our flowchart language. (You are probably learning to use a version of one or more of these.) The comments we will make about the compilers will be independent of the source language or machine language involved.

There are two major tasks to be accomplished in the typical compilation process. The first task is to assign memory space for all of the variables used in the program.

When the programmer refers to a variable A, he is referring to a memory cell which will contain the current value of that variable at execution time. When he refers to an indexed array of variables B[I] for I from 1 to 50, he is referring to one of a block of 50 cells reserved for data in the array at execution time. Constants used in the program will also have to be assigned locations in memory so that they are available for arithmetic operations.

The second major task is to convert the statements written in the source language into a machine language equivalent. This involves recognizing the different types of statements and generating appropriate instruction sequences for each statement. The compiler assigns memory space for the variables so that when the translated program is executed, each variable name in the source program corresponds to one or more locations in memory. If the source program is correct, the compiler will produce a program that can be executed. If the source program is incorrect, the compiler may or may not be able to translate it.

The compiler can detect only certain types of errors. It cannot, for example, detect the use of a wrong arithmetic operation. If the programmer writes $A + B$ when he means $A - B$, there is no way that the compiler can realize that an error has been committed. We call these *logic errors*. However, if the programmer mispunches a card so that the statement is not valid, the compiler will be able to detect an error. Thus if he writes $A \leftarrow B + \times C$, the compiler can detect an error. It cannot, however, correct the statement because it does not have any idea what the programmer intended. We call these errors *syntax errors*.

Syntax errors fall into three classes: fatal (which prevent the compiler from generating valid machine language), non-fatal (for which valid machine language can be generated, but which indicate some serious flaw in the program), and minor errors (which can be corrected by a "forgiving" compiler). An example of a fatal error is the "arithmetic assignment statement" "$A + B - C$". Since it does not include an assignment operator, it is not, in fact, an assignment statement. Nor does it look like any other valid statement, so the compiler will reject it as a fatal error. An example of a non-fatal error for which machine language can be generated arises when a section of program is unreachable. This could occur in our flowchart language if the programmer used an assignment box with no arrows entering it. This piece of the program could never be executed, and so there is something either wrong or superfluous in the program. However, the rest of the program can be compiled (assuming no other errors) and executed. Minor errors arise from misuse of detailed rules in the language. FORTRAN is a prime example of a language containing these. Many parts of a statement have to be separated by commas in FORTRAN, although there are a few cases where they are not used. The DO statement, for example, is written "DO # Var = #,#" where the # signs stand for any integers and Var stands for any integer variable name. There should be no comma between the first # sign and Var. Consequently, the statement DO #,Var = #,# is strictly invalid, but many compilers will comment and remove the offending comma.

The programmer should check error messages produced by the compiler carefully even if they are non-fatal because they are often

159

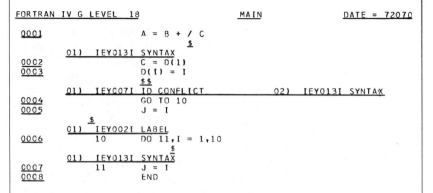

Notes: 1. Listing contains original program and compiler-generated comments. The latter are underlined.

2. The numbers in the left-hand column are numbers assigned to statements by the compiler.

3. The IEYxxxx is a reference number to a list of all error messages. The supplier of the compiler provides a book with a more detailed discussion of the cause of the error.

4. The $ character appears under the first (leftmost) character in error.

5. The name D in statement 2 was assumed to be the name of a function. In statement 3 it cannot be the name of a function, so the message means Identifier Conflict.

Fig. 4.4 Sample FORTRAN program with error messages

an indication of other errors. Frequently the compiler's diagnostic message will not seem to be meaningful because it has misunderstood the intent of the program. This will happen when the error causes it to interpret part of the program in a manner not intended by the programmer. A frequent example of this occurs in confusions between array names and function names. In our flowchart language we have used parentheses in function references such as SQRT(X), and brackets in indexed array references such as B[I]. This is in agreement with ALGOL usage. However, FORTRAN, PL/I and some other languages use parentheses in both cases. Since these languages require that arrays be declared explicitly, failure to declare an array will result in the compiler thinking that "B(I)" is a reference to a function named B. This may not cause an error message until there is an attempt to load the object program for execution, at which time it may not be possible to find a library program named B. (If there is such a library program, the error will not appear until execution time when the answers will be invalid.) On the other hand, if the programmer attempts to assign a value of B(I) in an assignment statement, the compiler will detect an error at the time it translates that statement and produce a diagnostic that says something about incorrect usage of functions. Figure 4.4 shows a sample output listing of a FORTRAN program with error messages.

QUESTIONS

1. What is an object program?

2. What are library programs?

3. What could happen when the computer fetches the content of a cell containing a data word and attempts to execute it as an instruction?

4. What is a source program?

5. What is (are) the job control card(s) that request(s) a compilation in the language you are using?

6. What is a compiler?

7. What are the two main tasks of a compiler?

8. What is a fatal error? Give some examples.

4.3 THE MONITOR

After a user program has been successfully translated by the compiler and loaded for execution, it becomes the duty of the monitor to provide certain basic functions needed during its execution and to detect its termination, which may occur either because of errors or because of the execution of a normal termination command. (We used STOP in our flowchart language.)

Many of the functions provided within the monitor handle input and output from the program. Although we have discussed input and output as if there were a single card reader for input and a single printer for output, a typical large computer system has many readers and printers, since they are among the slower hardware units, and many disk files, since a large amount of storage is needed. Usually several different jobs are being read and several different outputs are being written at the same time. This does not concern the average user who can continue to think of his program as if it were the sole occupant of the system and had control of the only reader and printer. In fact, the cards that contain his program and data have probably been read and stored on a disk file before compilation and execution of the program begins, and his program output is probably stored temporarily on a disk file so that it can be printed later. The monitor supervises these jobs. When the user requests the next input card, the monitor reads the data that is on that card image from its storage place on the disk file; when the user program attempts to print a line, the monitor stores it in a free area on the disk file for later printing.

On most computer systems, many conditions cause control to branch to the monitor program. They include gross numerical errors that result in numbers too large to be represented (overflow) and attempts to execute impossible operations—for example, an attempt to reference an area of storage not assigned to the user. These indicate program errors. We will discuss the problem of locating such errors in Chapter 6.

4.4 Input, Output and Storage Devices in a Large System Organization

A large computer system often serves a group of users with differing needs. A university installation, in particular, has to meet a wide range of demands. It may be providing a learning resource for its students, in which case it will be used for many short jobs—most of which do not execute correctly. It may be used to support research in many departments, in which case long calculations are performed—many requiring access to masses of data. (It is not unusual for a high-energy physics experiment to accumulate around 100 million characters of data.) Also, it may be used for data processing—of student and business office records, for example. To meet those needs, a computer must provide a range of devices appropriate to the demands. We have already studied simple card input and printer output, and briefly mentioned typewriter input/output. We have discussed main storage and how it can be supplemented by disk storage. In the following subsections we will look at these and other devices and the way in which they are controlled by the system in more detail.

4.4.1 Low Speed Input/Output Devices

Many computer systems have low speed input/output devices, called *remote terminals*, attached to the central computer. These terminals may be typewriter-like devices, or they may include some sort of visual output on a cathode ray tube of the sort used in television sets. (A typewriter terminal is shown in Figure 4.5; a cathode ray tube terminal is shown in Figure 4.6.) Both terminals have keyboards for program and data input. When the computer has readied the device to accept data, depressing a key transmits the code for that character to the computer memory. The computer can sense when this has been done and can either process that character or read another. A fast typist can seldom type more than 10 characters per

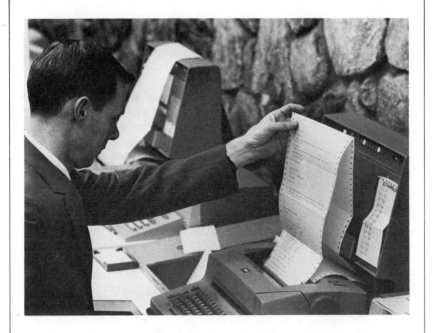

Fig. 4.5 IBM typewriter used as computer terminal in American Airlines Sabre System

Fig. 4.6 NCR 795 terminal

163

second. In the tenth of a second between characters a typical computer can execute 100,000 operations. Fortunately, the computer does not have to be idle between characters; in Section 4.4.3 we will see that it will switch to another user's program and do useful work there.

When the computer is ready to send output to either a typewriter or a CRT terminal, it transmits a character at a time. When that character has been typed or displayed, the computer is notified so that another character can be transmitted. This process is repeated until a complete message has been transmitted. Although the computer is operating a character at a time, the user need not be aware of the fact. System programs are provided so that he can read a complete line with a single input statement and type or display a complete line with a single output statement.

Whatever the design of a terminal, it can usually function in a number of ways. One way is by using an advanced keypunch that enables the user to input his programs and data directly into the disk files of the system. The major benefit of this is that it is usually possible to correct single lines or single characters in the copy of the program stored on the disk, and then to rerun the program without resubmitting the entire program through a card reader. A second way in which such terminals can be used is as direct input/output devices for the user program.

Telephone lines are an important mode of remote terminals operation. The character codes are transmitted between the computer and the terminals over wires at a fairly low speed. Since telephone lines provide this capability, it is possible to connect a number of them to a computer *input/output controller* (a device that sequences the reading and writing of characters) and to connect a number of remote terminals to the lines. Since all lines go to a telephone switching office, a user can dial the phone number assigned to the computer lines to automatically connect his terminal to the computer.

4.4.2 Large Storage Devices

Most large-scale storage devices use a magnetic material as the recording medium. The fastest, most expensive device is called Large Capacity Storage (LCS) by IBM, or Extended Core Storage (ECS) by CDC. It uses the same principle as most main memories. A core is a tiny ring of magnetic material as shown in Figure 4.7. It can be magnetized in either of two directions by passing currents in one or more wires through the core. The two directions are used to represent a 0 or 1. The state of a core can be sensed on another wire called a *sense wire* by detecting a voltage induced on it when the core changes state as shown in Figure 4.8. If a current is passed that sets the core to the zero state, a voltage is induced only if it

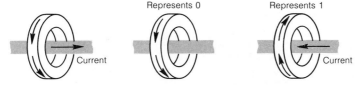

Fig. 4.7 Magnetic core

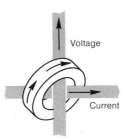

Fig. 4.8 Reading information from a core

were previously in one state. This destroys the stored information, but the memory unit automatically rewrites it for us so that it is not lost. The cores are very small and are wired in large arrays called *core planes* such as the one shown in Figure 4.9. Many of these planes are used in a core unit. A typical LCS unit contains about 10 million cores and can store over a million characters of information. Words can be read or written in a few millionths of a second.

If the magnetic recording medium is a coating on a non-magnetic base that can be removed from the storage unit and replaced, the storage unit can also be used for input/output. The disk storage unit is such a device. The magnetic material is on flat disk-shaped surfaces that rotate under a read/write head as shown in Figure 4.10. Tiny spots on the surfaces can be magnetized in one of two directions by passing currents through the head. These directions represent 0 and 1. The information can be read by sensing an induced voltage in the read winding when the magnetized spots pass under the head. The physical arrangement of a disk is shown in Figure 4.11. The disk pack consists of six disk platters, each with a coating on both sides. The outer surfaces are not used because they can be scratched too easily; only 10 surfaces are used to record information. The disk rotates at about 33 revolutions per second. The read/write heads are on a comb-type access arm that can be positioned to place the heads over two hundred different tracks on the disk surfaces. The disk pack can be removed and stored for a long time without deterioration of the information on it.

Whereas any word in main memory or an LCS unit can be read or

165

Fig. 4.9 Core plane

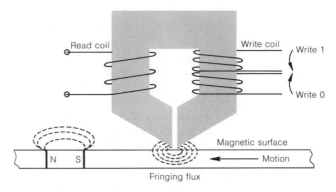

Read coil

Write coil

Write 1

Write 0

Magnetic surface

N S

Motion

Fringing flux

Fig. 4.10 Magnetic recording

written in the same amount of time, it may take a long time to reach a group of words on a disk unit. We first have to move the read/write heads over the right track, then wait for the disk to rotate so that the required information is under the head. This delay averages about a tenth of a second. However, once there, we can read data at about a million characters every six seconds.

There are many other arrangements of magnetic recording de-

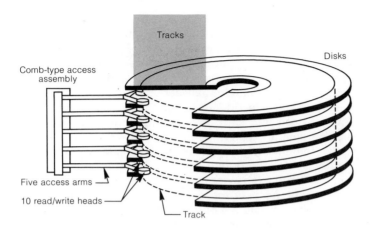

Fig. 4.11 Disk access mechanism and disk pack

vices—tapes, drums, and data cells, for example. The interested reader is referred to M. Bohl, *Information Processing* (Chicago: Science Research Associates, Inc., 1971).

4.4.3 Control of I/O by the Operating System

Earlier we discussed the system programs used to process a single job. Together with a program called the *scheduler* they form the *operating system*. The operating system attempts to make efficient use of the computer hardware by keeping units as busy as possible and by processing as many jobs in a given time as possible. It may also have to recognize the priority of some important jobs. To do this it will put jobs from several users in different parts of main memory. The CPU can only process one job at any one time. However, when a job performs a step that requires it to wait for completion of an input/output operation, the CPU can process a different job for a while. Either after a given time has elapsed or when an input/output unit signals that it has completed the operation (called an *interrupt*), the CPU can switch and process yet another job.

Each job in memory will have access to a number of input/output devices. A unit such as a card reader or printer can be used only by a single job, but storage units such as disk files can be used by several jobs, each using a different region. The system controls the actual input and output operations so that it can check to see that a job uses only the region or unit assigned to it. There are three major types of organization of operating systems. They are *batch*, *interactive*, and *real time*.

In batch operation the objective is to process as many jobs as

167

possible in a given time. Because it is desirable to keep the CPU running as rapidly as possible, as many jobs as will fit are loaded into the main memory. Rather than have one printer and one card reader for each job, all input/output for user jobs is done from disk files. Two system jobs, the *input processor* and the *output processor*, move this information between card readers and disk, or between disk and line printers, respectively. The *input processor* reads all jobs fed into card readers and stores them on the disk; at the same time it keeps a list of jobs to be done. The scheduler takes jobs from this list and loads them into main memory whenever space is available. The output from a job is put on the disk file by the monitor. When a job is terminated, the scheduler uses the space for another job and puts the output on a work list for the *output processor*, which prints the output when a printer is available. In a well-balanced system — that is, one with the right number of readers, printers, and disk files for the power of the CPU — units will be busy most of the time.

In an interactive system, the objective is to make it possible for a user to work directly with his program — making changes, recompiling and executing it, typing input only as input statements are executed, and receiving output immediately. Because each user interacts with the computer for a considerable length of time on one job — much longer than it would take his program to execute in a batch — many more programs must be in memory at one time. There must be at least one terminal connected to each program, so a typical interactive system will have 20 to 50 terminals.

In a real-time system, the computer is *online* to some device that must be serviced within a maximum time period. A spaceship control system is of this type. Real-time systems are frequently used in *process control*, which is the direct control by computer of a non-computer system, such as an electrical power station or a steel mill. Another example is an airline reservation system. Real-time systems are characterized by many input and output devices under the control of one program. A reservation system, for example, has many thousands of agent terminals scattered over the country. They are connected by telephone lines to one computer, which normally executes only one program.

In practice, many systems run two or even three of these modes of service. There could be a *background* batch processing set of jobs that are executed when there is nothing else to do. At the next level there could be an interactive system communicating with user terminals. The highest priority jobs must be the real-time jobs. For example, a computer doing batch and interactive processing might also be monitoring an experiment. When signals from the experiment indicate that data must be input or output, the computer must react quickly before the state of the experiment has changed.

QUESTIONS

1. What are the objectives of batch, interactive, and real-time operating systems?

*2. Why do batch systems not allow user jobs to read directly from card readers?

Flowchart Language II

5. Flowchart Language II

We defined various flowchart symbols in Chapter 3 and examined typical problem solutions that used them. The symbols introduced there are adequate to solve any problems we may meet. In this chapter we are going to introduce additional symbols that make a problem solution and its flowchart easier to prepare and follow. These symbols correspond to some concepts of program organization and problem solution that will be introduced in this chapter.

5.1 Program Loops

In Section 3.5 we examined program loops and saw that they arose in several ways. Among these were

- Loops that read data and terminate on some special condition — for example, a dummy final card with recognizable data such as a negative number.

- Iterative loops that solve a problem — perhaps by a trial and error process. These loops stop when the completed solution is sufficiently accurate.

- Counting loops in which a number of items are to be processed. This number is known at the start of the loop, so a counter can be used to count passages through the processing in the loop. The loop is stopped when the counter reaches a final value.

The counting type of loop occurs so frequently that we introduce special symbols for such loops. The important characteristics of this type of loop are

- A variable is used as a counter.
- An initial value is required for the counter (often 1).
- An increment amount is required for the counter (often 1).
- An end value is required for the counter.
- The section of code that is processed inside the loop must be specified.

If a counting type of loop were to be executed for values of I between J and N, that is, for I = J, J + 1, J + 2, . . . , N, we could write the flowchart shown in Figure 5.1.

This flow can be written in the more concise form shown in Figure 5.2, in which two new boxes have been introduced. The rectangle contains an assignment statement that specifies the variable used as a counter (called the *controlled variable*), the increment to be added after each execution of the loop, and the final value to be

173

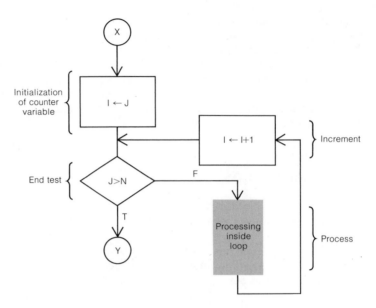

Fig. 5.1 Counting loop

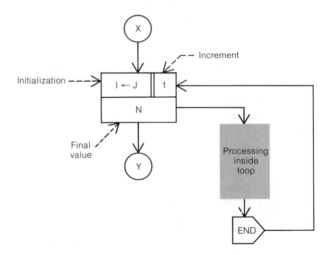

Fig. 5.2 Loop control box

used. For now we assume that execution stops when the value of the controlled variable exceeds the final value. The END box, although not strictly necessary, emphasizes that we have reached the end of the loop processing and are about to branch back to the incrementing stage.

174

It is very important to notice that the flowcharts in Figures 5.1 and 5.2 do *not* execute the loop if the initial value J exceeds the final value N as the first end test is made immediately after the initial assignment. This agrees with ALGOL and PL/I usage in FOR and DO loops, but not with FORTRAN usage in DO loops. In the latter, the loop is always executed once; the first end test is made after the first increment. It is also important to note that, whereas in Figure 5.1 the controlled variable I will have the value N + 1 when control reaches connector Box Y, we assume that the value of I is not known when control reaches connector Box Y in Figure 5.2. Our reason for this is that the same is true in many languages such as FORTRAN.

We can visualize the flow of control in a loop as shown in Figure 5.3. Either control passes straight down or it goes around the loop one or more times and then continues down.

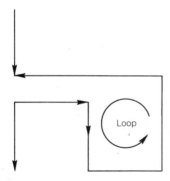

Fig. 5.3   Control flow in a loop

Example 5.1 — Adding Two Arrays

Suppose we wish to add A[I] to B[I] and store the result in C[I] for each I between 1 and 20.

The flowchart in Figure 5.4 achieves this.

Example 5.2 — Finding the Average and Variance

Suppose we wish to find the average and the variance of the N numbers A[I] through A[N]. (The variance is defined as the average of the squares of the differences between the A[I] and the average of the A[I].)

One solution uses two loops. The first loop computes the average and the second computes the variance. These loops occur sequen-

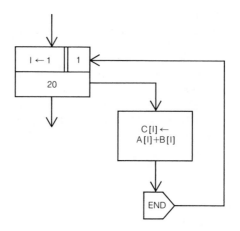

Fig. 5.4 Solution for Example 5.1

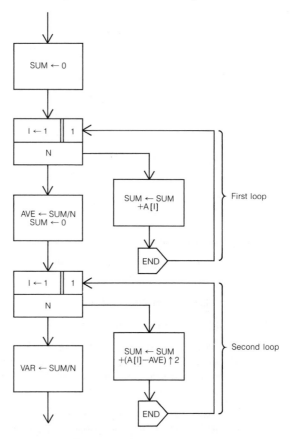

Fig. 5.5 Solution for Example 5.2

tially because the result of the first (the average) is needed in the second. The solution is given in Figure 5.5. Note that the loops are exclusive; that is, no part of one is inside the other.

Example 5.3 — Searching

Suppose we have an array of numbers A[1], A[2], . . . , A[N] and wish to find out if a given number B is equal to any one of the A[I], I = 1 to N.

To solve this we must compare B with each of the A[I]. This is shown in Figure 5.6. If B is not equal to any of the A[I], then control transfers to Y after the completion of the loop. If, however, B matches one of the A[I], then control transfers immediately to X with I containing a value that identifies the element of the array A matching B.

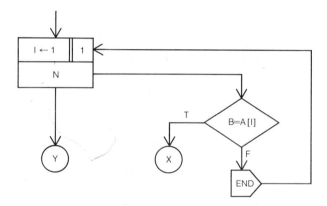

Fig. 5.6 Solution for Example 5.3

The last example introduces a new point. The transfer to X takes place from the middle of the loop when a matching entry is found. If we are content to find the first matching entry, we no longer need to continue the loop. That is, the section of flowchart connected to X will not eventually come back to the END box. We call such a transfer an *exit* from the loop. There can be any number of exits from the processing in a loop. However, **there may not be any paths entering the processing of a loop from outside of the loop**. A loop is defined by a loop control box and a matching END box as shown in Figure 5.7. The reason that paths may not enter the loop processing is that the initial conditions and incrementing must be started by passing through the loop control box.

177

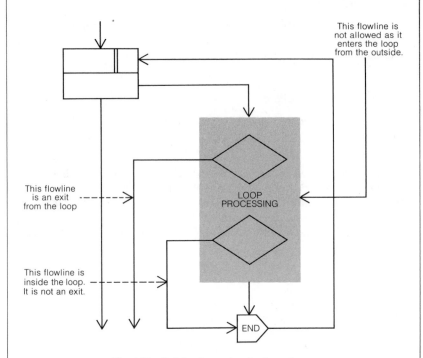

Fig. 5.7 Entries to and exits from loop

Example 5.4—Different Increments

So far we have used increments of one. In this example we use a different increment. Suppose the odd-numbered locations in the array I(J), J = 1, 2, ... contain bank account identification numbers and the next higher even-numbered locations contain the account balances in cents for those accounts. Thus if I(7) contains 1275317, the balance of the customer with that account number is stored in cell I(8). The problem is to print the balance of the account whose number is stored in IAC. Assume that there are 100 accounts, so the array I uses 200 cells.

The solution is to search through the odd-numbered cells to find the account number. A flowchart solution is shown in Figure 5.8.

Two things should be noticed about this flowchart. In Box 1 we specified an increment of 2 starting at 1, but the end test is 200. The variable K will never take on the value 200, since it assumes only the odd integers. However, the end test stops the loop when the controlled variable K passes the end test. Thus the loop is executed with values of K = 1, 3, 5, . . ., 199. When K is incremented to 201, the end test stops the loop. The second thing to be noted is in Box 4.

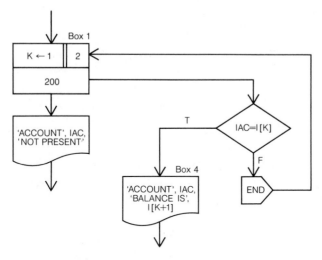

Fig. 5.8 Solution for Example 5.4

There the array variable I uses an index that is an expression, namely K + 1. We will allow expressions to be used to index into arrays, although some programming languages are more restrictive.

Example 5.5 — Polynomial Evaluation

Suppose we have the coefficients a_1, a_2, . . ., of the polynomial $p = a_n + a_{n-1}t + a_{n-2}t^2 + . . . + a_1t^{n-1}$ stored in the array A[1], A[2], . . ., and that we wish to compute p when t and n are given in locations with those names.

Problems of this sort arise when we want to estimate the value of common mathematical functions. For example, the logarithm of 1 + x is given by

$$0 + x - \frac{x^2}{2} + \frac{x^3}{3} - \frac{x^4}{4} + . . .$$

if x is less than one. We can approximate log(1 + x) by evaluating the first n terms of this sum for moderate size n.

If we evaluate p as it is written, we will use 2n − 3 multiplications; n − 2 to evaluate each power of t up to t^{n-1}, and n − 1 to multiply each of the a_i by t^{n-i} for i = 1, . . . , n − 1. Therefore, we factor the expression into the following form:

$$p = a_n + t \times (a_{n-1} + t \times (a_{n-2} + t \times . . . + t \times (a_2 + t \times a_1) . . .))$$

179

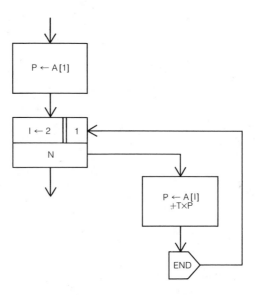

Fig. 5.9 Solution for Example 5.5

This can be evaluated by the steps

$$p \leftarrow a_1$$
$$p \leftarrow a_2 + t \times p$$
$$p \leftarrow a_3 + t \times p$$
$$\ldots$$
$$p \leftarrow a_n + t \times p$$

which uses only $n - 1$ multiplications. A flowchart is shown in Figure 5.9. This example uses the fact that if $N = 1$, the loop is not executed at all because in that case $P = A[1]$.

Example 5.6 — Sorting

Suppose we are given an array A[I], I = 1, 2, . . . , N that contains floating-point numbers. We wish to rearrange these numbers so that they are in order; that is, to that A[1] contains the largest number, A[2] the next largest, and so on, until A[N] contains the smallest.

We do this problem in two parts. First we find the largest of the N elements A[I], I = 1, . . . , N. Suppose this is A[J]. We exchange A[1] and A[J]. Now the first element is the largest and we are left with $N - 1$ elements in the sub-array A[I], I = 2, . . . , N. If we apply the same process to this sub-array we will put the next largest element into position A[2] and be left with a smaller sub-array A[I], I = 3, . . . , N. We can continue this way until we are left with the

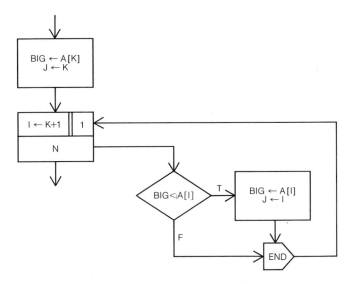

Fig. 5.10 Inner loop of sorting problem

sub-array A[I], I = N, which has only one element in it. It, by definition, is in order, and will contain the smallest element from the
original array because we removed the largest remaining element
at each previous stage.

In a problem of this sort, it is usually easier to study the central
section first. We want a loop to find the largest element of the
array A[I], I = K, . . ., N where K is some integer between 1 and
N − 1, and to save the value of J for which A[J] is the largest. The
solution to this part is shown in Figure 5.10.

To do the complete sort we execute the program section shown
in Figure 5.10 for K = 1, and then exchange A[J] with A[K]. Next we
execute the program section with K = 2 and exchange A[J] with
A[K]. This is repeated for K = 3, . . ., N − 1. Evidently, we can use
a program loop that contains the program section of Figure 5.10
in the loop processing. This is shown in Figure 5.11.

The control structure in Figure 5.11 is called a *nested loop*.
The inner loop, which controls variable I, is totally contained
(nested) within the outer loop, which controls variable K. The nesting is very apparent when we sketch the control flow as in Figure
5.12.

The solution in Figure 5.11 requires a long time for execution.
The inner loop is executed for I from 2 to N the first time, for I from
3 to N the second time, and so on. Thus, it is executed a total of
(N − 1) + (N − 2) + (N − 3) + . . . + 2 + 1 times. This is a total of

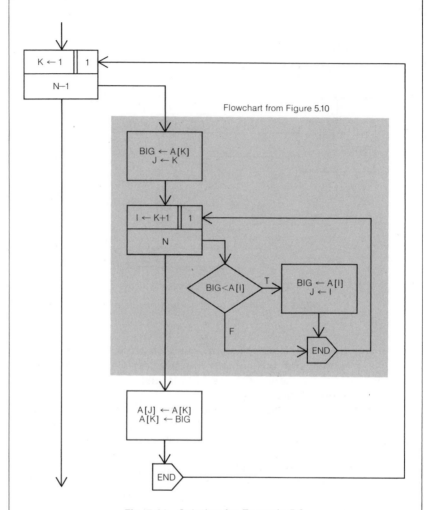

Flowchart from Figure 5.10

Fig. 5.11 Solution for Example 5.6

$N \times (N - 1)/2$ times‡ so, for example, if N is 100, it is executed 4950 times. This is independent of the original order of the items. Even

---

‡This can be seen by writing down the series once in the order given and once in reverse to get:

$$(N - 1) + (N - 2) + (N - 3) + \ldots + \quad 3 \quad + \quad 2 \quad + \quad 1$$
$$\quad 1 \quad + \quad 2 \quad + \quad 3 \quad + \ldots + (N - 3) + (N - 2) + (N - 1)$$

If we add, we find that twice the value of the series is

$$N \quad + \quad N \quad + \quad N \quad + \ldots + \quad N \quad + \quad N \quad + \quad N$$

There are $N - 1$ terms present, so the sum of twice the series is $N \times (N - 1)$. Hence the value of the series is $N \times (N - 1)/2$.

182

if they were already in order and needed no sorting, 4950 passes through the inner loop would be required.

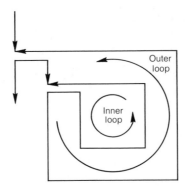

Fig. 5.12 Nested loops

Example 5.7 — Bubble Sort

This method requires fewer steps if the data is partially in order. We search down the array A[I], starting from I = 1 and continuing until we find an element out of order. Thus if A[1] ≥ A[2] ≥ . . . ≥ A[K], but A[K] < A[K + 1], the (K + 1)ᵗʰ element is the first element out of order. We then search back from A[K], moving elements down one slot until we find the right place to put A[K + 1]. This is diagrammed in Figure 5.13.

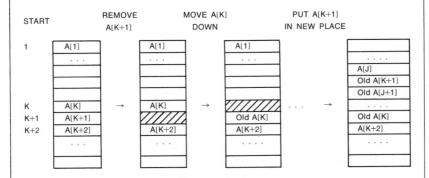

Fig. 5.13 Bubble sort

The name of the method arises from the fact that the element A[K + 1] is allowed to rise up to its place in order, like a bubble in a bottle of fluid. The inner loop for this process is shown in Figure 5.14.

Notice that we are using a negative increment in the loop. Because of this, we do not expect the loop to stop until the counter K is reduced *below* the end test value of one. Second, notice that the loop has an exit to Box 9. If this is taken, the right place for the old value of A[K + 1] is in cell A[I + 1]. If the loop terminates normally, the right place for the old value of A[K + 1] is at the top of the array. In this case we must ensure that I contains zero before going to Box 9 since we do not know the value of the controlled variable I after a normal termination.

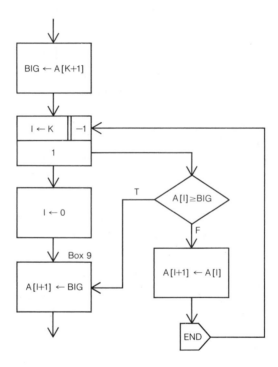

Fig. 5.14 Inner loop

After the process in Figure 5.14 has been executed, the first K + 1 elements of A are in order. The search can then continue down the table to see if other elements are out of order. The full program is given in Figure 5.15. If the array is already in order, the TRUE exit will never be taken from Box 2, so one pass through the data will be sufficient to "sort" it.

Of course, the worst case will still take N × (N − 1)/2 passes through the inner loop. This case occurs when the original data is in reverse order, as the following example shows.

Suppose the array A contains the three elements 1.7, 2.3, and 8.7. The values of the important variables and the flow through Figure 5.15 are shown in Table 5.1.

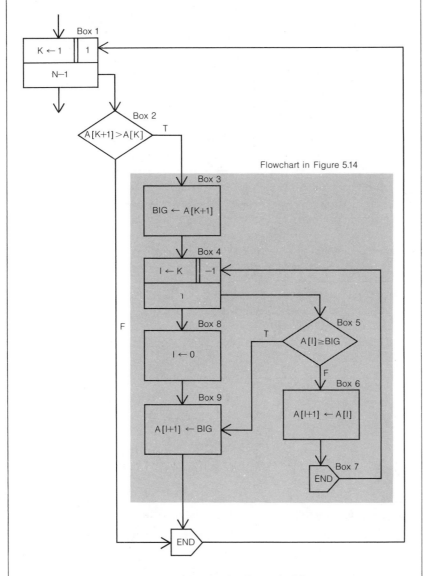

Fig. 5.15 Solution for Example 5.7

TABLE 5.1

COUNTING LOOP

Box to be Executed	Values of Variables (Only Changes Shown)						
	K	I	BIG	A[1]	A[2]	A[3]	
1	1			1.7	2.3	8.7	
2							
3			2.3				
4		1					
5							] 1st pass of inner loop
6					1.7		
4		0					
8		0					
9				2.3			
1	2						
2							
3			8.7				
4		2					
5							] 2nd pass of inner loop
6						1.7	
4		1					
5							] 3rd pass of inner loop
6					2.3		
4		0					
8		0					
9			8.7				
1	3						

Questions

1. Consider the following program (next page):

   *a. If, initially, K = 1 and L ≥ J are positive, how many numbers are printed?

   *b. How many numbers are printed if L ≥ J and K > 0?

   *c. How many numbers are printed if K ≠ 0?

186

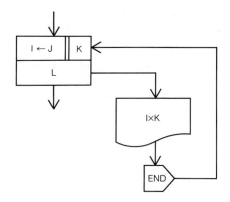

2. Consider the following program:

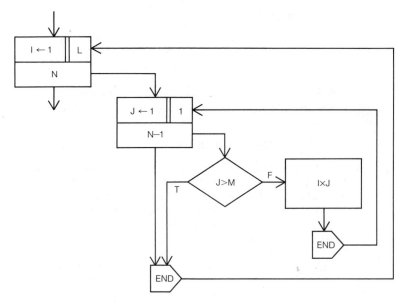

a. If L = 1 and M ≥ N − 1, how many numbers are printed?
b. If L > 0 and M ≥ N − 1, how many numbers are printed?
c. If L > 0, how many numbers are printed?

Problems

*1. The array A[I], I = 1, . . . , N contains N numbers. Give a flow-chart segment that computes the difference between the smallest and the largest.

187

2. Using only one loop, give a flowchart segment that finds the second largest number in the array A[I], 1 = 1, . . ., N. Assume that N ≥ 2.

*3. Give a complete flowchart that reads N cards, each containing two numbers A[I] and B[I], I = 1, . . . , N, in that order. Then compute the means

$$AX = \frac{1}{N} \sum_{I=1}^{N} A[I] \; \left(\text{This means } \frac{1}{N} \; (A[1] + A[2] + \ldots + A[N]).\right)$$

and

$$BX = \frac{1}{N} \sum_{I=1}^{N} B[I]$$

Finally compute and print the *correlation*

$$C = \frac{1}{N} \sum_{I=1}^{N} (A[I] - AX) \times (B[I] - BX)$$

4. An array X[I], I = 1, . . . , M, contains floating-point numbers. Give a flowchart segment that computes the sum of the N largest. Assume that 1 ≤ N ≤ M.

5. Give a complete flowchart that handles the following problem:

A bank wishes to read cards that contain details of transactions and requests for information. Each card contains three numbers. The first indicates the type of transaction or request, the second the account number of the customer, and the third the amount of the transaction. The following cases are to be accepted:

First number on card	Action
1	Add the amount of the customer's account.
2	Subtract the amount from the customer's account.
3	Print the balance in the customer's account. (The third input number is ignored.)
4	Print a list of all customers in ascending order of account number, list the balance in each account, and print the sum of all balances. (The second and third input numbers are ignored.)

| 5 | Open a new account with the third number as the initial balance. |

If an addition or subtraction is attempted on a nonexistent account, an appropriate message should be printed. If a subtraction is made that would make the balance negative, the transaction should not be performed, but an appropriate message should be printed.

Initialize your data so that the bank has no customers.

5.2 INPUT/OUTPUT

In this section we examine some additional features of input and output boxes, and see how they might be applied in various problems. So far we have assumed that an input box contains a list of cell names. These names were either simple variable names such as A or X, or elements of arrays such as B[I], where I is the name of a cell that had already been assigned a value. It is possible that the read statement that includes B[I] in its list could also assign the value to I, as long as it does that first. Thus, the flowchart in Figure 5.16 reads an integer and assigns that value to I; it then reads a floating-point number into B[I]. If the input card contained "5, 15.71," the result of the read operation above would be to set I to 5 and B[5] to 15.71.

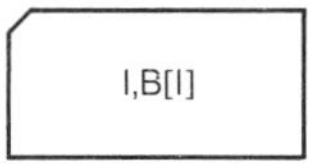

I,B[I]

Fig. 5.16   Reading an integer and using it as an index

Example 5.8 — Inserting into an Array

Suppose we have taken a series of temperature readings at some of the points shown in Figure 3.48 (page 146), and we have recorded the I, J, and K of the points, and the temperatures T[I, J, K]. We wish to read these temperatures into the proper places in the array T.

Since we do not know how many cards to expect when we write the program, we assume that each card has the numbers I, J, K, T[I, J, K], and zero punched on it in that order, except for the last card which has I, J, K, T[I, J, K], and a one punched on it. A program to read in this data is shown in Figure 5.17. If temperature readings are taken at all points, we can save ourselves punching all of the I's, J's, and K's by using three loops nested inside each other. If I

189

runs from 1 to NI, J from 1 to NJ, and K from 1 to NK, we can use the program shown in Figure 5.18.

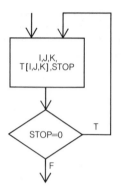

Fig. 5.17   Example 5.8 (1)

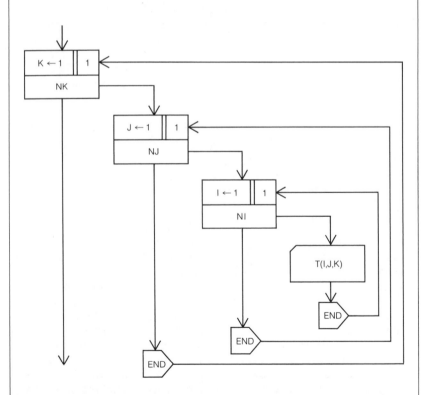

Fig. 5.18   Example 5.8 (2)

However, it is a rather lengthy way of expressing a fairly simple task. We could write simply

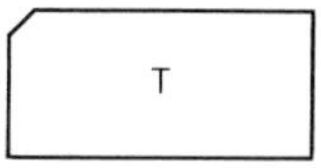

As long as it is known that T is an array of NI × NJ × NK variables, this can be interpreted as meaning "read in all of the elements of T." There will have to be a *declaration* of the number of elements in the array T and we will have to know in which order they are read. We assume that they are read in the order that they are stored. Since this depends on the language that is used, we will not be specific here. You must use the order in the language you are using. (We will also ignore the question of how the size of the array is declared, as this is a relatively unimportant detail.)

We could also express this read operation by use of the repetitive specification shown in Figure 5.19. This uses the idea of an *indexed list*, written as

("variable list", "controlled variable" ← "initial" TO "final")

It is equivalent to a list consisting of the "variable list" being written out, first with the "controlled variable" equal to the value of "initial," then to this value plus one, plus two, and so on, up to the value of "final." Thus

$$(T[I, J, K], I \leftarrow 1 \text{ TO } NI)$$

is equivalent to the list

$$T[1, J, K], T[2, J, K], \ldots, T[NI, J, K]$$

This itself can be used as an element in the "variable list" of

$$(\text{"variable list"}, J \leftarrow 1 \text{ TO } NJ)$$

which is similar to nesting ordinary loops.

Thus ((T[I, J, 1], I ← 1 TO 3), J ← 1 TO 2) is equivalent to the list

$$T[1, 1, 1], T[2, 1, 1], T[3, 1, 1], T[1, 2, 1], T[2, 2, 1], T[3, 2, 1]$$

Finally, this doubly indexed list can be used as a "variable list" in another loop, as in Figure 5.20. (Programming language also allows for increments of other than one. You should find details in your language manuals.)

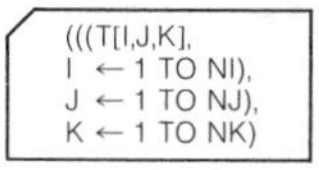

Fig. 5.19   Repetitive specification

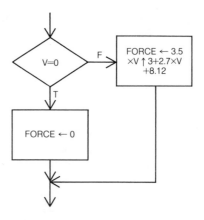

Fig. 5.20   Computation of force

An indexed list can be a part of another variable list. Thus, the sequence A[1, 1], A[1, 2], B[1], A[2, 1], A[2, 2], B[2], . . ., etc., can be specified in an input or output list by ((A[I, J], J ← 1 TO 2), B[I], I ← 1 TO N).

Question

1. What is the order of reading the elements of T in Figure 5.19 if NI = 3, NJ = 2, and NK = 2?

Problems

*1. Write one input statement to read the numbers N, I, and the variables A[I, J] for J = 1 TO N.

2. Draw a flowchart that reads the list (I, A[I,J], J = I TO N) without using an indexed list in your read box.

5.3 Procedures–Functions

In Section 3.7 we introduced a number of additional operations which, although not basic, can be expressed in terms of the basic arithmetic and decision operations. Examples of these additional operations, called *built-in functions*, included COS(X) and MAX(A,B). Since these built-in functions are frequently used by programmers, it is worthwhile to provide them within the system. The user does not have to reprogram such an operation each time he needs it in a procedure.

Frequently, the user with a complex problem can identify sections of code that are needed in many places in his solution. Suppose, for example, an engineer has a problem in which the frictional force on a body moving with speed V is given by $3.5V^3 + 2.7V + 8.12$ if V is not zero, or by 0 if V is zero. The flowchart section shown in Figure 5.20 would have to appear at each place that the force is needed in the procedure. If this occurred in many different places, the engineer would soon wish that he had a built-in function named FRICT that computed the frictional force directly, so that he could write FORCE ← FRICT(V). Consequently, we allow the user to define his own functions by means of flowchart procedures.

The important characteristics of a function are:

- It has a name—FRICT in this example.
- It has parameters—V in this example.
- It has a rule for computing the value of the function from the value of the parameters—given by flowchart 5.20 in this example.

We will define a function by a flowchart of the form shown in Figure 5.21.

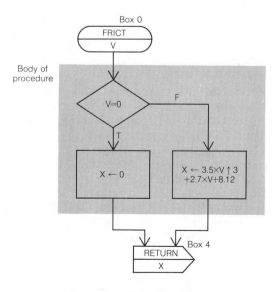

Fig. 5.21 Defining a function

193

This flowchart introduces two new boxes. Box 0 contains the name of the function being defined in its upper half and a list of parameters in its lower half. (Parameters are also called *arguments*.) Box 4 is a RETURN box that tells the computer the computation of the function FRICT is complete. Its value is given in the lower half of the RETURN box. (In this case it is X.) The function is defined by the actions given in the body of the procedure.

When a flowchart such as this forms part of the solution to a problem, we interpret it to mean that the user may now use the name FRICT as a function of one parameter, just as the built-in function COS is a function of one parameter. A function can be used in any place that a "right-hand side value" can be used because it can be processed to yield a value. Thus we can use a function as part of an expression in an assignment statement such as "$A \leftarrow P \times FRICT(Q)$", or in a logical expression such as "$17.5 < FRICT(R \times 2.5)$." Notice that the *actual parameter value* specified when we use the function need not be the name used for the parameter when we define the function. Thus, when the engineer writes FRICT(Q), it is equivalent to writing $(3.5 \times Q \uparrow 3 + 2.7 \times Q + 8.12)$ if Q is not zero, or to writing 0 if Q is zero. That is, the actual value of the parameter (Q) is substituted for the parameter (V) used in the definition. We say that V is a *dummy variable* because it is a place holder for a value to be fed in when the function is used.

When the engineer uses the function FRICT, he does not want to be concerned with the way it works or with the names of variables he happened to use when he defined it. If he should happen to be using a variable named X in a section of program where he also uses the function FRICT, he does not want that variable changed by the use of FRICT. (Such a change is called a *side-effect*.) Therefore, variables used inside a function definition are normally assigned to memory locations local to that definition. The variable X in Figure 5.21 is part of the code for FRICT and cannot be referenced in any other flowchart. (In a later section we will see how to override this by use of global variables. The usage here is similar to FORTRAN; in PL/I and ALGOL it is necessary to declare specifically that variables are local to a function.)

A function is a complete piece of program known as a *procedure*. When it is used we say that it has been *called* or *invoked*. The program that uses it is said to *call* it. The computer transfers control from the calling program to the called program when the value of the function is to be calculated. The called program is executed until a RETURN box is encountered. One and only one expression must appear in the bottom half of this box since the result of a function must be a single value that can be returned as the value of the function.

Example 5.9—Greatest Common Divisor

*The greatest common divisor of two integers J and K is the largest
integer I that divides both J and K exactly. There is a unique such
integer, since 1 divides both J and K, while any number larger than
either number certainly does not divide both. There are a finite
number of integers between 1 and the minimum M of J and K. The
largest positive integer less than or equal to M that divides both
J and K is the required answer.*

This argument shows both that the problem has a solution and
gives one method of solution by an enumerative method. Although it
is not a good method, we will use it as an example of a function. We
will give a better solution in a second example.

The task is to define a function IGCD(J,K) whose value is the greatest common divisor of I and J. A solution is shown in Figure 5.22.
Note that two parameters, J and K, are used. A function may use any
number of parameters. This solution checks each value of I starting
from MIN(J,K) working down until it finds a value that exactly divides
both J and K.

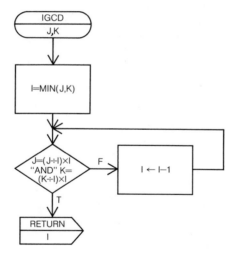

Fig. 5.22 Solution for GCD

Example 5.10—Euclidean Algorithm

*The Euclidean algorithm is a faster method for finding the greatest
common divisor of two numbers J and K. It works as follows:*
1. *Suppose J ≥ K. (If not, exchange them.)*
2. *Divide J by K to get a remainder L and quotient M.*

195

If L is zero, K divides J. Since K is the largest integer that
divides itself, K is the greatest common divisor of J and K.
If L is not zero, we have from the definition of the quotient
M and the remainder L that

$$J = K \times M + L \text{ and } L < K$$

Therefore any integer that divides J and K also divides L,
while any integer that divides K and L also divides J. Hence
the greatest common divisor of J and K is also the greatest
common divisor of K and L. If we replace J by K and K by
L, we now have the same problem to solve, but with
smaller numbers. Thus we can repeat the process. Eventually the number K will be reduced to the greatest common divisor, at which time K will divide J exactly.

The solution is shown in Figure 5.23.

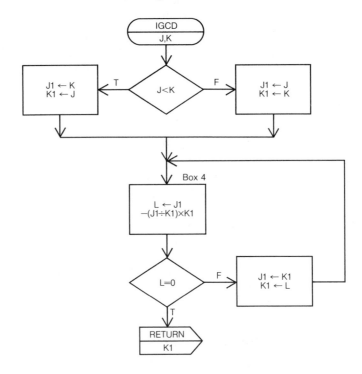

Fig. 5.23 Solution for Example 5.10

The solution given in Figure 5.23 uses three local variables, L,
J1 and K1. J1 and K1 were used to hold the larger and smaller of
J and K. It appears that we could have used J and K themselves by
simply switching them if J is not larger than K. There is a very im-

196

portant reason for not doing this. J and K stand for variables in the calling program; if we change them in the function procedure, the corresponding variables would be changed in the calling program. We do not like to have variables changed by procedures unnecessarily.

The difference in speed between the two solutions is illustrated by the case IGCD(55,95), which has an answer of 5. The loop in flowchart 5.22 will be executed for I = 55, 54, . . ., 6, and 5 for a total of 51 times. The states of J1, K1, and L after the five executions of Box 4 in the loop of Figure 5.23 are shown in Table 5.2. Thus the method in Figure 5.23 is about ten times faster than that in Figure 5.22 in this case.

TABLE 5.2

STATES OF J1, K1, AND L
AFTER LOOP EXECUTION

Loop Pass	J1	K1	L
1	95	55	40
2	55	40	15
3	40	15	10
4	15	10	5
5	10	5	0

Example 5.11—Binary Search

Suppose we have an ordered linear array $A[I]$ such that $A[1] < A[2] < A[3] < . . . < A[N]$, and we wish to find an index I such that $A[I] = B$. We would like this in the form of a function ISRCH(A, N, B) whose value is the index I if such exists, or zero otherwise.

Example 5.3 used the straightforward method of looking at each entry until either a match was found or all entries had been checked. That is called a *sequential search*. Because the array A is in order, we can use the much faster *binary search* method.

This method is very similar to the method of bisection discussed in Example 3.3. We start with two indices, L = 1 and M = N. If there is an I such that $A[I] = B$, then $L \leq I \leq M$. We choose an integer K about midway between L and M, say $K = (L + M) \div 2$. We compare $A[K]$ with B. If they are equal, we have found a suitable value of I. If $B > A[K]$, then we know that if there is an I it satisfies $K + 1 \leq I \leq M$. Hence we set L to K + 1 and continue the process. Similarly, if $B < A[K]$, we know that if there is a suitable I it satisfies $L \leq I \leq K - 1$, so we set M to K — 1 and continue. The process must stop when a match is found, or when we reach the state $L > M$. There is no I satisfying $L \leq I \leq M$ any longer, so the entry is not in the table.

197

Effectively, this method divides the table into two pieces at each step and determines which piece could contain the value B. Its flowchart is shown in Figure 5.24.

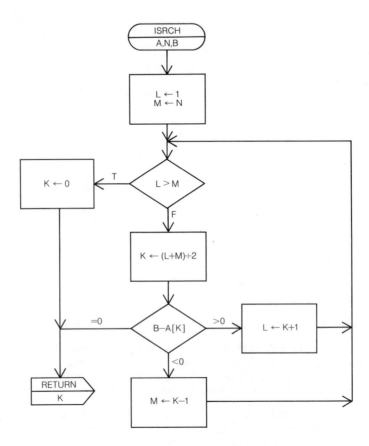

Fig. 5.24 Solution for Example 5.11

Questions

1. How many values can be returned by a function procedure?

2. Consider the function on page 199:

   *a. What is the value of the expression F(3)?
   b. What is the value of F(6)?
   c. What does the smaller flowchart assign to A?

198

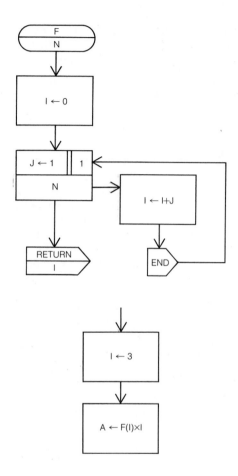

Problems

*1. Write a function flowchart for MAX(A, B), assuming that it is not available as a built-in function.

2. Write a function flowchart that has the same effect as that in question 2 and that does not use a loop.

*3. Write a function flowchart SEARCH whose value is an integer I such that B = X[I]. B is an input parameter. X is an array of N elements. If there is no I such that B = X[I], the value of SEARCH should be 0.

4. The smallest common multiple (SCM) of two integers I and J is defined to be the smallest integer such that both I and J divide

the SCM exactly. Devise an algorithm to find the SCM and express it by means of a function procedure flowchart that defines ISCM(I, J) to be the SCM of I and J. Do not worry about efficiency.

5. If you already have a function IGCD(I,J) that finds the greatest common divisor efficiently, how can it be used to find the SCM efficiently?

5.4 PROCEdURES–SubRoUTiNES

Functions are normally used in situations in which a single output value is calculated for use in an expression. However, situations also arise in which multiple output values are needed. For example, we might frequently want to test the contents of two cells, place the larger number in a third cell, and then place the smaller in a fourth cell. In this case we would wish to give the procedure two values as input and get back two values as output. Consider the procedure ORDER defined by Figure 5.25. It has four parameters A, B, X, and Y. These are four cells in the calling program. The procedure operates on these cells, leaving its two results in cells corresponding to X and Y. There is no single result, so there is no expression in the return box. It makes no sense to invoke the procedure by writing P ← ORDER(C, D + 5, R, S). "ORDER" has no function value. Instead we use a *call box* that suggests a transfer to the subroutine. It is shown in Figure 5.26. The name of the procedure is given in the top half of the box; the list of parameters is given in the lower half.

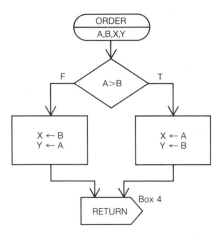

Fig. 5.25 The procedure ORDER

200

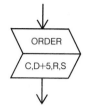

Fig. 5.26 Call box

This type of procedure is called a *subroutine*. Its output is provided by some of the parameters (in this case by X and Y) in the definition. If we invoke ORDER by the flowchart in Figure 5.26, the output is placed in cells R and S of the calling program. We call the parameters X and Y *output parameters*. It is obvious that the actual values used for output parameters when a subroutine is invoked must be the names of cells so that the output values can be stored.

In the example above, A and B are input parameters, so they can be given values by any expression when the subroutine is called. Thus the actual values of input parameters can be anything allowed for the right-hand side of an assignment statement, while the actual values of output parameters can be anything allowed for the left-hand side of an assignment statement.

A parameter can be both input and output. Suppose, for example, we need to sort the entries in a number of arrays into numerical order. We might then write a subroutine called SORT with parameters B (an array) and N (an integer). The subroutine is to sort the N elements B[1] to B[N] into order. Thus the array B is an input parameter, as is the integer N. The array B is also an output parameter. Note that a whole array can be passed as a parameter. It appears in the *call sequence* as the name of an array.

When a procedure refers to an actual parameter value in the call sequence, it must know in what way it is represented. Thus, if the actual value of a parameter is an integer, the called program must use it as an integer. If the parameter name B (for a real) is used in a definition of a procedure, the calling program must supply a real as the actual parameter value. We will also require that if a parameter in the procedure definition is an array the actual value be an array.

Example 5.12—Subroutine SCALE

We want to prepare a subroutine SCALE that will divide all N elements of a linear array by the element of largest magnitude, so that the resulting array has all elements in the range −1 to +1.

201

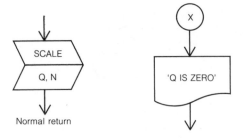

Fig. 5.27 Connector box for special return

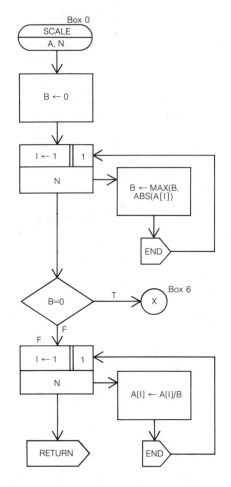

Fig. 5.28 Desired flowchart for Example 5.12

The solution is straightforward. We first find the value of the largest element in one loop, then divide by it in a second loop. If all elements are zero, however, the largest is zero. Since it is not possible to divide by zero, we want to take a special exit from the subroutine if this occurs. If the subroutine is invoked as shown in Figure 5.27, we want to go to the connector labeled X if all elements are zero.

The flowchart for the subroutine is as shown in Figure 5.28. The connector in Box 6 is given the name of a connector in the main flowchart. If the case of all zeros occurs, the transfer to X will cause a special exit to Box X in the main flowchart of Figure 5.27 instead of the normal return to the next box.

If the subroutine is programmed as in Figure 5.28, an exit to X will occur if $B = 0$ no matter where it is called from.

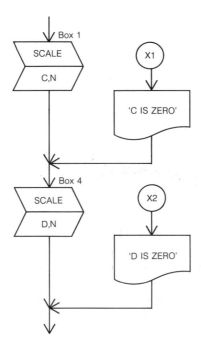

Fig. 5.29   Scaling the arrays C and D

Suppose we wish to scale the arrays C and D if possible, or print messages if either is not possible. That is, we would like to write the flowchart in Figure 5.29. We want to make a special exit to X1 in the first case and X2 in the second. We do this by making X a parameter (called a *label parameter*) in Figure 5.28. Box 0 in that figure is changed to

The X is a label because it is the name used in a connector box. Then Boxes 1 and 4 in Figure 5.29 can be changed to those in Figure 5.30. Needless to say, when labels are in the parameter list of the definition, the actual parameter values supplied must also be labels.

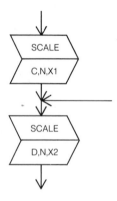

Fig. 5.30   Modifying figure 5.29

Example 5.13 — Store Accounts

We wish to write a program to handle the customer charge accounts for a store. This is an example of a problem that is first studied by a person called a systems analyst. *He must interact with the owner or manager of the store and the accountants to see what is needed for efficient operation and what information must be generated for proper accounting procedures.*

Let us suppose that he has decided that the following processes are required:

1. Add a new customer's name to the list of accounts.
2. Charge a customer a specified amount for a purchase.
3. Record a payment from a customer.
4. Generate monthly bills for all customers.
5. Delete a customer's name from the list of accounts and generate a bill for him.

204

The input to the program is to be a set of cards. The first item on the card will be an integer between 1 and 5, identifying the type of process as defined above. The second item will be the customer name except in case 4, when it will not be used. The third item will be the amount charged in case 2, the amount paid in case 3, and zero in all other cases. The fourth and final item will be the stock number of the item purchased in case 2 and zero in all other cases.

The computer must store a list of all individual purchases made so that an itemized bill can be generated. Therefore two two-dimensional arrays will be used. AMOUNT[I,J] and ITEM[I,J] will contain the amount and the stock number of the Jth purchase by the Ith customer, respectively. (Most programming languages require that the maximum size of arrays be known when the program is written. If you are going to implement this example on a computer, assume some numbers reasonable for the size of memory you have available.) Customer payments will also be recorded as a payment in AMOUNT. The corresponding position in ITEM should be a −1. The number of entries in AMOUNT and ITEM for customer I will be stored in N[I]. The outstanding balance for the Ith customer will be stored in BALANC[I]. For example, if the tenth customer has made purchases of $10.13 for item 11 and $25.11 for item 93, and paid $16.21 on his bill, his account information could read

```
BALANCE[10]  = 19.63
N[10]           3
AMOUNT[10,1] = 10.13      ITEM[10,1] = 11
AMOUNT[10,2] = 16.21      ITEM[10,2] = −1
AMOUNT[10,3] = 25.11      !TEM[10,3]   93
```

The customer names will be kept in a linear array NAME of character strings. This array is to be kept in alphabetical order so that an alphabetical list of customers can be printed. This means that each time a new customer is to be added or removed from the list of accounts, many entries in the NAME array will have to be moved as well as the corresponding entries in the BALANC, N, AMOUNT, and ITEM arrays. To avoid moving the latter we will add one more linear array called NCUST (customer number). When the first customer is added to the account list, his name is stored in NAME[1] and his customer number, which is 1 as he is the first customer, is stored in NCUST[1]. AMOUNT[1,J], ITEM[1,J], N[1], and BALANC[1] contain his account information. If his name is SMITH and he charges $10.27 for item 5, his account would read

NAME[1]=SMITH,NCUST[1]=1,BALANC[1]=10.27,N[1]=1,
AMOUNT[1,1]=10.27,ITEM[1,1]=5

Now suppose a second customer named JONES is added. His name will go in NAME[1], pushing SMITH to NAME[2]. His customer number, 2, will go in NCUST[1], pushing the old value of NCUST[1], 1, up to NCUST[2]. However, we need not move the information in the remaining arrays as we can use NCUST to give the index into the remaining arrays. Thus, if at any stage a customer's name is in NAME[J], we can access his balance by writing BALANC[NCUST[J]].

Now we can outline the steps needed to perform each process.

1. Add a new customer's name to the list of accounts.

   Search through the list of names from the beginning until the first larger name is found. If the name is present, print an error message. Move every entry in NAME and NCUST from this name down one place, and put the new name in the vacated spot. Assign the next available customer number to this customer. Set N and BALANC entries to zero for this customer number.

   Evidentally we must also keep a record of the number of entries NN in the array NAME and the next available customer number NCN.

2. Charge a customer's account.

   Search for the name. Suppose it is NAME[J]. If it is not present, print an error message. Otherwise, let K = NCUST[J]. Increase N[K] by one, add the amount to BALANC[K], and store the amount and item number in AMOUNT[K,N[K]] and ITEM [K,N[K]].

3. Record a payment.

   Handle as for a charge with item number equal to −1, but deduct the amount from the balance.

4. Generate a list of bills.

   Use a loop, generating one bill in each loop, listing the charges, payments, and balance. At this time the list of amounts and items should be cleared by setting N to be zero.

5. Delete a customer's name and generate a bill.

   Search for the customer's name. If it is not present, print an error message. Otherwise, print a bill, then remove the name and move all later entries in NAME and NCUST up one.

A solution for a problem like this should use many subroutines. First, common areas of code should be identified and defined as subroutines. In this case we see that a search operation is used in four of the cases, and printing a bill is used in two of the cases. Therefore, we define two subroutines.

1. SEARCH—parameters NM, NAME, NN, I, J meaning:
   NM   The name being sought

206

NAME   The array to be searched
NN   The number of entries in the array
I   The index of the first entry in NAME greater than or
           equal to NM. Set I to NN + 1 if no entries satisfy this.
           (Output parameter)
J   0 if NM is not in NAME, 1 otherwise. (Output param-
           eter)

2. BILL—parameters NM, K, N, BALANC, AMOUNT, ITEM, meaning:
    NM   Name of customer to be billed. K is his customer
             number. N, BALANC, AMOUNT, and ITEM are as
             defined above. The subroutine should also set
             N[K] to zero to clear the list of charges.

Secondly, we should define subroutines for various sections of
the program so that relatively independent sections are in different
subroutines. This makes for a better description of the program. In
this case subroutines can be defined for each of the basic actions
as follows:

3. NEW—parameters NM, NAME, NN, NCN, NCUST, N, BALANC,
   meaning:
    NM   the name to be added to the array NAME.
             Appropriate changes must be made to other arrays.

4. CHARGE—parameters NM, A, I, NN, and all arrays, meaning:
    NM   The name to be charged the amount A for item I if
             $I \geq 0$ or to be credited to the amount A if $I < 0$.

   This subroutine can also be used for recording payments.

5. MONTH— Parameters NN and all arrays, meaning:
              Generate bills for all NN customers.

6. DELETE— Parameters NM, NN, and all arrays, meaning:
              Bill customer NM and delete from arrays NAME and
              NCUST. Reduce NN by one.

The main program is shown in Figure 5.31. It sets NN to zero and
NCN to one initially. Obviously, this is done only once—the first
time the program is run. When a run has processed all input cards,
the current states of NN, NCN, and all arrays have to be saved,
usually on a disk file or similar device, so that they can be restored
to the same values when a later run is to be started. The subroutines
SEARCH and DELETE are shown in Figures 5.32 and 5.33, respectively. Not all parameters have been listed because of lack of avail-

able space. The remainder of the subroutines are left as the inevitable problems for the student.

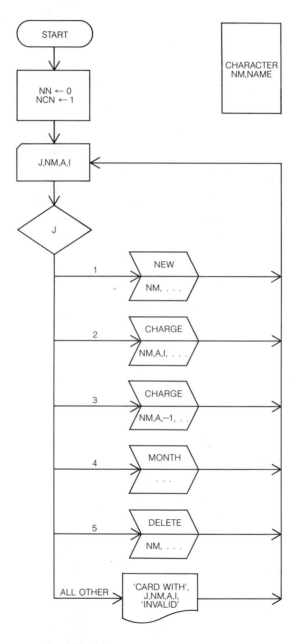

Fig. 5.31   Main program for Example 5.13

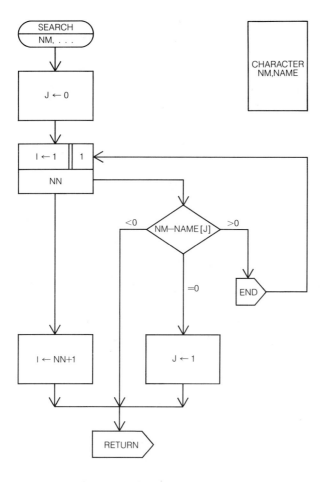

Fig. 5.32 Subroutine SEARCH

The previous example illustrates an important approach to the programming of large problems: they are broken down into a group of small subroutines and functions. This should be done before formal flowcharts are drawn. Frequently, a "high-level" flowchart is drawn for the overall system first. This flowchart uses English language descriptions of the tasks to be performed and does not include detailed information. For example, we might say "Charge the customer" in one box and "Credit the customer" in another. A flowchart similar to Figure 5.31 could then be drawn. Next we decide how to handle these operations, come to the conclusion that both of these actions can be handled by one subroutine (CHARGE in that example), and then decide on the parameters needed.

209

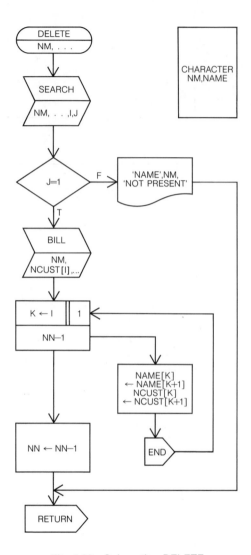

Fig. 5.33 Subroutine DELETE

Questions

*1. What are actual parameter values?

2. Why must a constant not be used as an actual parameter value for an output parameter?

3. What can be used as an actual parameter value for an output parameter?

210

Problems

*1. Write a subroutine NORM(AM, SD, A, N) that computes the mean
AM of the array A[I], I = 1, . . ., N, and the standard deviation
SD of the same array, where

$$AM = \frac{1}{N} \sum_{I=1}^{N} A[I]$$

$$SD = \sqrt{\frac{1}{N} \sum_{I=1}^{N} (A[I] - AM)^2}$$

2. Write a subroutine STNDRD(A, W, T, N, M) that has the following actions:
The array A[I, J] contains the score on the Jth test for the Ith student. There are M tests and N students. Normalize the scores
on each test to a mean of 0 and a standard deviation of 1.0 by
first forming

$$AM = \frac{1}{N} \sum_{I=1}^{N} A[I, J]$$

and

$$SD = \sqrt{\frac{1}{N} \sum_{I=1}^{N} (A[I, J] - AM)^2}$$

and then forming

$$B[I, J] = \frac{A[I, J] - AM}{SD} \qquad I = 1, . . ., N$$

if SD $\neq$ 0, and B[I, J] = 0 if SD = 0

Repeat this for J = 1, . . ., M.
Then form the weighted sum of the normalized scores and return the result in T, where

$$T[I] = \sum_{J=1}^{M} B[I, J] \times W[J]$$

3. Write the subroutines BILL, NEW, CHARGE, and MONTH required in Example 5.13.

*4. When a customer's name is removed by DELETE in Figure 5.33,
the space that customer was using in the arrays BALANC, N,
AMOUNT, and ITEM is not made available for use by customers
added in the future. This means that as names are added and
deleted, the size of these arrays (NCN) slowly increases, even
though the total number of customers (NN) may never exceed

some reasonable number. Can you think of a way of re-allocating customer numbers that are no longer in use, so that the array space can be reused?

5. Modify the subroutine SEARCH in Figure 5.32 so that it uses the binary search method (see Example 5.11).

5.5 Local and Global, Static and Dynamic Storage

When the CPU encounters a call on a procedure, it prepares information about the parameters and puts it in some memory cells. It then transfers to the code for the called procedure and executes that code. Both the calling and the called procedures will have their own data areas in memory and will be restricted to using their areas for their local variables. This is shown in Figure 5.34.

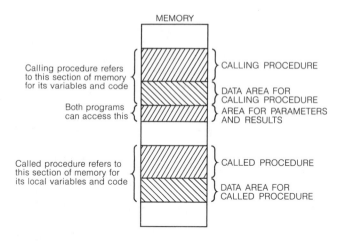

Fig. 5.34 Memory allocation for procedures

We have allowed two types of variables in a procedure—local variables totally internal to the procedure and parameters intended for passing input data between procedures. The restriction that prevents a procedure from accessing local variables associated with other procedures is one of convenience only; it is obvious that the machine language code for a procedure could use memory addresses referring to any part of memory. When a compiler translates a POL such as FORTRAN into machine language, it enforces this restriction by assigning different memory space to variables in each procedure so that they are different from variables of the same name in the other procedures.

Example 5.14—Normalization of Scores

Suppose we have a one-dimensional array A that contains student scores on a test. We wish to find constants X and Y, where Y is positive, such that if we form

$$B[I] = (A[I] + X) \times Y$$

the smallest of the "normalized" scores B[I] will be 0 and the largest will be 100. The parameters to the subroutine should be A, B, and N (N is the number of scores).

If the smallest of the A[I], I = 1, . . . , N is C, then we can take X to be −C. This makes A[I] + X zero when I is such that A[I] is minimum. If the largest element of A[I] is D, we can take Y to be 100/(D + X). Then (A[I] + X) × 100/(D + X) will be 100 when A[I] takes on the maximum value D. There is a problem if D + X is zero. This occurs if all of the A[I] are equal, in which case it is obvious that we cannot find an X and Y to accomplish the goal. For this case we must modify the problem statement and add an error exit to the parameter list. A flowchart for the solution is shown in Figure 5.35.

When we use this example, we may wish to write

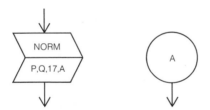

At the time we write this we must be aware that the array P will be input to the procedure, and that either the results will be returned to Q or an error exit will be made to A. However, we do not wish to concern ourselves with the fact that variables with the names A, B, C, D, I, N, and X are used in the procedure NORM. Because these are either variables local to the procedure or parameter names, we do not have to worry about them.

Communication between a called procedure and a calling procedure is normally via the parameter list. However, problems sometimes arise in which large amounts of data must be accessed by both the calling and the called procedure. (We say that they have a large *data-base* in common.) It can be very inconvenient to have to put every variable required by both procedures in the parameter list. We had to use very long parameter lists in Example 5.13. There-

213

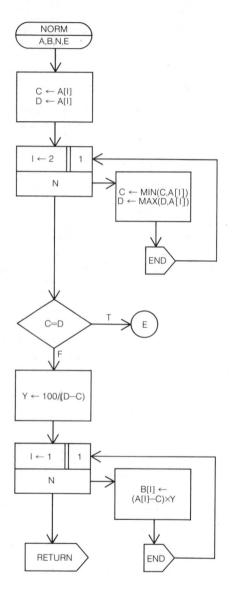

Fig. 5.35 Solution for Example 5.14

fore we use *global variables*. A variable that is global in a procedure is one that appears in the calling procedure. If, in Example 5.13, the variables NN and NCN and the arrays NAME, NCUST, BALANC, N, AMOUNT, and ITEM were global to all subroutines, it would not

214

have been necessary to put them in the parameter lists.

The declarative statement GLOBAL must be put in a declaration box along with the other declarations. Thus, if in Figure 5.35 we had added the box

GLOBAL C

the variable C would be assumed to be one of the calling procedure variables. An example where this might be used follows.

Example 5.15—Linear Interpolation

A section of highway is to be built and an array H contains the elevation above sea level of the highway at 1000-foot intervals from the city A. Thus the first entry H[1] contains the elevation at the city itself, the second entry H[2] contains the elevation at a point 1000 feet from the city and so on. We wish to use a function E(X) which will give us the elevation of a point P that is X feet from the city.

Since we have only the elevations at a finite number of points we must decide what to do if X is not one of those points. We will use *linear interpolation*; that is, we will draw a straight line between the two nearest points and find the elevation of that straight line. (This is equivalent to assuming that the road has a constant slope between two consecutive 1000-foot points. It provides an *approximation* to the actual elevation, which we don't know.) The required elevation is illustrated in Figure 5.36. First we must find N. This we can do by dividing X by 1000 and taking the integer part. The elevation of the point to the left of P is stored in H[N + 1], that of the point to the right of P in H[N + 2]. The elevation of P is the height from P to Q plus the height from Q to sea level at X. The latter is H[N + 2], while, using simple geometry, we see that

$$\text{height } PQ = \text{height } AB \times \frac{\text{distance } RQ}{1000}$$

$$= (H[N + 2] - H[N + 1]) \times \frac{X - 1000N}{1000}$$

215

The elevation is therefore

$$H[N+1] + (H[N+2] - H[N+1]) \times \frac{X - 1000N}{1000}$$

A flowchart is shown in Figure 5.37. The exit to label parameter W occurs if the input value X is not between 0 and $1000 \times (M - 1)$.

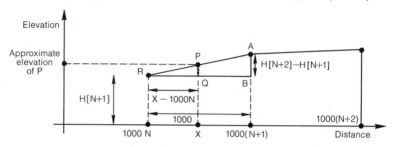

Fig. 5.36 Linear interpolation

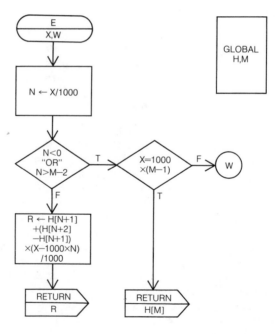

Fig. 5.37 Solution for Example 5.15

M is assumed to contain the number of elements in the array H. If X is less than zero, it refers to a point on the other side of the city; if it is greater than $1000(M - 1)$, it is off the end of the road we have prescribed. In neither case can we compute an elevation. Both H and M are global. They are not put in the parameter list because they refer to variables of the same name in the calling procedure. Global variables provide a more rapid and concise mechanism for communication between procedures than do parameters, because the passing of parameters requires time and memory space. However, parameters are more flexible. The function E defined by Figure 5.37 can operate only on the array H with M entries. If M and H had been put in the parameter list, it could have been used for linear interpolation in any table. If we had written a procedure to deal with similar arrays for many different roads, we would have preferred to use parameters rather than global variables.

5.5.1 Static and Dynamic Storage

We have stated that the local variables associated with a procedure are stored in an area of memory reserved for that procedure. Many procedures will be written for use in a typical problem. Some of the called procedures will be the calling procedures of other procedures, just as we nested one loop inside another. If each procedure has its own data area, a lot of memory space may be allocated, although only those areas associated with *active procedures* may be in use. (An active procedure is one that has been called and has not yet returned to the calling procedure.) An alternative method for allocating data areas is to assign a space in memory for general use by all procedures and to allocate space from it when a procedure is first called. This is called *dynamic allocation*. Suppose, for example, we have the series of subroutines S1, S2, and S3 and a main procedure S as shown in Figure 5.38. Suppose we also have other subroutines S4, . . . , SK as part of the total program, and that subroutine SI uses NI local variables, for I = 1, 2, . . . , K. If we assign fixed areas of storage for local variables separately to each subroutine, we will need space for N1 + N2 + . . . + NK variables. This is called *static allocation*. If, however, we assign space dynamically, we will need storage for only N1 + N2 + N3 variables at the time that subroutine S3 is being executed. This space can be allocated as each subroutine is called. When S1 is called from the main procedure, space for N1 variables can be allocated from the available space. When S1 calls S2, space for the N2 local variables in S2 can be allocated from the next available space, and so on. When a return from a procedure is executed, the space that it uses can be made available for use by procedures called subsequently.

One characteristic of dynamic storage allocation is that the values of variables are not retained from one use of a procedure to another because the memory locations used in the procedure may be used

217

by another when the first is not active.

Dynamic storage is adequate for many problems. Thus examples 5.14 and 5.15 could use dynamic storage for their local variables since values are assigned to the local variables each time the procedures are entered. There are, however, cases in which we must have static storage.

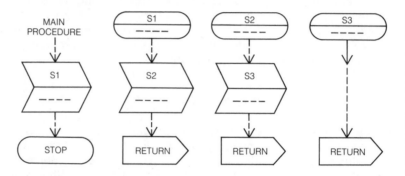

Fig. 5.38 Series of subroutines and main procedure

Example 5.16—Page Layout

Suppose we are generating a long list of numbers and we wish to print these 5 per line, 50 lines per page, with an integer at the start of each line in the sequence 1, 6, 11, . . . , etc., and a page number at the head of each page. It is often simpler to write a subroutine, say PRINT(X), which will accept the next number in the list (the parameter X) and put it in a position on the page. Every fifth call should cause this subroutine to print a line of the last 5 numbers. Every 50th line, a new page should be started and numbered.

The technique used is as follows: If this is the first call or the first call after the last line of the previous page was printed, a new page is started. A line count is then set to 1.

An array B[J], J = 1, . . . , 5 is used to save up to 5 numbers. The counter J is increased on each call until it reaches 5. Then a line is printed and J is reset to zero.

When a line is printed, the integer to be printed at the start of each line is incremented by 5. A line count is also increased by one. When it is greater than 50, a signal that we should start another page is given. When a new page is printed, the page count is increased by one.

A flowchart is shown in Figure 5.39. This subroutine contains two *entry points* besides PRINT. These will be discussed shortly.

In the procedure given in Figure 5.39, the local variable I may be

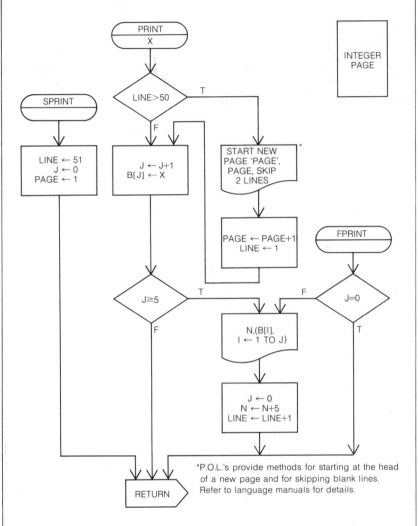

Fig. 5.39 Solution for Example 5.16

dynamic, but the local variables B, J, LINE, PAGE, and N must
be static because their values after one execution of PRINT are
needed to control the next execution of PRINT. In some languages
(FORTRAN) all variables are static. In other languages (PL/I,
ALGOL) all variables are dynamic unless it is stated otherwise. We
will assume the latter case and require a declaration STATIC . . .
to override the dynamic property. Thus Figure 5.39 should have its
declaration box modified as shown in Figure 5.40. It is also necessary to set some initial values into the variables J, LINE, and PAGE

219

(0, 51, and 1, respectively). The additional entry point SPRINT (Start PRINT) is used for this purpose. SPRINT can be called in the same way as any other subroutine. In this case it has no parameters, but this is not a requirement of entry points. The entry point FPRINT (Finish PRINT) prints the final line containing less than five values, if there is one.

INTEGER PAGE

STATIC B, J,
LINE, PAGE

Fig. 5.40   Static declarations

Problems

*1. Write a subroutine GROUP(A, B, I) that is to be called each time a new value of A is calculated. The subroutine should accept five successive values of A and form their sum and the sum of their squares. It should then store these in B[I, 1] and B[I, 2] and increment I by one.

2. Write a print subroutine with one parameter A. Each time a new value of A is calculated, the subroutine will be called. The subroutine should print three numbers across a line but there is a snag. The numbers are computed in a diagonal order. The order in which the A's are computed is shown below.

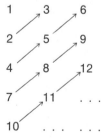

etc.

Therefore the partial contents of several lines must be saved.

3. Modify the solution to Example 5.16 so that the SPRINT entry point has parameters specifying the number of values to be

printed on each line and the number of lines to be printed on each page.

Questions

*1. What are the advantages of local storage?

2. Why do we use global storage in some cases?

*3. What are the advantages of dynamic storage?

4. When do we need to use static storage?

5.6 Access of Parameters

In earlier sections we gave a deliberately simplified idea of the way in which a calling procedure communicates parameter values with a called procedure. We implied that the called procedure could refer to the actual parameter values directly. In fact, there are several ways in which parameters are passed between procedures, and different POLs use different methods. In this section we will discuss three basic techniques that can be used: *call by address*, *call by value*, and *call by name*. For simple usages there is no difference between the results of these three techniques. However, when a variable name appears as more than one actual parameter value or appears in an actual parameter value and is also global to the called procedure, the different techniques yield different results. In order for you to be able to determine the effect of any particular usage, we will discuss some of the details of implementation.

First we will examine both the types of parameters that can be used in a procedure and the kinds of actual parameter values that can be matched with them. Again, each POL may allow more or less of these types. The restrictions we will develop here are logical restrictions, that is, ones that must be enforced to make sense out of the call and return. (Consult a language manual for a specific POL to see what additional restrictions are enforced.)

In the definition of a procedure, its parameters are *dummy variables* because they stand for (or are placeholders for) constants, variables, or expressions that will be fed into the procedure when it is called. We classify the parameters by the way they are used in their procedure according to their structure, their type, and their access.

By *structure* we mean are the parameters single variables (that is, names of single cells in memory) or arrays? (Some languages

221

may also allow more complex structures, which will be discussed in Chapter 7.)

By *type* we mean do the parameters refer to data consisting of integers, real numbers, labels, functions, or subroutines — or, of course, any of the other allowed data types in a given language, such as LOGICAL and COMPLEX?

By *access*, we mean are the parameters used as input to the procedure only, or output from the procedure (and possibly input as well)?

Every parameter must have one and only one of the attributes from each of the groups *structure*, *type*, and *access*. Thus a parameter could be a single real variable used as input only. Many of the possible combinations are disallowed in some languages. In FORTRAN, for example, labels, functions, and subroutines may be used as parameters only if they are single variables used for input. That is, the flowchart in Figure 5.41 is acceptable whereas the two in Figure 5.42 are not. In Figure 5.42a the label parameter X is an array. This is not permitted in FORTRAN (although it is acceptable in PL/I). In Figure 5.42b, the actual parameter value F in the call of procedure E2 is used as a function name in the next box. In the subroutine E2, the corresponding parameter G is assigned the value SIN. We are thus trying to use a function name as an output parameter. This is neither permitted in FORTRAN nor PL/I.

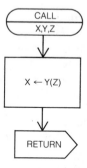

Fig. 5.41 Acceptable flowchart

Actual parameter values have *structure* and *type*. The permissible types of actual parameter values are exactly the same as the permissible types of parameters. In most languages, the type of the parameter and the type of the actual parameter must match. That is, if the parameter is used as an integer, the actual parameter value must also be an integer. We can see why this restriction is desirable if we consider our hypothetical machine. Suppose we have a function F(I) that expects an integer value for the parameter I. If, in the

222

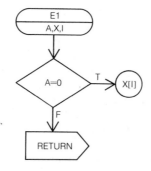

Fig. 5.42a Use of label parameters unacceptable in FORTRAN (1)

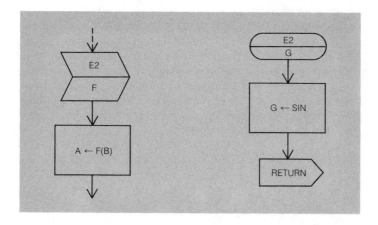

Fig. 5.42b Use of label parameters unacceptable in FORTRAN (2)

calling program, we write F(1.0), the actual parameter value 1.0 will be passed in the representation 05110000 ($= +0.1 \times 10^1$) in our machine. The function will take this to be an integer, that is, the number $+5110000$.

The structure of actual parameter values includes constants, expressions, single variables, array elements, and arrays. If a parameter is an array, then the corresponding actual parameter value must also be an array. This is evidently necessary because if the subroutine accesses the Ith element A[I] of the parameter A, the calling program must provide an array of cells corresponding to the array A. Many POLs will also restrict the parameter and the actual parameter value to be of the same dimension, that is, to have the same number of indices, each with the same range. (However, when we come to techniques for implementation, we will see that

223

this restriction can often be sidestepped with useful results.) If a parameter is a single variable, then the actual parameter value must have one of the first four types of structures. That is, it must represent a single entity rather than an array.

If a parameter is used for output, it is evident that the actual parameter value must represent a cell or set of cells in memory. That is, the first two types of actual parameter value structures (constants and expressions) may not be passed as output variables.

In many translators these restrictions are not checked. Hence the user can commit logical errors that lead to nonsensical execution time results. Consider the flowcharts in Figure 5.43. If the equivalent of this program were to be run under most FORTRAN systems, the main program would cause the number 2.0 to be printed! This occurs because the main program is compiled with 1.0 and 2.0 in cells in its area of memory. When the subroutine WRECK is called, it gets the value 2.0 for parameter B and stores it into parameter A. Since A is an output parameter, its value will be stored back into the cell that originally contained 1.0. Thus the result of calling WRECK at execution time in the manner above is to store the value 2.0 in the cell the compiler has assigned to hold the constant 1.0. When the code corresponding to $Z \leftarrow 1.0$ is executed, the right-hand side will be copied from the cell the main program believes to contain 1.0, resulting in 2.0 being assigned to Z.

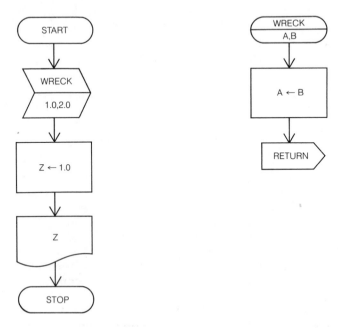

Fig. 5.43 Invalid use of parameters

Call by Address (also known as Call by Location)

The most common and one of the simplest forms of linking the actual parameter values to the parameters is by passing the address of the actual value from the calling program to the called program. The called program can then access actual values directly in the place they are stored and return results to these locations (in the case of output parameters).

The address usually passed is given in Table 5.3. If labels of procedure names are passed as actual parameter values, the address can be the address of the location in memory where the labeled section of code or procedure starts. However, if label or procedure type variables are allowed, the address passed will have to be the address of a location containing the address of the start of the section of code or procedure. (Label variables are the names of cells in memory that contain the address of a labeled section of code.) Call by address is used for arrays in most FORTRAN compilers.

TABLE 5.3

FORM OF ADDRESS PASSED AS PARAMETER

Structure of Actual Parameter	Address Passed
Constant	Address of that constant in the calling program
Single Variable	Address of that variable in the calling program
Expression	Address of a temporary location
	Before the actual call, the calling program computes the actual parameter value and stores it in this temporary location.
Array Element	Address of that element.
Array[a]	Address of the first element in the array.

a. Some POLs pass the address of a "description" of the array used for the actual parameter. This description includes the address of the first element and the size of the array (number of indices, and range of each).

If an array is passed by passing the address of its first element, it is often permissible to pass the address of a single element in a larger array, even one with a different number of dimensions.

225

Example 5.17—Summing Columns of an Array

Suppose the array SCORE[I,J] contains the score of the Iᵗʰ exam for the Jᵗʰ student in the class. Suppose that arrays are stored by column, that is, element SCORE[I + 1, J] is one location beyond SCORE[I,J] in memory. We wish to find the total score of the Jᵗʰ student; that is, we wish to form SCORE[1,J] + SCORE[2,J] + . . . + SCORE[N,J]. The function shown in Figure 5.44 will accomplish this if call by address is used in the system and if the address of the first element of an array is passed when an array is used as an actual parameter value.

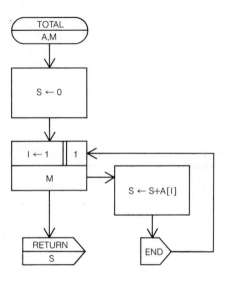

Fig. 5.44 Solution for Example 5.17

This function can be called by writing TOTAL(SCORE[1,J],N). The address of the element SCORE[1,J] is passed to the function that assumes this is the address of the first element of the array A. When it accesses the element A[I], the address of SCORE[1,J] plus I − 1 is computed. Since SCORE is stored by columns, this is the element SCORE [I,J].

Call by Value

When actual parameter values are *called by value*, the actual values are passed across to the procedure at the time of the call. Call by value requires that separate memory locations be provided by the called subprocedure for the values of the parameters during the

226

execution of the subroutine. These locations must be loaded with
the actual parameter values at the start of the procedure, and the
values of output parameters must be copied back at the end. This
is handled by the compiler. Call by value is an option in ALGOL and
is standard for single values in many FORTRAN compilers. However, ALGOL does not copy the values back afterwards, so call by
value parameters can only be used as input parameters in ALGOL
procedures.

Call by Name

Call by name is the type of parameter linkage provided by an ALGOL
compiler unless the call by value option is requested for specific
parameters. In the call by name linkage, it is as if **the string of
characters given as the actual parameter value replaces the name
of the parameter throughout the use of the procedure**. (There will
be a slight modification to this statement later.) Let us illustrate
this by example.

Example 5.18 — Summing a Vector

*Suppose we are using call by name. The function in Figure 5.45
forms the sum of $N - L + 1$ elements, each named A.*

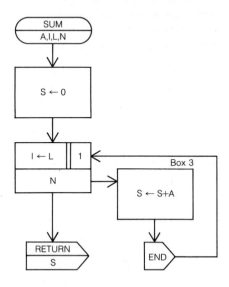

Fig. 5.45   Call by name example

On the surface it appears that this does nothing more than form
$(N - L + 1) \times A$. However, suppose we write SUM(B[I],I,L,N). If call

227

by name is used in the POL, this is equivalent to replacing the A in Box 3 by the character string B[I]. Then the function returns the value B[L] + B[L + 1] + . . . + B[N]. Similarly, if we wrote SUM (C[I,J],J,1,M) the function returns the value C[I,1] + C[I,2] + . . . + C[I,M]. With this simple function we can then write a procedure for multiplying an N by N array E by a linear array F to get a linear array G, as shown in Figure 5.46.

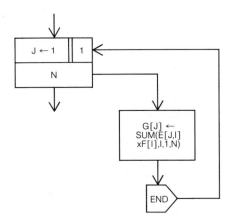

Fig. 5.46   Use of SUM procedure to form square array times linear array

Suppose we had written SUM(S[I],I,1,N). Then our rule states that Box 3 in Figure 5.45 contains S ← S + S[I]. This would apparently lead to an error, as the same name cannot represent both a single variable and an array. However, this is not a problem here; S in Figure 5.46 is a variable *local* to the procedure SUM. It bears no relation to any variables in the calling program, even if they have the same name. Thus Box 3 really says, in this case,

"S in procedure SUM ← S in procedure SUM
+ S[I] in calling procedure."

The results of using call by name can be determined most easily if the technique used in the computer is understood. The usual technique is for the calling procedure to pass an address of a *parameter subroutine* for each parameter. The parameter sub-routines are part of the calling procedure. When the called procedure needs a particular parameter, it calls the corresponding parameter subroutine, which returns the address of a memory cell that contains the parameter. The address can be used by the called program to either access data or to return results. Thus in Example 5.18 above, with the call by SUM(A[J],J,1,M) we would have the arrangement in memory shown in Figure 5.47.

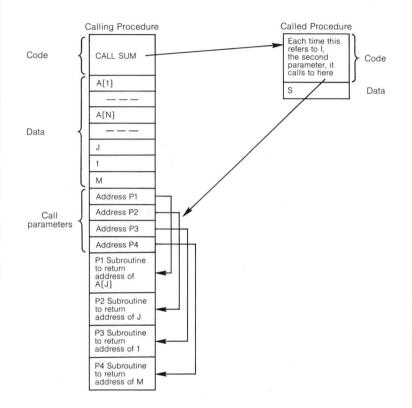

Fig. 5.47 Memory arrangement for call by name

When we understand this process we can answer the question "What happens if we call the function in Figure 5.48 by PROD(A[I] + B[I], I, 1, N)?" It is not quite as if we had written A[I] + B[I] in place of A because that would have changed Box 3 to P ← P × A[I] + B[I]. Rather it is as if Box 3 read P ← P × (A[I] + B[I]). Each time that a parameter is needed in call by name, its actual value is re-computed. (This is necessary only if it is an expression or an array element indexed by a variable.)

229

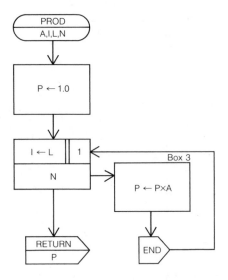

Fig. 5.48 The function PROD

Example 5.19—Differences Between Address, Value, and Name

We will illustrate the way in which the different techniques of parameter access can give different results. (This example is not supposed to do anything useful.) Consider the procedure in Figure 5.49. Suppose we use this by writing A ← R (B, B, B + C). Suppose the initial values of B and C are 1.0 and 2.0, respectively.

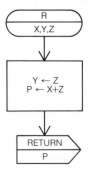

Fig. 5.49 Example 5.19

Consider first call by address. The calling procedure passes across the address of the actual parameter B for parameters X and

Y and passes across the address of a location containing B + C; that is, 3.0 – for Z. Thus the function first stores the value 3.0 in cell B (Y ← Z); then it stores the sum of B and 3.0 into the local cell P (P ← X + Z). The result returned is therefore 6.0.

Now consider call by value. First cells X, Y, and Z, local to the function, are assigned the values 1.0, 1.0, 3.0, respectively. Now the function stores 3.0 in Y (Y ← Z) and 4.0 in P (P ← X + Z). The result returned is 4.0.

Finally let us consider call by name. It is as if we performed the steps B ← B + C followed by P ← B + B + C. The effect of these is to store 3.0 in B and 8.0 in P. Thus the result 8.0 is returned.

Problems

1. Determine how your compiler actually handles parameters by trying various examples such as Example 5.19.

2. Consider

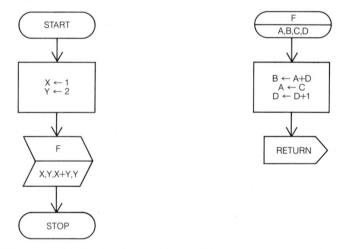

What are the final values of X and Y if parameters are handled

a. by value
b. by address
c. by name

5.7 Recursive Procedures

We have already mentioned that one procedure may call another, which in turn may call yet another, and so forth. If, in this chain of calls, the same procedure appears more than once—that is, if it has effectively called itself—we say we have used the procedure *recursively*. FORTRAN does not allow recursion. PL/I allows procedures to be recursive, but such use has to be explicitly declared. ALGOL assumes that all procedures are recursive.

We will illustrate the use of recursion by means of examples and then discuss some of the implications of recursive procedures.

Example 5.20—Binary Search

We previously discussed the binary search method in an ordered table and wrote straightforward procedures that implement it. We will now implement it by means of a recursive subroutine SEARCH with parameters B, A, L, M, and I. This subroutine should locate the variable B in the ordered table $A[L]$, $A[L + 1]$, . . . , $A[M]$ and return with I such that $A[I] = B$ if a match is found, or return with $I = 0$ if no match is found. The reason for having the parameters L and M will be apparent below. If there are N entries $A[1]$ to $A[N]$ in the table, we expect the subroutine to be called initially with parameters B, A, 1, N, and I.

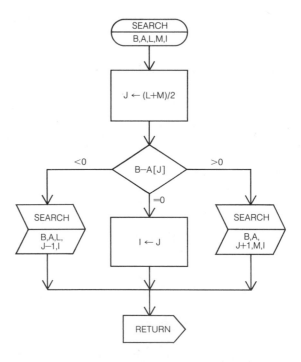

Fig. 5.50 Solution for Example 5.20

The basic technique of the binary search is to compare the searched item B with the middle entry $A[(L + M)/2]$. If there is a match, we have found the entry; otherwise we continue to search into either the first or the last part of the table. This is shown in Figure 5.50. (There is a serious error in this solution that will be pointed out later.)

Figure 5.50 defines a recursive procedure. We can understand recursive procedures by imagining that many different copies of the procedure are available. The first call on the procedure transfers to the first copy. If that copy calls the same procedure, it transfers to the second copy. Each copy has storage for its own local variables. Similarly, if copy #2 calls the same procedure, it transfers to the third copy. A trace of the values of L, M, and J is shown in Table 5.4 for the case $A[K] = K$ for $1 \le K \le 7$ if the initial call uses the parameters B, A, 1, 7, I, where $B = 3$. A match is found in the third call.

TABLE 5.4

TRACE OF VALUES A, M, AND J

Call on Subroutine No.	L	M	J
1	1	7	4
2	1	3	2
3	3	3	3

Table 5.5 shows a trace for the same problem with $B = 8$. When we reach the call on subroutine #4 with parameter values 8 and 7 for L and M, respectively, subroutine #4 will compute $J = (8 + 7)/2 = 7$. Since $B - A[7]$ is positive, yet another call on SEARCH is made with L and M equal to 8 and 7 again. We are now in an infinite loop.

TABLE 5.5

A TRACE WITH $B = 8$

Call on Subroutine No.	L	M	J
1	1	7	4
2	5	7	6
3	7	7	7
4	8	7	7
5	8	7	7
— (ad infinitum)	—	—	—

233

The problem occurs because we did not ensure that only a finite number of calls on SEARCH are possible. We require that at some point a call on SEARCH must cause it to go to a RETURN box without recursively calling SEARCH again. We can take care of the problem in this example by noting that if L > M, there are no entries in the table to be searched; hence B is not present. Therefore we modify flowchart 5.50 to that shown in Figure 5.51. If L > M, we set I = 0 and return immediately.

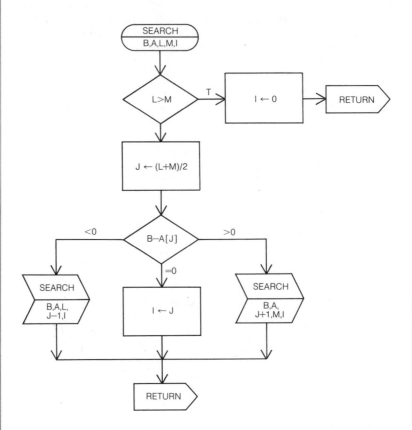

Fig. 5.51   Modified flowchart of Figure 5.50

The major advantage of recursion is that it makes the statement of an algorithm more concise. The example above does not illustrate this adequately. We will have to wait until Chapter 7 to introduce more meaningful examples. By then we will have introduced more complex data structures. Recursion usually pays off more in non-numerical processing. The major disadvantage is one of lack of speed in some simple numerical problems. We will illustrate this with one of the common examples of recursion.

Example 5.21—Factorial by Recursion

We wish to define a function FACT(N) whose value is N × (N − 1) × (N − 2) × . . . × 2 × 1 if N > 1, or 1 if N ≤ 1.

We note that FACT(N) = N × FACT(N − 1) if N > 1. Thus we can use the recursive procedure shown in Figure 5.52.

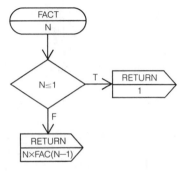

Fig. 5.52   Recursive procedure for factorial

The *iterative* method shown in Figure 5.53 leads to a more complex flowchart, but it will execute more rapidly on most systems. We can see this when we study the actual technique used for recursion. When the procedure in Figure 5.52 is first called, a section of available memory space is assigned for use in this invocation of the procedure. If the procedure calls itself, the next available section of memory space is assigned for use in the second level of invocation. These sections of memory correspond to storage in different copies in our analogy. Performing the call and assigning this memory usually take considerably more computer time than the time required to perform the overhead of the loop in Figure 5.53; hence the recursive approach is often slower. However, for non-numerical problems a nonrecursive approach is usually so much more complex that the small additional computer time is a good investment, since the procedure can be written and debugged more rapidly.

235

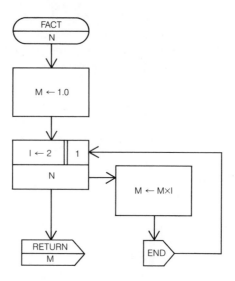

Fig. 5.53 Iterative procedure for factorial

PRObLEMS

1. If flowchart SEARCH in Figure 5.51 is called with actual parameter values CONS, X, 1, 10, I, and if the array X contains the ten
   values −7.5, −5.2, −4.1, −1.7, 0.5, 1.2, 1.7, 1.9, 2.1, and 2.8, how
   many calls are made on SEARCH to locate CONS if:

   *a. CONS contains 0.5
    b. CONS contains 1.7
    c. CONS contains −8.3

2. Write a recursive function procedure IGCD(I,J) to evaluate the
   greatest common divisor of I and J.

ERRORS,

OR "WHEN THE PROGRAM RUNS, ARE THE ANSWERS RIGHT?

6. Errors, or "When the Program Runs, are the Answers Right?"

The solution of a problem requires that we formulate an algorithm, program it in a suitable language, and check that the algorithm and program are correct. The latter step is the most difficult and time-consuming of all three.

Errors in programs are called *bugs*. Finding and fixing errors is called *debugging*. It is a three-stage process consisting of *detection*, *isolation*, and *correction*. First, we must determine whether the program works or not. If it does not, we have detected at least one error. Then we must isolate the error; finally we must correct it if possible. If the fault is in the program, the bug must be removed; if it is in the algorithm, the algorithm must be modified; if the fault is that the problem statement makes a solution impossible, we must consider restating the problem so that it has a solution.

Very few general remarks can be made about errors in problem statements. Their effect is often similar to the effects of program bugs. For example, a problem that required determination of a value X, such that $X^2 = 2$ exactly, has no solution. Any attempt to solve the problem may result in a program that never stops. The effect of this is hard to distinguish from the effect of the *infinite loop* shown in Figure 6.1. This infinite loop is a program bug in which there is a loop with an end test that is never satisfied.

In Chapter 4 we classified errors into syntax errors—those that are detected by the compiler—and logical errors—those that are not detected by the compiler. The compiler isolates most errors it detects. If we refer back to Figure 4.4, we see that error messages identify the point at which the compiler was first aware of the error. This was the point where the error occurred except in the case of the misuse of the array D, which should have been dimensioned at the start of the program. Finding and correcting syntax errors is not difficult with the aid of appropriate language implementation manuals.

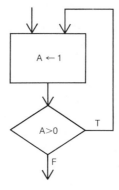

Fig. 6.1   Infinite loop

239

In this chapter we concentrate on other types of errors. They arise in a number of ways, including

- Incorrect expressions—for example, $X - Y$ instead of $X + Y$

- Incorrect program flow—a program branch goes to the wrong point in the program

- Failure to account for some cases of data—for example, the distance between two points on a line is found by subtracting their position coordinates and the possibility of negativity is ignored

- Failure to properly initialize data—for example, a search algorithm requires data to be in order, but the data is not ordered before searching

- Numerical errors—arithmetic operations work with only a finite number of digits of accuracy. Also, some problems can only be solved approximately.

In the next section we will look at the problem of detecting and isolating errors; in the final two sections we will look at some of their causes in detail.

6.1 DETECTION AND ISOLATION

Some errors are detected by hardware or the monitor program. These are of two types.

- An attempt to use non-existent or unassigned computer resources—for example, reference to memory with an address larger than available on the computer, or attempted use of an input/output unit not assigned to the program

- An attempt to generate a number that is out of range. This leads to overflow if the magnitude of the answer would be too large or an underflow if it would be too small.

When such an error occurs, program execution is stopped and the monitor program gives the user as much diagnostic information as possible, including an indication of the cause of termination and where in the program the error was detected.

Underflow may be an acceptable result in some cases. If two small numbers are multiplied, the result may underflow. The user may be happy to accept an answer of zero, even though all significant digits have been lost. Therefore most systems provide monitor subroutines that can be called to specify what is to happen in the case of overflow or underflow. These subroutines should be used with caution because valuable diagnostic information may be lost if overflow is ignored. An indication of when overflow first occurs is much more useful for debugging than a set of meaningless results.

Unfortunately, the hardware and monitor programs do not usually isolate the error even when they detect it. The cause of an overflow may have been an erroneous calculation very much earlier. Consequently, we need techniques for systematically checking each section of a program to determine if it is working.

Most program flowcharts contain many branches, and the path that is followed by the computer will depend on the input data. For example, if we are computing income tax, the tax rule applied may depend on the income. Consequently, to check a program we will have to check all cases (all forms of input) that can arise. We would like to make the statement that all possible branches of the program have been checked, so that it is guaranteed to work for any input data. We will sidestep the question of whether or not it is possible to make a guarantee that a program is correct; it is a question that is currently receiving a lot of attention from researchers in the field of computer science. Instead, we face the question of how we make tests of the program so that we can be reasonably sure that it is working, without absorbing enormous amounts of both programmer and computer time in the checking process.

We should endeavor to execute not only each branch of the program, but also each combination of branches that can occur in the algorithm. Figure 6.2 shows a small section of a program flow. In this figure we see four branches, labeled A, B, C, and D, whose execution depends on the results of decision boxes. In order to check each branch, we must give data to the program so that each of the branches A, B, C, and D is executed. This needs at least two tests; one, say, to execute A and C, and another to execute B and D. Four combinations of branches can occur, AC, AD, BC, and BD. Each should be tried if it is possible for the combination to occur in practice. The reason for testing the combinations is that there may be an error, for example, in Box A of Figure 6.2, that causes problems if Box D is executed immediately afterwards. For example, Boxes A and B may assign values to the variables P and Q, but the assignment to Q may have been erroneously omitted in Box A. Box C may use the value P, while Box D uses the value of Q. If the combination of A and D is not checked, the error may not come to light until the program is being used in production, that is, when it is being used to get answers to actual problems.

How can we check branches and combinations of branches? We must compute the results of performing the required operations on test data by some other means to check the results determined by the program. There are two major types of test data that can be used. Sometimes we generate very small problems that can be

241

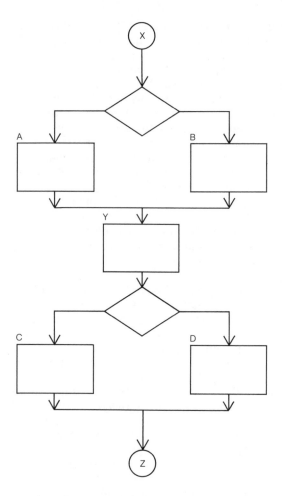

Fig. 6.2 Section of a program flow

solved by hand methods. However, it is obvious that this is not practical for large programs. The other source of test data comes from problems with known answers. If the program is a numerical one, for example, the solutions to some cases may be known from analytic means.

If the answers to the problem for the test data do not agree with the answers known from other sources, then we must find out the reason. One technique is to insert output statements that print intermediate results at a number of key points. The intermediate results also have to be computed by hand and compared with the printed results. The first discrepancy determines the section of the code that is causing the trouble. Thus, if in Figure 6.2 the results were printed before and after Box Y and were seen to be correct before Box Y and incorrect after, we would know that there is some form of error in Box Y.

The major drawbacks to this process are the problems of generating all intermediate results by hand and generating test cases to cause all combinations of branches to be followed. If the program is large, there will be many branches and many possible combinations. For this reason it is often wise to break the program down into smaller pieces and to check each piece thoroughly. The example in Figure 6.2 could be broken before or after Box Y. Input data could be generated for the first section and the output from it printed. Similarly, input data could be generated for the second section and read by some additional read statements used for debugging purposes only. The results from this input could be printed at Box Z to check the second section. The advantages of checking this way are that it is both easier to plan test data for a small section of a program and easier to compute the results from that test data by hand without error. Furthermore, it reduces the number of combinations of branches that have to be considered. For example, if we had five sections, each with two branches, there would be 32 combinations of branches, but if the sections were checked separately, only ten paths would have to be considered!

The process of breaking a program into a number of smaller segments is called *segmentation*. A convenient mechanism is to use subroutines as was done in Example 5.13. When this method is used, it is necessary to consider all possible forms that the input for each section can take. In many programs, certain forms of intermediate results will not be possible because of the nature of the solution. Thus if a calculation involves finding a set of distances, they will naturally be positive numbers. However, when writing another section of the code that will use these distances as input, it is wise to allow for cases that may not be expected. If it is really believed, for example, that a set of numbers will never be negative, it may not be necessary to test the section of the code with negative numbers. On the other hand, it is wise to program checks that will detect the "impossible" cases. If they arise, an immediate indication of an error is available.

The hand calculation of intermediate results is a time-consuming, tedious process. Another technique that can be used in some classes of problems is that of substituting the answer back into the problem. If it is of the form, "Find the xxx that satisfies the condition yyy," it is sometimes possible to verify whether the computed answer xxx does or does not satisfy the condition yyy. A numerical case where this is possible is in the solution of equations. The answers can be substituted back into the original equations to verify that they are satisfied. Unfortunately, in large numerical problems they will not be satisfied exactly, for reasons to be discussed in

Section 6.3. They should be approximately satisfied, however, and if they are not, it is an indication of an error. Usually this check will be programmed as part of the computer solution. If the time for checking that the answer satisfies the initial problem is short compared to the time required for solution, it is worthwhile to leave the check section in the final production program. It will detect errors that might still be present but that have not been uncovered by the test data used. It will also detect machine errors, which, although not frequent, do occur.

The techniques discussed above allow small sections of code to be checked so that errors can be isolated. We can think of the process of isolation as similar to the method of bisection discussed in Example 3.3. If intermediate results are correct at one point and incorrect at a later point, an error exists between the two points. By subdividing the program section into two or more subsections and checking the results at those division points, the error can be further isolated.

Usually, when the section is only ten or twenty lines of code in length, the error can be spotted by reading the program; however, every programmer has encountered the frustration of looking at a small section of code and being unable to see why it produces the answers obtained.

There are several ways of proceeding at this point. The first is *desk checking*. This involves sitting down with ample paper and space and pretending to be the computer executing the program step by step. This may not uncover the error, because people are prone to repeat their errors. A friendly programmer can be helpful at this point. You can set out to prove to this friend that the computer hardware must be making errors because you can show why this program cannot compute the results that are obtained. Frequently, verbalizing the steps in the program enables you to see your error. If that fails, a computer *trace* can be used. A trace is an execution of the program by the computer in a mode that prints the results of each step. These can be examined to locate the first error. However, if a lot of computation is involved, the results of a trace may be too long. An alternative is to take a series of *snapshots* at points in the program section. A snapshot is a listing of the values of variables at a point in the middle of program execution. You can specify which variables you wish to have printed. These, together with a *dump*, which is a listing of the state of the memory at the termination of execution, can provide valuable information.

It must be realized that it is not currently possible to guarantee the validity of a sizeable program. In programming, you will have to learn to balance the additional cost of checking the program further against the potential damage if errors remain uncovered. Perhaps a criterion to bear in mind is "Would I be prepared to fly in a plane if part of it were designed by my program?"

6.2 Non–Numerical Errors

A section such as this can only mention a few errors that can arise. Its purpose is to acquaint the beginning programmer with some of the most frequent errors.

6.2.1 Array Subscripts Out of Range

These are annoying errors because they can cause a program failure long after the erroneous subscript was used. If there is a compiler that compiles code to check subscript ranges during execution, it is advisable to use it for debugging.

When the programmer uses an indexed array, an address function is implied. Thus, reference to the value of B[I] implies a reference to location $B + I - 1$, where B is the address of B[1]. The compiler assigns a block of storage for the elements of B based on the space required. If the programmer generates a value for the subscript I that is out of the range allowed (that is, if I does not correspond to a cell B[I] for which storage was allocated by the computer) the implied address, $B + I - 1$, will not be a part of the desired block—it will refer to some other area of memory. This could be an area that is used for other data in the program, an area that is used for storing the program itself, or one not even assigned to the program by the system. If the programmer attempts to read from location B[I], he will obviously not get the number that he intended since he is using a subscript that was not intended when he declared the size of his array. (Although we have not required that array sizes be declared in our flowchart language, most programming languages do require this.)

If the programmer attempts to read from a location not in the area assigned to his program, the monitor will terminate program execution. If on the other hand he attempts to write into a cell with an out-of-range subscript (this can happen either with an assignment statement, an input statement, or a function/subroutine), the program can cause other serious problems. Storing something into a program area of memory can cause error symptoms that are very difficult to analyze. Usually the result will be a termination on an invalid operation code because the chances are small that an arbitrary piece of data will represent a valid operation. However, the time of the termination may occur long after the actual error of overwriting occurred. Storing into a data area will overwrite another piece of data; consequently, it will not contain what it was believed to contain. In this situation the programmer may spend many hours trying to find out why data has been changed.

Fortunately, many compilers can compile code to check when a subscript is out of range. For example, WATFOR and WATFIV will

245

detect out-of-range subscripts immediately. PL/I can provide this as an option. Unfortunately, the code to detect these conditions slows down the object program considerably, so these checking features should be used only during the debugging phase of a program.

6.2.2 PARAMETERS TO FUNCTIONS AND SUBROUTINES

Actual parameter values supplied when functions or subroutines are called must satisfy some requirements determined by the use of the parameters. Frequent errors that can be difficult to detect include: reordering of the parameters—the subroutine expects A, B and is passed B, A; the use of two few parameters—this happens when there are a large number of parameters; and use of the wrong type of data—passing an integer when the subroutine expects a floating-point number. Problems occur when the user overlooks the fact that a parameter is an output as well as an input parameter, so that an unexpected change is made, or when he overlooks a side-effect—that is, a change made by the subroutine in global storage.

A sensible step in checking a program is to examine each subroutine or function call carefully to check the actual parameter values and to put a comment near a subroutine or function call if it has side-effects, so that they will not be overlooked.

6.2.3 INITIALIZATION OF DATA

When the program is first loaded, the memory may contain anything (although some systems will set all locations to some standard value). However, the program should not rely on the memory containing known information, since the system may change after the program has been written. If variables are to be set to some standard value initially, the programmer should so set them. Some languages include initialization statements. (FORTRAN has the DATA statement while PL/I has the INITIAL declaration.) However, the programmer should be very careful to make sure that he does not execute more than once the sections of code that assume the initialization without being sure that the variables are indeed re-initialized. In many cases it is better to set the variables to their desired initial state immediately before that state is required. This warning applies particularly to program loops. Usually the start of the loop is preceded by a number of lines of code that initialize various variables to a starting value. It is very easy to make the mistake of transferring back to the start of the loop, forgetting to re-initialize variables when it is required.

246

6.2.4 Incorrect Loop Tests

A fourth common error causes an incorrect number of passes through a loop. The programmer may incorrectly initialize the starting value or incorrectly calculate the final test value, often resulting in one too few or one too many executions of the loop. This is a frequent source of out-of-range subscript errors.

Questions

1. What is a snapshot?

2. Identify three ways of comparing the input and output of a program to determine its validity.

Problems

*1. The following program is tested. It is supposed to read a set of positive numbers and compute their average. The end of the input deck of cards is indicated by a card with a negative number. When it is executed with the input data 3.5, 2.7, 2.2, −1.0 (on separate cards), it prints the answer 2.1. What is the error?

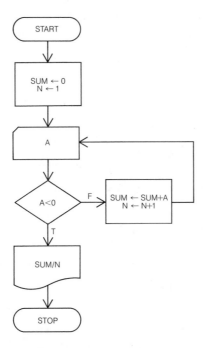

2. The following program is supposed to read two sets of positive numbers, each terminated by a card with a negative number, and print the largest number in each set. It is run with the data (on separate cards) 1, 7, 5, 2, −1, 3, 8, 1, −2. It does not print anything; it stops trying to read a card. When this error is fixed, it correctly prints the answers 7 and 8. However, it is found not to work on other data. What are the two errors?

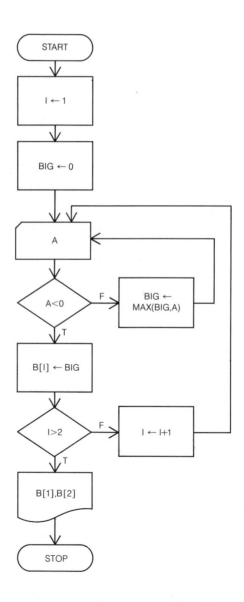

6.3 Numerical Errors

This section takes a brief look at numerical errors. These errors initially arise from two sources. The first source is called *rounding* error, and is due to the fact that only a finite set of all of the real numbers can be represented in the computer as floating-point numbers. Therefore we must approximate most data input to the problem and the results of most arithmetic operations. The second source is called *truncation* error. It has nothing to do with the use of truncation as a means of converting real numbers to representable floating-point numbers, but refers to the approximation of functions that can be computed exactly only by means of an infinite sequence of operations. For example, sin(y) is given by the series

$$y - \frac{y^3}{3!} + \frac{y^5}{5!} - \frac{y^7}{7!} + \dots$$

If a finite number of terms of this series are used to compute SIN(Y), the error due to truncating the series is called the truncation error, The errors introduced by rounding and truncation are initially small, but sometimes their effect is amplified by subsequent operations.

The purpose of this section is to point out some of the pitfalls in numerical computation, not to discuss numerical methods. If you are going to do a lot of numerical work, you should also look at Chapter 9, which suggests solutions to some of the pitfalls. If you are not particularly concerned with numerical computations, you should still be aware of the traps awaiting the unwary, although you normally need not be unduly concerned with them.

6.3.1 Errors in Arithmetic [Rounding Errors]

Errors in arithmetic arise when initial data or intermediate results cannot be represented exactly in the computer. Because machines are usually more precise than we are, we often assume that the computer is accurate enough for anything we need to do. Our hypothetical computer discussed in Chapter 2 carried five digits of precision in floating point. Since numbers we measure in experiments are seldom accurate to more than three digits, surely five are sufficient? Besides, most available computers carry from seven to sixteen digits of precision. Surely that is enough, even if our experimental data is good to six digits? Many times it is, but we must be aware that things can go wrong.

The number of digits of precision carried in floating-point is fixed. Our hypothetical computer has five. The *weight* of these digits varies with the exponent of the number. Thus, if a number is rounded to put it in the form

$$\pm.nnnnn \times 10^e$$

the rounding error will be a maximum of $\pm.000005 \times 10^e$. Its actual value will depend on the exponent e. When an arithmetic operation results in an answer that cannot be represented exactly, additional round-off errors are introduced. These depend on the exponent of the answer.

One immediate consequence of this is the phenomenon known as *cancellation*. This occurs when two numbers of nearly equal size are subtracted. Consider, for example, the problem of subtracting $\frac{129}{388}$ from $\frac{162}{485}$. The correct answer is $\frac{3}{1940}$. If the numbers are formed correctly rounded to five significant digits, the arithmetic process yields

$$.33402 \times 10^0 - .33247 \times 10^0 = 0.15500 \times 10^{-2}$$

whereas the answer is $.15464 \times 10^{-2}$ correctly rounded to five digits. What has happened? When the fractions were represented to five-digit precision, rounding errors were made. 129/388 is 0.3324742 . . ., so a rounding error of $.0000042 \ldots \times 10^0$ is committed. Similarly a rounding error of $.0000006 \ldots \times 10^0$ is made in representing 162/485 to five digits. When these two numbers are subtracted, their first two digits cancel, decreasing the exponent of the result by 2. The total rounding error is $(.0000006 - .0000042) \times 10^0$, which is $(-.00036) \times 10^{-2}$, and so it shows up as early as the fourth place of the answer. The problem of cancellation is illustrated in Figure 6.3.

A standard example is the sum of three numbers. Suppose we form $A + B + C$ by first adding A to B, then by adding C to the result. Suppose the values of A, B, and C are $-.12344 \times 10^0$, $+.12345 \times 10^0$, and $+.32741 \times 10^{-4}$, respectively. $A + B$ is $.00001 \times 10^0$, or $.10000$

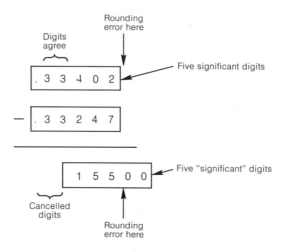

Fig. 6.3 Cancellation

250

$\times 10^{-4}$ after normalization. When C is added to this, we get .42741 $\times 10^{-4}$. Suppose, on the other hand, we first add C to B, then add the result to A using five-digit floating-point arithmetic. B + C is .123482741 $\times 10^0$, which is .12348 after rounding. When A is added to this, we get .00004, which is .40000 $\times 10^{-4}$ after normalization. Thus the result (.42741 $\times 10^{-4}$ or .40000 $\times 10^{-4}$) is very dependent on the order of the arithmetic. Although exact addition is *associative*, that is, (A + B) + C = A + (B + C), the result of machine computation depends on the size of intermediate results.

Example 6.1

A common example of the buildup of round-off errors is in the repeated addition of the same number to a running total. Suppose in the nth pass through a program loop, we need the value n/6. One way of doing this is to initialize a variable to 1/6 and to add 1/6 to it after each pass. In order to be able to see what happens after only a few passes, let us examine the behavior of a machine with only two significant digits of accuracy in floating point. One-sixth is represented by .17 $\times 10^0$ if rounding is used, by .16 $\times 10^0$ otherwise.

Let us look at the states of the variable in the first twelve passes in each case. They are shown in Table 6.1. Once the total reaches 1.0, future additions of 1/6 can only add .1 or .2 because the intermediate result has an exponent of one. If the passes through the loop continued until the total were 10, further additions would not change the result, as 10 + .16 is still 10 to two significant digits. It is true that modern computers have more than two significant digits, but it is also true that we often make more than twelve passes through a loop.

One way to overcome this effect is to form an integer N that is equal to the number of passes through the loop and to divide that by 6. It takes a little more computer time since division is slower than addition in a computer, but it is much more accurate since the maximum error is a rounding error in the last significant digit of the answer. This example points out that the fastest program may not be the most accurate.

Example 6.2—Variance Calculation

This illustrates the effects of cancellation. If the N numbers in a set are S[1], S[2], . . . , S[N], then their mean (or average) is

$$A = (S[1] + S[2] + . . . + S[N])/N$$

and their variance is

$$V = ((S[1] - A)^2 + (S[2] - A)^2 + . . . + (S[N] - A)^2))/N$$

251

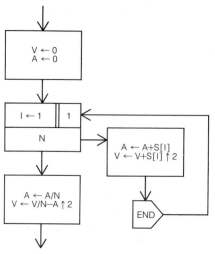

Fig. 6.4 Short solution for Example 6.2

The variance is a measure of how scattered variables are. If they are all the same, the variance is zero. Earlier we calculated the variance exactly as shown above. (See Example 5.2.) It takes $2N - 2$ additions, N subtractions, N multiplications, and 2 divisions spread over two loops. Alternatively, we can rewrite V as

$$V = ((S[1]^2 - 2S[1] \times A + A^2) + \ldots + (S[N]^2 - 2S[N] \times A + A^2))/N$$
$$= (S[1]^2 + S[2]^2 + \ldots + S[N]^2)/N - 2 \times A \times (S[1] + S[2] + \ldots + S[N])/N + (A^2 + A^2 + \ldots + A^2)/N$$

The second term contains $(S[1] + S[2] + \ldots + S[N])/N$ which is exactly A, while the last contains N instances of A^2. Hence

$$V = (S[1]^2 + S[2]^2 + \ldots + S[N]^2)/N - 2 \times A \times A + A^2$$
$$= (S[1]^2 + S[2]^2 + \ldots + S[N]^2)/N - A^2$$

A program to compute this is shown in Figure 6.4.

This approach requires $N - 1$ fewer subtractions and one more multiplication than the earlier method, and only uses one loop, resulting in a faster program. However, if the average (A) is large but the variance (V) is small, this faster method may be much less accurate. Consider an example using a three-digit computer that rounds correctly. Suppose we wish to find the variance of the five numbers 4.3, 4.4, 4.5, 4.6, and 4.7. Using the earlier method, we first sum them to get 22.5. On dividing by 5 we get the correct average of 4.5. No rounding errors are introduced if three digits are used. Next we calculate the sum of squares of the differences as shown in Table 6.2. Therefore the computed variance is .1

TABLE 6.1

RUNNING SUM OF 1/6

Pass	Sum Correctly Rounded	Sum Truncated	True Answer Rounded
1	$.17 \times 10^0$	$.16 \times 10^0$	$.17 \times 10^0$
2	$.34 \times 10^0$	$.32 \times 10^0$	$.33 \times 10^0$
3	$.51 \times 10^0$	$.48 \times 10^0$	$.50 \times 10^0$
4	$.68 \times 10^0$	$.64 \times 10^0$	$.67 \times 10^0$
5	$.85 \times 10^0$	$.80 \times 10^0$	$.83 \times 10^0$
6	$.10 \times 10^1$	$.96 \times 10^0$	$.10 \times 10^1$
7	$.12 \times 10^1$	$.11 \times 10^1$	$.12 \times 10^1$
8	$.14 \times 10^1$	$.12 \times 10^1$	$.13 \times 10^1$
9	$.16 \times 10^1$	$.13 \times 10^1$	$.15 \times 10^1$
10	$.18 \times 10^1$	$.14 \times 10^1$	$.17 \times 10^1$
11	$.20 \times 10^1$	$.15 \times 10^1$	$.18 \times 10^1$
12	$.22 \times 10^1$	$.16 \times 10^1$	$.20 \times 10^1$

TABLE 6.2

VARIANCE CALCULATION BY OLD METHOD

$(4.3 - 4.5)^2$	$= .4 \times 10^{-1}$
$(4.4 - 4.5)^2$	$= .1 \times 10^{-1}$
$(4.5 - 4.5)^2$	$= 0$
$(4.6 - 4.5)^2$	$= .1 \times 10^{-1}$
$(4.7 - 4.5)^2$	$= .4 \times 10^{-1}$
Total	$= .1 \times 10^0$

TABLE 6.3

VARIANCE CALCULATION BY NEW METHOD

I	S[I]	S[I]²	Rounded to Three Digits	Sum So Far, Rounded to Three Digits
1	4.3	18.49	18.5	$18.5 = S[1]$
2	4.4	19.36	19.4	$37.9 = S[1] + S[2]$
3	4.5	20.25	20.3	$58.2 = S[1] + S[2] + S[3]$
4	4.6	21.16	21.2	$79.4 = \ldots$
5	4.7	22.09	22.1	$102. = \ldots$

$\times 10^{-1}/5 = .2 \times 10^{-1}$. Again, no rounding errors are committed so the answer is exact. On the other hand, the second method will square each of the S[I]'s and round the answers to three digits. This process and the total is shown in Table 6.3. This time we calculate V using three-digit rounded arithmetic to get

$$V = \frac{102.}{5} - (4.5)^2 = 20.4 - 20.3 = .1$$

This is in error by 400%! An extreme example, yes—but one to remind you, once again, that the fastest way is not always the best.

6.3.2 TRUNCATION ERRORS

Truncation errors are those errors that arise because an infinite process necessary to compute a function must be truncated after a finite number of steps. We have already mentioned the example of sin(y). Many of the simple functions are given by power series. For example

$$\exp(y) = 1 + y + \frac{y^2}{2!} + \frac{y^3}{3!} + \ldots$$

If we want to know how many terms to use, we must decide how much accuracy we need, and on the range of y to be allowed. If, for example, we are interested in $-1 \leq y \leq 1$, the difference between exp(y) and $1 + y + \ldots + y^n/n!$ is certainly less than

$$E = \frac{1}{(n+1)!} + \frac{1}{(n+2)!} + \ldots$$

Since

$$1 + 1 + \frac{1}{2!} + \frac{1}{3!} + \ldots = e = 2.7182818 \ldots$$

we can calculate E for various n to be

$$E = 2.7182818 \ldots - (1 + 1 + \frac{1}{2!} + \ldots + \frac{1}{n!})$$

Values of E are shown in Table 6.4.

A person designing a function procedure for EXP could pick a value of n from a table such as this. (Not all functions can be treated this simply.)

TABLE 6.4

VALUES OF MAXIMUM ERROR IN APPROXIMATION

n	2	3	4	5
E	0.218 . . .	0.0516 . . .	0.00991 . . .	0.00151 . . .

Even if computer arithmetic were infinitely accurate, stopping the calculation of a series after a finite number of terms leads to truncation errors. These errors also occur in some of the other examples we have discussed. The method of bisection, for example, computes more accurate approximations to the solution of an equation by moving upper and lower bounds closer together. However, no matter how much accuracy is achieved in the arithmetic or how many steps are taken, the two bounds will always be separate, so we will not get an exact answer unless we are lucky and happen to hit the answer when one of the midpoints is formed.

Questions

*1. What is a rounding error?

2. What is cancellation?

*3. How can cancellation magnify the effect of a rounding error in the final answer?

4. What is truncation error?

5. Compute the mean and variance of the numbers 4.9, 5.05, 4.98, 4.89, and 5.02 using correctly rounded three-digit arithmetic by the techniques used in Tables 6.2 and 6.3.

6.3.3 Amplification of Errors

Most problems start with data that is in error. It may come, for example, from incorrect measurement in experiments. Obviously, errors in data will lead to errors in answers. Rounding and truncation errors also lead to errors in answers. Even though all such errors are of limited size—for example, less than 0.1%—it does not follow that the errors in the final answer will be similarly restricted in size. Indeed, in Examples 6.1 and 6.2, final errors were much larger because of cancellation. Even in methods of solution that involve no truncation error, and in which arithmetic is done arbitrarily accurately, errors in initial data can be magnified out of all proportion.

Such problems are said to be *ill-conditioned*. In such problems, no method can lead to an accurate answer, so we cannot come up with a solution to the difficulty. However, it is important that we know when it can arise so that we know when our answers will be nonsense.

An example of an ill-conditioned problem is the case of a man trying to decide where his moon-bound rocket is going to land, assuming that it is aimed from the earth and that no midcourse corrections are allowed. The dependence of the final destination on the initial angle and velocity is critical, since a small variation will leave the rocket wandering in space or crashing into the sun, 9×10^7 miles off course!

In this section we start with a simple example of an ill-conditioned problem. We then investigate a method of solution of a problem that is initially well-conditioned but can be changed into an ill-conditioned problem if care is not exercised. In this case a good problem is ruined. This should not happen.

Consider the system of two equations in two unknowns

$$.992u + .873v = .119 \qquad\qquad (6.1)$$
$$.481u + .421v = .060$$

These can be seen by inspection to have the answer $u = 1$, $v = -1$. Suppose that these numbers are the result of measurements of an experiment, and are good only to $\pm.001$. Thus the right-hand side of the first equation might be .120 rather than .119. Let us solve the *perturbed* problem.

$$.992u + .873v = .120 \qquad\qquad (6.2)$$
$$.481u + .421v = .060$$

The answers are

$$u = .815$$
$$v = -.789$$

to three digits, about a 20% change caused by a 1% change in the problem. It is easy to construct examples in which the change in the answer is arbitrarily as large. For example

$$.400y + .400z = .800 \qquad\qquad (6.3)$$
$$.401y + .400z = .801$$

has the solution $y = z = 1$
whereas

$$.400y + .400z = .800 \qquad\qquad (6.4)$$
$$.401y + .400z = .800$$

has the solution $y = 0$, $z = 2$. A change of one part in 800 gives a 100% change in the answer.

What is happening in these examples? A pictorial representation makes it obvious. The set of values of y and z for which

$$.400y + .400z = .800$$

form a line on a y versus z graph as shown in Figure 6.5. This line represents all those points (y,z) that satisfy the first of equations (6.3). If we recognize that the initial data has errors, so that the

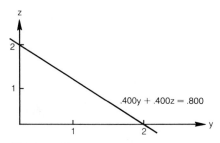

Fig. 6.5 Graph of .400y + .400z = .800

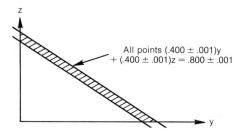

Fig. 6.6 Region of solution

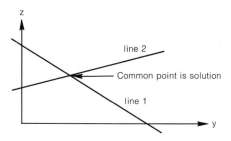

Fig. 6.7 Solution of a pair of equations

equation might really be .400y + .400z = .801, we see that points on this perturbed line could equally well satisfy the first equation *within the accuracy we were able to measure*. When we consider all possible equations that could replace the first one if we allow each of the coefficients to be perturbed by any amount up to its maximum error, we see that the set of points that satisfy the first equation (or rather, satisfy what we know about it) form a region like the "thick line" shown in Figure 6.6. (Actually, the thickness of that line is exaggerated; it is only about .004 units thick.)

The second equation also represents a line if the coefficients are known exactly (see Figure 6.7), or a "thick line" if there are errors

257

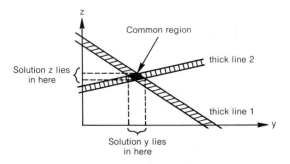

Fig. 6.8 Area of possible solution

in the coefficients. The solution of a pair of equations, each of which represents a line, is the point common to both lines, as shown in Figure 6.7. When we draw the lines with thickness, a possible solution will be any point in the common region as shown in Figure 6.8. It is not possible to determine y and z more accurately than shown if the given data is approximate. This is all right if the lines are only about .004 thick and as shown. The uncertainty in y and z is only about .007. However, suppose that the two lines are nearly parallel, as shown in Figure 6.9. In that case, the common region is very large, even though the lines are not very thick—that is, even though the initial data is fairly accurate. The examples we gave above both represented nearly parallel lines. Nothing can be done to determine the answer more accurately than it is determined by the original problem. If the answer is very sensitive to changes in the original data, the problem is ill-conditioned.

If we are given a well-conditioned problem, we should be able to determine the answers accurately. Sometimes a bad choice of method will make the solution very sensitive to round-off or truncation errors, or even to errors in the initial values. This is particularly true when we solve linear equations. Let us consider an example using three-digit floating-point arithmetic.

$$.512y - .920 \times 10^{-3}z = .511 \qquad (6.5)$$
$$.117 \times 10^{-2}y + .648z = .649$$

The two lines represented are almost at right angles, so the problem is well-conditioned. (The answer is $y = z = 1$ to three digits.) The usual method of solution is to use the first equation to express the first variable (y) in terms of the other variables. In this case we divide the first equation by .512 to get

$$y - .180 \times 10^{-2}z = .998 \qquad (6.6)$$

and then subtract $.117 \times 10^{-2}$ times equation (6.6) from the second of equations (6.5) to get of y. Thus, we have

258

$$.117 \times 10^{-2}y + .648z \qquad\qquad .649$$
$$=$$
$$-.117 \times 10^{-2}(y - .180 \times 10^{-2}z) \quad -.117 \times 10^{-2} \times .998$$

If we do this arithmetic rounded to three digits we get

$$.648z = .648$$

or $z = 1.00$. Equation (6.6) then tells us that

$$y = .998 + .180 \times 10^{-2} = 1.00$$

Suppose, however, that we had written equations (6.5) in the reverse order

$$.117 \times 10^{-2}y + .648z = .649 \qquad (6.7)$$
$$.512y - .920 \times 10^{-3}z = .511$$

We divide the first of equations (6.7) by $.117 \times 10^{-2}$ to get

$$y + 554z = 555 \qquad (6.8)$$

Now we subtract .512 times equation (6.8) from the second of equations (6.7) to get rid of y:

$$.512y - .920 \times 10^{-2}z \qquad .511$$
$$=$$
$$-.512(y + 554z) \qquad -.512 \times 555$$

If we do three-digit rounded arithmetic we get

$$-284z = -283$$

or

$$z = .996$$

Substituting this into equation (6.8) we find

$$y = 555 - 554 \times .996 = 555 - 552 = 3.00$$

The answer for z is reasonable (0.4% error, which is all we can expect in view of the initial error). The answer for y is hopeless, and yet the problem is well-conditioned. What has happened? The answer is that we have turned it into an ill-conditioned problem in the middle of the solution by making a bad choice of which equation to handle first. Small rounding errors or initial errors then perturb the solution of this new ill-conditioned problem. We can see what is happening if we use a graphical interpretation.

When we divide an equation in order to make the coefficient of one of the variables equal to one, we do not change the line it represents, so this step has little effect. When we subtract a multiple of one equation from another, we get a third equation. It also represents a straight line. Any values of y and z that lie on both of

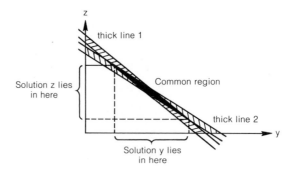

Fig. 6.9 Area of possible solution with nearly parallel lines

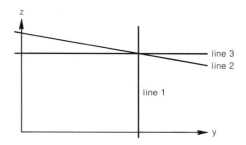

Fig. 6.10 Effect of elimination of variable

the original lines must also lie on this third line since if both of the original equations are satisfied, so is the third. Hence this line passes through the intersection of the other two as shown in Figure 6.10. We can then replace the problem of finding the common point of line 1 and line 2 by the problem of finding the common point of lines 1 and 3. We chose line 3 so that y did not appear in its equation. Hence it is parallel to the y axis. In Figure 6.10, line 1 is nearly vertical, so our new problem appears to be well-conditioned.

In the problem of equations (6.5), the first equation corresponds to a nearly vertical line, the second to a nearly horizontal line. When we eliminate y from the second equation to get a horizontal line we still have lines nearly at right angles, so we still have a well-conditioned problem. However, when we reversed the order and kept the second and third lines by eliminating the first equation, we gave ourselves an ill-conditioned problem. This is shown with "thick" lines in Figure 6.11. The original region of uncertainty is ABCD. Line 3 must contain this region since any solution of the original problem must lie in the thick line 3. If lines 1 and 3 are now used to find the solution, the minimum region of uncertainty is AECF. However, if lines 2 and 3 are used, the region is much larger, namely AGCH.

260

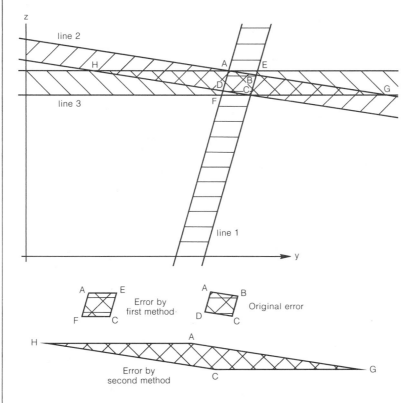

Fig. 6.11 Regions of uncertainty

Questions

1. What is an ill-conditioned problem?

2. Is the problem of computing the hypotenuse of a right-angled triangle, given the other two sides, well-conditioned?

Problems

*1. Solve the equations

$$-.263a + .527b = .392$$
$$.826a + .412b = .851$$

by hand methods using three-significant-digit rounded floating-point arithmetic.

2. Solve the equations

261

$$.215x + .430y = .258$$
$$.461x + .917y = .553$$

by hand methods using three-significant-digit rounded floating-point arithmetic. Are your answers accurate? Is the problem well-conditioned?

DATA
STRUCTURES

7. DATA STRUCTURES

In the introduction we stressed that the solution of a problem consists of finding a method for converting the input structure of the data to the intermediate and output structures required. In numerical problems the structure of the data is fairly straightforward, so we do not usually stress this aspect. However, in nonnumeric problems the data structure is of paramount importance.

Consider, for example, the problem of organizing a computer-based airline reservation system. The inputs to the system are lists of flights between cities and lists of passenger names with their reservation requests. The outputs from the system are passenger lists for the flights and seat availability information. The computer program must store the input data in a form that shows the relations between items. In this case the data structure must indicate which reservations a passenger holds and what passengers are booked on each flight. It is also desirable that the data be stored in a way that makes it possible to perform the required computations rapidly. For example, the data could be stored exactly as input. However, finding out if there were any seats left on a given flight would require a search through all the data—a very slow process. Therefore the input data should be restructured so that it is possible to access required information rapidly. The internal form of the data should also be structured so that the data can be changed if that is a part of the problem. For example, the data stored in an airline reservation system will be continually modified as new passengers are added, others change their reservations, and flights depart. Thus there are three key considerations in the design of an internal data structure:

- Relations between items of data
- Rapid access of related data
- Ease of modification of data

In this chapter we will examine a number of problems and see how certain forms of structure can be used in their solution. During this examination we will categorize the types of structures into broad classes such as strings, lists, trees, and so forth. There is nothing magic about this categorization and there are no rules for saying "for problems of type X use a structure of class Y." The types of data structure available are as varied as the programmer cares to invent; the structure used in any solution should be tailored to the individual problem. We will see how some operations are facilitated by particular classes of data structures.

7.1 STRINGS

Many non-numerical problems deal with character strings. For example, in an airline reservation system, each reservation contains a passenger name, phone number, and list of flights booked. One of the operations needed is the ability to search through the passenger names in order to locate the name of a passenger who wishes to change his reservations. Two search methods were discussed earlier—the sequential search on page 177 and the binary search on page 197. The latter required that the table be in alphabetical order. In the discussion of those search methods the table of items was assumed to consist of a set of single-word entries in a linear array that was referenced through indexing as A[I]. In a passenger list each entry consists of many characters, so they will occupy several words. The way in which these entries are stored can have a significant effect on the speed of the program.

When a table of information, such as a passenger list, is to be searched, the part of the information to be matched with the item being looked up is called the *key*. Thus in the passenger list the name is the key for each entry. A table is ordered if it is in alphabetic (or numeric) order on its key.

The major problem when searching a table like a passenger list (apart from its size) is the fact that some entries are longer than others. We say that the entries are of *variable length*. If the entries are character strings (and we will assume that they are for now) the total number of characters in the string is not the same for all entries. This raises the question of how the character strings are stored. They could be packed several characters per word (four in our hypothetical computer) or stored one character per word. Which of these cases is used is relatively unimportant for our study of the problems, so we will assume that one character is stored per word. Placing four characters in each word would obviously reduce the memory space required. If that were done, we would simply work with multiples of four characters rather than with single characters.

The two searching methods discussed earlier required that we access the data in different ways. In a sequential search we access the next entry; in a binary search we access the midpoint of the remaining portion of the table. Both methods can be implemented using arrays.

To find the Ith member of an array A[J], J = 1, . . . , N, we must know how much space is used in each entry. Previously we assumed that one word was used for each element of A, so that the address function $A + I - 1$ was implied by the expression A[I] where A is the address of A[1]. When we store character strings, more than one word will be needed for each member of the array. If exactly M contiguous words are used for every member of an array A, the corresponding address function would be $A + (I - 1) \times M$. Thus, if we took M to be the maximum length of all entries, we could use M words for each entry. Strings that were shorter than M words could

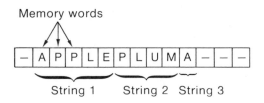

Memory words

Fig. 7.1 Storing characters of a string

be padded on the right with blanks so that they used exactly M words.

This scheme allows the Ith element in an array of character strings to be located directly. Either a sequential or binary search could be written for such a scheme. The drawback of the scheme is that it may use a lot of extra storage space because each element uses a space long enough to accommodate the longest string. Furthermore, we must know the length of the longest string before we can construct the table. If new entries are to be added to the table from time to time, we may not be able to determine the maximum length at the time the table is constructed. Therefore we should consider other ways of storing and manipulating variable-length strings of characters.

We will continue to assume for now that a single string of characters is stored in contiguous locations in memory. Suppose we used only enough locations to store the characters of the string and put the next string in the table immediately after the first, as shown in Figure 7.1.

When we are dealing with these strings, we need to know two things: where each string starts and where it ends—that is, how long it is. There are two common ways of indicating the length of a string in memory. We can store the length of each one in a word at the start of the string, or we can put a special mark at the end of it. This special mark is a digit combination that does not represent any of the characters being manipulated. These two methods are illustrated in Figure 7.2.

If the strings are stored next to each other as in Figure 7.2, we can tell where one element starts when we know where the preceding element stops. For the sequential search this is sufficient. If we know where the start of the table is, we can compare the first element with the entry being sought; if a match does not occur, we move on to the second element and so on. The entries in a table of this form are sequentially accessible only. Fortunately, that is all we need for the sequential search.

Suppose we wish to *index* into the list, that is, to treat it as an array and to process the Ith entry for any I. (We used this in the

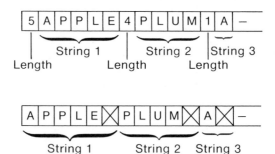

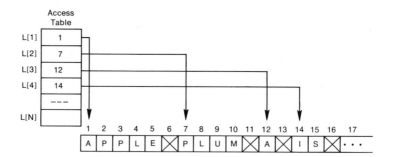

Fig. 7.2 Indicating string length in memory

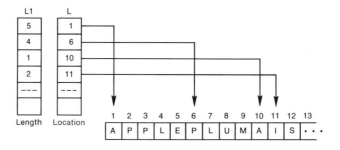

Fig. 7.3 Access table

Fig. 7.4 Storing the length of the Ith string in a separate array

binary search solution.) The only way we could do so using the data structure in Figure 7.2 is to count our way from the beginning—a very slow process. To avoid this we must create an array that tells us where the Ith member is located. Such an array is called an *access table* or *directory*. It is a fixed-length array L (typically of integers) such that the Ith member of the array L[I] contains the address of the Ith element of the table. This is shown in Figure 7.3. If the length of each string is given numerically, it is simpler to also store the length of the Ith string in a separate array, say L1. This is shown in Figure 7.4. If we were programming this in a POL, the array element L[I] could contain the index of the start of the Ith string in some other array. Thus if C is an array of single characters, C[L[I]] would be the first address of the Ith character string.

A flowchart for a binary search using the access table technique is shown in Figure 7.5. The name to be located is assumed to be in

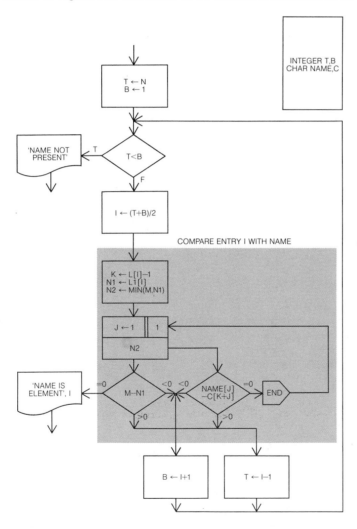

Fig. 7.5 Binary search using access table technique

269

NAME[I], I = 1, . . . , M. The Ith character string is assumed to be stored in C[J], J = L[I], . . . , L[I] + L1[I] − 1. (That is, the length of the string is stored in the array L1.) There are assumed to be N entries in the table. T and B are the top and bottom of the remaining portion of the table to be searched. The shaded part of the chart compares the Ith entry with NAME a character at a time. The first inequality found determines that the table entry is not equal to the name. It also indicates whether NAME (if in the table) is above or below that entry. If the character strings (the table entry and NAME) are equal up to the length of the shortest of the two, then the longer is alphabetically larger. For example, FULLY must follow FULL. Character strings are equal only if they are the same length and match in all positions.

Questions

*1. If a set of different length strings is to be accessed sequentially, what is the most compact way of storing them?

2. If it is necessary to access a member of a set of different length strings by its index (that is, to access the Ith member) what way of storing them will allow the fastest access and yet use the smallest amount of storage space?

3. What is the answer to question 2 if the strings are all of the same length?

Problem

1. Suppose the array C[I] contains characters or integers, one per word, representing character strings and their lengths, as shown in the upper part of Figure 7.2. Write a function flowchart that returns the index I of the start of a string that matches a parameter B. B is an array whose first entry B[I] is the length of a string whose characters are in locations B[2], B[3], ... Return the value 0 if the string cannot be found. The end of the array C is indicated by a zero entry in C; that is, if C contains the two strings AB and C1X, its entries are

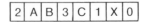

7.2 Lists

In many problems a table of information has to be changed from time to time. Examples of this include names of airline passengers, the records that a bank keeps on its customer accounts, and the tables of names of books, periodicals, and reports available in an information retrieval system. Let us examine the application of various data structures to the problem of changing data. In this section we will consider tables that might be used in a sequential search. The table entries are not in any particular order.

Suppose, first, that the table is stored in an array. Adding a new item to an unordered table is straightforward if there is enough room at the end: we add the new entry on the end of the existing set. However, deleting an entry creates a problem unless it is the last one because it leaves a hole that can only be filled by moving up all following entries, as shown in Figure 7.6. It is necessary to fill the hole so that a sequential operation accesses the datum MURRELL immediately after accessing the datum MORGAN. This moving is a time-consuming process we wish to avoid.

An alternative is to structure the entries as a *list*. Each entry contains, in addition to the data, a clue to the location of the next item in the list. This could be its actual memory address or an index into an array that contains the data. In either case we will call the extra datum that gives the location of the next item a *pointer*. Because we can find our way from one entry to the next, we do not leave "holes" when we delete an entry. Figure 7.7 shows the table of information used in Figure 7.6 stored with pointers. These pointers contain the index of the next entry in the table. The pointer stored in the last entry in the table is shown as NULL in Figure 7.7. This is a value that is recognized as an end-of-list indicator. It could be, for example, zero.

The process of removing an entry from the list consists of copying the value from the pointer in that entry into the preceding entry.

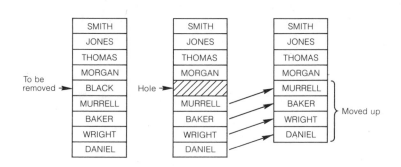

Fig. 7.6 Deleting an entry in an array

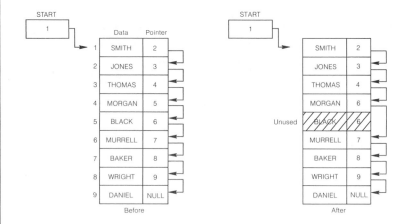

Fig. 7.7   Information stored with pointers

In the example in Figure 7.7 the value of the pointer in BLACK (which is 6) is copied into the pointer from MORGAN. If the last entry, DANIEL, had been removed instead of BLACK, we would have copied NULL into the pointer from WRIGHT. If we had removed the first entry, the new first entry would be JONES rather than SMITH. To implement this, we save the start of the list in another variable shown as START. Initially, for Figure 7.7, this contains 1. If we removed SMITH it would contain 2.

In the future we will draw lists as shown in Figures 7.8 and 7.9. We do not know or care where the pairs are in relation to each other because the pointer indicates where the next item on the list is located. Lists such as this can be used for ordered or unordered data. Even if the list is ordered, however, we cannot use a binary search since it is scattered through memory and we cannot access its midpoint directly.

When an entry is to be added to a list we insert it into the chain of pointers that connect the list elements. We can put it at any point we wish. If there is no reason to put it in any particular place, the front of the list is the easiest place to reach. Adding a new entry

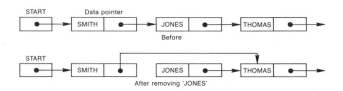

Fig. 7.8   Removing an item from a list

272

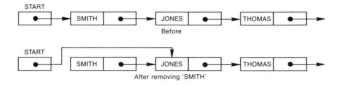

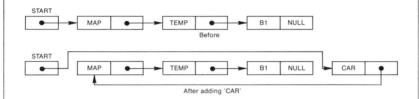

Fig. 7.9 Removing the first item from a list

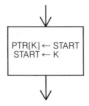

Fig. 7.10 Adding a new entry to the beginning of a list

'CAR' to the front of a list containing MAP, TEMP, and B1 is shown in Figure 7.10. No data has to be moved. The pointer that was in START is put into the new entry and START is set to point to this new entry.

If each list entry consists of a pair of entries DATA[I] and PTR[I] in the arrays DATA and PTR, the index I of the next entry can be stored in PTR. If the entries MAP, TEMP, and B1 are in DATA[3], DATA[10], and DATA[7], respectively, START will contain 3, PTR[3] will contain 10, and PTR[10] will contain 7. If the new entry CAR is in DATA[K], the program to add CAR to the beginning of the list is

```
PTR[K] ← START
START ← K
```

In some applications it is desirable to add the new entry to the end of the list—for example, if the list must be kept in order of construction. So that we can find the end without chasing down the chain from the front, it is also desirable to carry a pointer to the last item in the chain. Figure 7.11 shows this mechanism being used to add the string 'CAR' to the end of the list. The END pointer tells us where to put a pointer to the new entry. The pointer in the new

273

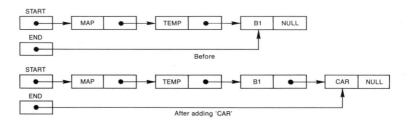

Fig. 7.11 Adding a new entry to the end of a list

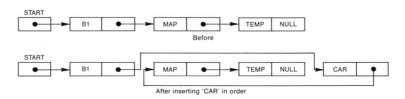

Fig. 7.12 Adding a new entry in order

entry is set to NULL, and END is set to point to the new entry. If CAR is in DATA[K], this process can be accomplished by the assignment statements PTR[END] ← K, PTR [K] ← NULL, and END ← K.

If a table is to be kept in sorted order, it is necessary to search sequentially to find the appropriate position for the new entry. However, it can then be inserted without moving existing information. We need only set the pointer of the preceding entry to point to the new one, and set the pointer of the new one to point to the next one. This is shown in Figure 7.12.

Each entry in the lists in Figures 7.8 through 7.12 is shown as a doublet. The first part contains the data. Suppose that a table is already constructed but new data must be added. We must find storage space for the new entry before we can add it to the table. The simplest method is sequential assignment of storage. In this method we initially assign an area of memory for storing the table and note that the first word in this area is currently available. As each entry is placed into the table, the first available locations in the area assigned are taken for the entry. This is shown in Figure 7.13. AVAIL contains the address of the first available location in the storage area. When 'CAR' is logically inserted at the front of the table containing MAP and B1, AVAIL and START are both updated appropriately.

When an entry is removed from the list, the storage it occupied is lost unless it happens to be physically the last. Thus, if 'B1' is removed from the list in Figure 7.13b, we get the list shown in Figure 7.14.

274

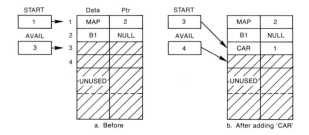

Fig. 7.13 Available memory locations

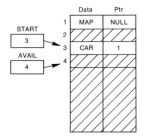

Fig. 7.14 Lost storage

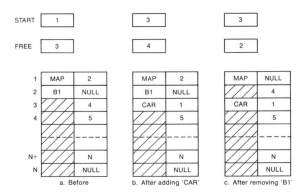

Fig. 7.15 Use of free storage pointer

   DATA[2] and PTR[2] are unused, but there is no simple way of reusing them for the next entry. We can solve this problem by keeping the unused space on a *free storage list*. A cell, say, FREE, can contain a pointer to an unused element. That element can contain

275

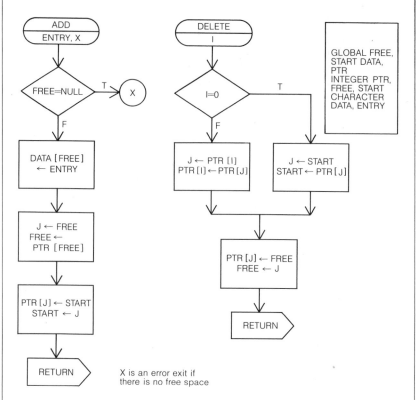

Fig. 7.16 Flowcharts for ADD and DELETE

a pointer to another unused element, and so on. Initially, all available storage space must be put on the free storage list. This can be done by setting FREE to 1, PTR[I] to I + 1 for $1 \leq I \leq N - 1$, and PTR[N] to NULL. When an element is added to the list, space can be taken from the beginning of the free storage list. When an element is removed, the space can be added to it. The steps to add 'CAR', then remove 'B1' are shown in Figure 7.15. Flowcharts for this process are shown in Figure 7.16. Subroutine ADD puts the data ENTRY into the table. DELETE removes the entry given by PTR[I]. If I is zero, the entry is pointed at by START; that is, it is the first on the list.

7.2.1 Lists of Character Strings

In the first part of this section we assumed that the character string data was stored in an array DATA. This assumes that each string occupies the same amount of memory space, which causes the problem of excess space discussed in Section 7.1. In order to avoid this, the access table technique discussed in Section 7.1 could be used. Then we would use the triplet L (location of first character), L1 (length of string), and PTR (index in access table of next entry). If an entry were to be deleted from the access table, the space occupied by the string would be available for reuse. Unfortunately, we could only use it for storing a new string that was not longer than the previous one stored there.

This problem arises because we are still storing the strings in contiguous locations. To overcome it we must structure the storage for the string so that it occupies a list of fixed-length groups. One way of doing this is to store each string entry itself as a list, as shown in Figure 7.17. (This shows one character per word; however, we could have stored four characters per word equally easily.) Each character and a pointer to the next character are stored in a doublet. All doublets for a character string constitute one entry in the access list. The list of entries that makes up a table is stored using two pointers in each entry. The first points to the start of the entry itself, the second to the next entry in the access list. The length of the string is no longer needed, since the end of the string is given in the list structure. The three entries 'MAP', 'TEMP', and 'B1' are shown in Figure 7.18.

Fig. 7.17   Storing a string entry as a list

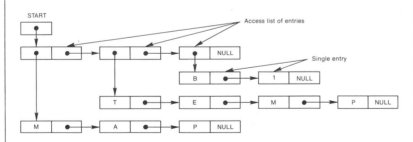

Fig. 7.18   List of strings

This data structure can be implemented using two words for each element.‡ Since each element is of the same length, we can keep a

---

‡On many computers, different parts of one word can be used to store both parts of the doublet. For example, we could store the character in the first two digits of a word in our hypothetical computer, and the pointer in the last five. Some programming languages allow the user to make such decisions.

277

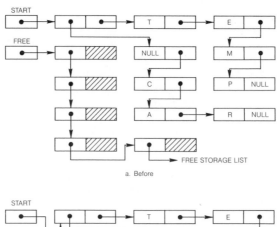

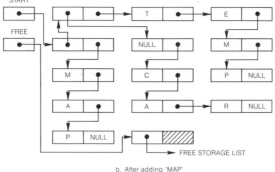

a. Before

b. After adding 'MAP'

Fig. 7.19 Updating a list of strings

free storage list, which consists of a set of pairs of words. As many
pairs as necessary must be taken for a new element. An example
is shown in Figure 7.19. The new entry 'MAP' is added to the front
of a list containing 'CAR' and 'TEMP'. Four doublets are removed
from the free list. One is used to store the access list entry, the other
three for the entry. It is assumed that the first word can be used to
store either a pointer if the doublet is used for an access table
entry, or a character if the doublet is used for a character string
element.

QUESTIONS

1. What is a list?

2. What is a free storage list?

3. When the storage structure is designed for a problem, one

characteristic is important if a free storage list is to be used effectively. What is it?

Problems

*1. Suppose that there is a list stored in memory in the following format:

The array DATA contains the stored data (regard these as floating-point numbers for this problem). The array IPTR contains integers that are the indices of the next elements of the list. Location START contains the index of the first element of the list. Location END contains the index of the last element of the list. Location FREE contains the index of the first element on the free storage list. The NULL pointer is indicated by a zero. Thus if the list contained the two data entries 1.5 and 3.7, the contents of various cells might be

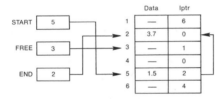

Write subroutines to perform each of the following functions. Consider first which variables you would like to make global and which should be parameters.

a. Add a new entry to the end of the list. The data to be added should be a parameter. The subroutine should get a free place to store it. An error exit should occur if there is no more space.
b. Remove an item from the list and return the space to the free storage list. What parameter is most desirable for this task?
c. Search for an entry whose data is equal to a parameter. What results should this return in view of problem 1b?

2. A company manufactures a number of different products. Their products can be viewed as character strings. It also has warehouses around the country, and each product is stored in some of them. Consequently, a list of warehouses will be associated with each product. That list will contain the warehouse names and the quantity of the product in storage in the corresponding warehouse.

279

The company wishes to write programs to change the data corresponding to the following actions:

(i) Ship quantity X of product Y to warehouse Z.
(ii) Ship quantity X of product Y from warehouse Z.

a. Suggest a data structure for the information, assuming that the products of the company may change from week to week, that the company may purchase additional warehouses or sell existing ones, and that most products are stored in most warehouses.

b. If there is a position (X,Y) associated with each warehouse, show how it can be put in the data structure and write a program to find the nearest warehouse to the point (X_0, Y_0) that contains at least X units of product Y.

3. Consider the following problem: an airline wishes to program a reservation system. The data to be stored in the computer will include:

(i) All flights for the next 60 days, stored by flight number and date.
(ii) The names of all passengers holding reservations on those flights, together with a variable-length character string of data about each passenger.
(iii) The number of unreserved seats on each flight. This data will be continuously changing as seats are sold or cancelled and as the date changes.

a. Design a method for storing the data given that the airline will need to be able to:

(iv) Find out if there are any unsold seats on a given flight.
(v) Print a passenger list for a given flight.
(vi) Access the reservation for a given passenger when the flight number, date, and passenger name are specified.
(vii) Change the character string of data about any passenger.

b. Suggest some useful subroutines that would help in the programming of a total system.

c. What changes would you make to your proposed data structure if the airline also wished to find out quickly the next date after a given day on which there were unsold seats on a specified flight number?

d. Suggest other ways in which the airline may wish to access and manipulate the data.

7.3 TREES

In the previous section we dealt with a data structure called a *list*. It was developed to handle variable-length tables in which we wished to add and remove items and which we were content to access sequentially. In this section we will introduce a structure called a *binary tree*. Later, we will introduce more general forms of trees and study their application to problems.

We saw that we could not perform a binary search on a list. In the binary search method we go to the middle entry in the table. If this is not the entry being sought, we go to the middle of the top or bottom half of the table, depending on whether the middle entry is larger or smaller than the one being sought. This is diagrammed in Figure 7.20.

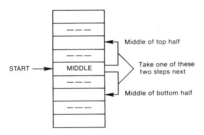

Fig. 7.20 Binary search

This figure suggests that we could use a pointer to tell us where the middle of the table is located and then use two pointers to tell us where the middle parts of the two halves of the table are located. If, after going to the middle of one half of the table, we find that the entry is not the desired one, we wish to continue to the middle of a half of the half. Again, we could find that entry if we had two pointers. This is shown in Figure 7.21 for a table with seven entries in alphabetical order. NULL pointers have been omitted for clarity. Each entry now consists of three items: the data (which may be of variable length and could also be stored as a list) and two pointers, one to the earlier part of the table, and one to the later part. This structure becomes clearer if drawn as in Figure 7.22. Each entry is shown as the triplet LEFT, DATA, and RIGHT. LEFT is a pointer to the part of the table to the left of the entry, RIGHT a pointer to the part of the table to the right of the entry. This type of data structure is called a tree. If it is drawn ''up the other way'' as shown in Figure 7.23, the analogy is obvious, but we will normally draw trees as in Figure 7.22.

Much of the terminology of tree structures is based on horticulture. As shown in Figure 7.23, the bottom (top in Figure 7.22) of a

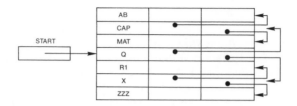

Fig. 7.21 Search with pointers

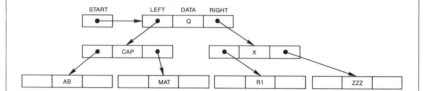

Fig. 7.22 Expansion of Figure 7.21

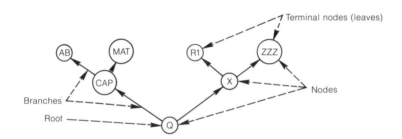

Fig. 7.23 Tree

tree is called the *root* of the tree. The places where we have entries
are called *nodes*. The pointers from one node to another are called
branches, while the nodes with no pointers leaving them are called
terminal nodes (or *leaves*). Formally, a tree is a set of nodes connected by branches such that there is one and only one way of going
from one node to another via branch connections, and which has a
distinguished node called the *root node*.

The tree shown in Figure 7.22 is ordered. Its important feature is
that all nodes connected via the left pointer of a given node are
alphabetically less than the given node. Similarly all nodes connected via the right pointer are alphabetically greater. If we wish to
search for a given item, say 'R1', we start at the root and compare
'R1' with the entry at the root. Since 'R1' is larger, it is either not
in the tree or connected to the right pointer. Therefore we proceed

282

to the entry to the right of the root. There we find that 'R1' is less than the entry 'X'. We therefore proceed via the left pointer and arrive at R1 in the next entry.

Example 7.1 — Searching a Binary Ordered Tree

A function procedure for searching a tree of the form shown in Figure 7.22 is shown in Figure 7.24. The tree is assumed to be stored in arrays LEFT[I[, DATA[I] and RIGHT[I] for I = 1, . . . , N. The integers in LEFT and RIGHT are the indices in the arrays of the entry indicated. Zero is used as a NULL pointer. DATA and NAME are assumed to be suitably declared as character strings. The procedure returns the index of the entry if it is found, or zero if it is not present.

A trace of this flowchart in the search of the tree in Figure 7.22 for the names CAP and S (the latter is not present) is shown in Tables 7.1 and 7.2. We assume that the tree of Figure 7.22 is stored as shown in Figure 7.25.

Although the table is "balanced" in the example above, it is not necessary that the root node contain exactly the middle entry or that

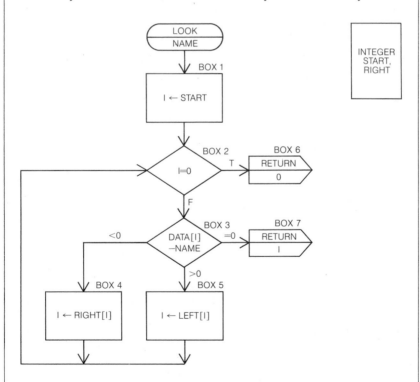

Fig. 7.24 Binary tree search

START

1

INDEX	LEFT	DATA	RIGHT
1	2	Q	5
2	3	CAP	4
3	0	AB	0
4	0	MAT	0
5	6	X	7
6	0	R1	0
7	0	ZZZ	0

Fig. 7.25 Storage of Figure 7.22

TABLE 7.1

SEARCH FOR CAP

Box Executed	Value of I	Data[I]	Name	
1	1	Q	CAP	
2	—	—	—	
3	—	—	—	
5	2	CAP	—	
2	—	—	—	
3	—	—	—	
7	—	—	—	Returns 2 (Index of CAP)

any node contain the middle entry of the section of the tree below it (that is, the *subtrees* connected to it via the left and right pointers of that node). But all entries accessible via the left pointer of any node must be alphabetically less than the entry in the node, and all entries accessible via the right pointer must be alphabetically greater, as shown in Figure 7.26; that is, the tree must be *ordered*. If this relationship is maintained, then the search algorithm given in flowchart 7.24 will work.

As an example, the data given in Figure 7.22 could be stored using the tree structure given in Figure 7.27. The tree is still ordered so that when we search for 'R1', we can compare it with 'MAT' in the root node and immediately determine that it must lie in the subtree to the right of that node if it is in the table. The difference between trees 7.22 and 7.27 is only one of average execution time. Suppose each of the seven entries were to be looked up. The number of levels

284

TABLE 7.2

SEARCH FOR S

Box Executed	Value of I	Data[I]	Name
1	1	Q	S
2	—	—	—
3	—	—	—
4	5	X	—
2	—	—	—
3	—	—	—
5	6	R1	—
2	—	—	—
3	—	—	—
4	0	—	—
2	—	—	—
6	—	—	— Returns 0 (Not Found)

TABLE 7.3

LEVELS OF SEARCH NECESSARY

| Entry | Number of Levels of Search | | |
	Figure 7.22	Figure 7.27	Figure 7.28
AB	3	3	1
CAP	2	2	3
MAT	3	1	4
Q	1	4	7
R1	3	3	6
X	2	4	5
ZZZ	3	2	2
TOTAL	17	19	28
AVERAGE	2.43	2.71	4

of the tree that must be searched is shown in Table 7.3. We can see that a balanced tree leads to fewer operations on the average if any item is equally likely to be referenced. The extreme case occurs when all nodes have a null subtree on one side, as shown by the example in Figure 7.28. The number of levels of search necessary for this case is also shown in Table 7.3. The tree in Figure 7.28 is equivalent to a list since there is only one branch from each node.

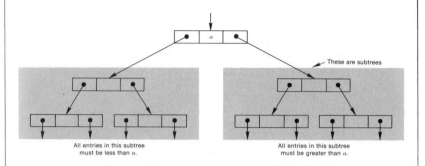

Fig. 7.26   Subtrees of ordered tree

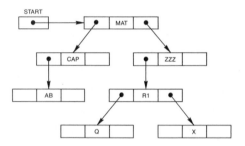

Fig. 7.27   Storage of data of Figure 7.22

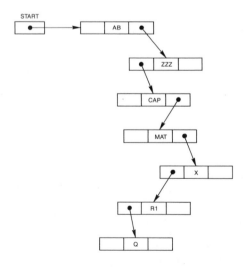

Fig. 7.28   Alternative tree for Figure 7.22

286

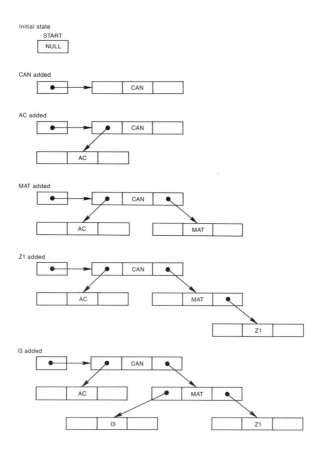

Fig. 7.29 Successive stages of tree building

Consequently, a search in this tree is equivalent to a sequential search, so we expect the average time to be about N/2 where N is the number of entries.

Because a binary tree does not have to remain balanced, it is simple to add a new entry. Suppose we have the configuration shown in Figure 7.27 and we wish to add the string 'CAR'. We search down the table looking for it until we reach a null pointer. If we were to find CAR, we could hardly add it because our structure does not allow for repeated entries. In this example we find a null pointer when we attempt to go right from 'CAP'. This occurs as a result of the following sequence of steps:

1. Compare CAR with MAT. CAR is less, so go left.
2. Compare CAR with CAP. CAR is greater, so go right.

287

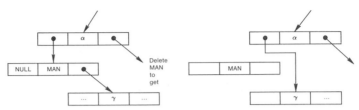

Fig. 7.30 Deletion from ordered tree

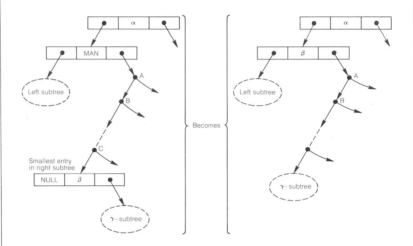

Fig. 7.31 Deletion when replacement necessary

3. Right contains a null pointer, so stop and put CAR on the right of CAP.

Successive stages, starting from an empty table and adding the strings CAN, AC, MAT, Z1, and I3, are shown in Figure 7.29.

As new items are added to a tree, storage space for the triplets can be obtained from a storage allocation mechanism such as that described in Section 7.2 using a free list (in this case of triplets). If items are to be deleted from a tree, the space made free can then be returned to the free list.

Deletion from an ordered tree is more difficult. Unless the deleted entry is a terminal node, some reorganization of pointers is necessary. If either the right or left pointers of the deleted entry are NULL, the problem can be handled as in a list. (See Figure 7.30.) In all other cases we must replace the deleted entry with an entry from either its left or right subtree. Suppose we decide to use an entry from the right subtree. It must be the smallest entry in that subtree, as shown in Figure 7.31. A flowchart for removing the entry whose value is in NAME is shown in Figure 7.32.

288

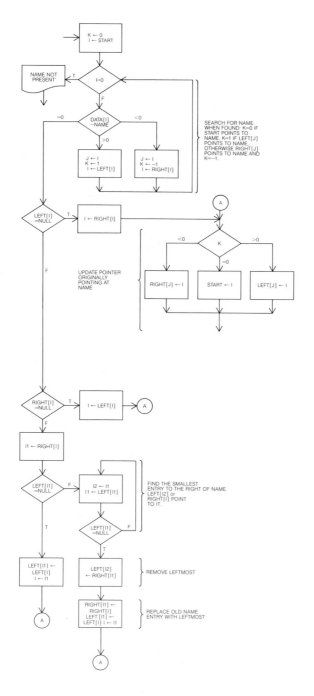

Fig. 7.32 Flowchart for removing entry from ordered tree

7.3.1 ACCESSING A TREE IN ORDER

We sometimes wish to examine entries in a tree in a particular order. In our example the obvious order is alphabetic. This can happen if we wished to print the contents of a tree, as would happen if this mechanism were used to store the names of customers of a bank. It is obvious in what order we should print the nodes of a tree, but how do we construct an algorithm?

Let us consider the tree in Figure 7.33: a, b, and c are the addresses of locations where the tree elements are stored (or their indices in an array used for storage). We start at the node containing 'B', but before we can print that, we must print all entries in the subtree to the left of 'B'. Therefore we move left to 'A'. Since that has no subtree to its left, we can print 'A'. Now, since there is no subtree to the right of 'A' we must move back to 'B' to print it. How can we get back to 'B'? We have no pointer to show us the way back. When we moved down to 'A' from 'B', we should have saved the address b of 'B'.

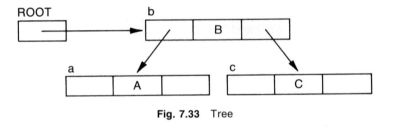

Fig. 7.33 Tree

Now consider the tree in Figure 7.34. We move left to 'A2' from 'B', saving its address b. There is a subtree to the left of 'A2', so we must

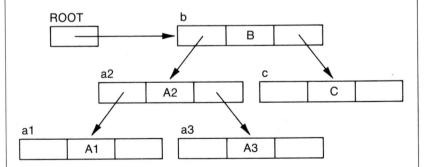

Fig. 7.34 Tree

290

print that subtree before printing 'A2'. Hence we move left from 'A2', saving its address a2. As we go deeper into a tree, we will accumulate more and more addresses that must be saved in order to find our way back. How should we save these? One way is to use a *stack*. A stack is a data structure that can be thought of as a pile of memory cells. Each time we want to enter some data into the stack, we put the data into a memory cell and put that cell on top of the pile. When we want to get something from the stack, we take the data from the top cell of the pile and "discard" that cell. Thus the last item to be put into a stack is the first item to be removed. (For this reason, it is also called a Last In First Out queue, or a LIFO queue.) This structure is exactly what we want, because as we go deeper into the tree, we can put the address of the entry we are leaving on top of the stack. When, for example, we have reached 'A1' in Figure 7.34, the stack will be as shown in Figure 7.35. When we wish to return to the next higher level, 'A2', its address is in the top of the stack. After we remove it, the address of the level above, namely 'B', is at the top of the stack.

TOP LEVEL	a2
BOTTOM LEVEL	b

Fig. 7.35 Stack with two entries

Suppose we have just printed 'A1'. We return to the next higher level by removing the address a2 from the top of the stack. Now we can print 'A2'. Next we wish to go to the right subtree of 'A2' and print it. What should we save in the stack in order to return? After we have printed the right subtree, we do not wish to return to A2 because we have already printed it. Rather we wish to go to 'B' to print it. Thus when we go down to the right of 'A2' we need not put a return into the stack. The address b already there is the appropriate place to which to return.

An algorithm for printing an ordered tree can now be expressed in English. In this algorithm, the stack is assumed to be initially empty. PTR points to the entry on which we are currently working. It is given by the flowchart in Figure 7.36. This high-level flowchart uses some English language statements such as "Remove top level of stack and put in PTR." These actions can be performed by subroutines or functions.

A trace of flowchart 7.36 is given in Table 7.4 for the tree shown in Figure 7.37. This figure does not show the left and right pointers explicitly, but it does show the indices of the tree elements that determine the value of the pointers. Lack of an arrow indicates a NULL pointer.

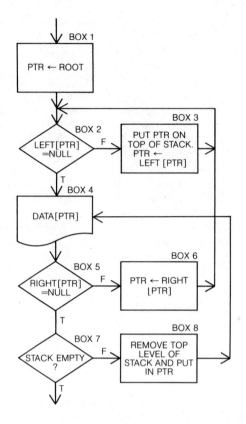

Fig. 7.36 High-level flowchart for printing tree

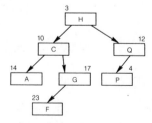

Fig. 7.37 Tree

TABLE 7.4

DATA VALUES AFTER EXECUTION OF FIGURE 7.36

Box No.	Value of Data after Box has been Executed					
	PTR	Left[PTR]	Right[PTR]	Printed Value	Stack	
					Top	Second . . .
1	3	10	12		—	
2						
3	10	14	17		3	
2						
3	14	NULL	NULL		10	3
2						
4				A		
5						
7						
8	10	14	17		3	—
4				C		
5						
6	17	23	NULL			
2						
3	23	NULL	NULL		17	3
2						
4				F		
5						
7						
8	17	23	NULL		3	—
4				G		
5						
7						
8	3	10	12		—	
4				H		
5						
6	12	4	NULL			
2						
3	4	NULL	NULL		12	
2						
4				P		
5						
7						
8	12				—	
4				Q		
5						
7						

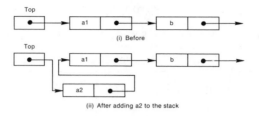

Fig. 7.38   Stack implementation

7.3.2 Stack Implementation

Of course we do not actually move memory cells around in order to put them on top of the stack. One way of implementing a stack is to use a list. A pointer to the top cell of the stack is stored in a fixed cell; the top cell of the stack carries a pointer to the next lower cell, and so on. When a new top level is added, it is put on the front of the list. This is shown in Figure 7.38. The top level is removed by removing the first entry in the list.

7.3.3 Threaded Lists

If it is necessary to trace through a tree in order frequently, it is worth storing the trace path. One way of doing this is to add an extra pointer to each tree node, which can point to the next node on the trace path. The tree shown in Figure 7.34 would then be stored as shown in Figure 7.39.

The trace pointers use extra storage space. If we examine Figure 7.39 we see that trace pointers go up the tree toward the root only when the right pointer is NULL. Otherwise, they point to the left-most subnode accessible from a node. Therefore we can store the trace pointers that point only *up* the tree, providing that we also indicate whether the right pointer is used to point out the right sub-

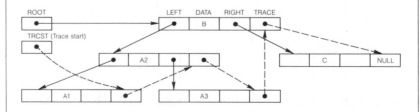

Fig. 7.39   Threaded list in a tree

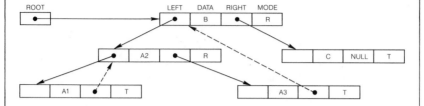

Fig. 7.40 Storing the tree with upward trace pointers

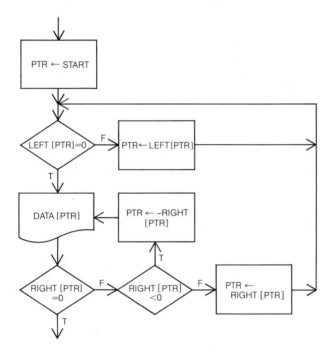

Fig. 7.41 Flowchart for printing tree in order

tree or the trace path. This can be stored in one digit, a zero or a one, using much less space than needed for another pointer. Figure 7.40 shows the same tree stored in this way. MODE is either an R — indicating that the third element of the triplet is a right pointer — or a T — indicating that it is a trace pointer. One way of storing this in many POLs is to use a positive index for one type of pointer index and minus the index for the other type. A flowchart for printing a tree in order is shown in Figure 7.41. It assumes that the index of a trace pointer is stored negatively and that a NULL pointer is represented by zero.

295

PROBLEMS

*1. Assume that an ordered binary tree is stored in the arrays LEFT, DATA, and RIGHT, and that the index of the root of the tree is in location START. Write a subroutine to add the data in cell A to the tree. Assume that free storage is on a free storage list starting at the index given in location FREE, and that it is linked by pointers in the array LEFT. (For example, if the indices of free storage locations are 5 and 3, then FREE might contain 5, in which case LEFT(5) would contain 3 and LEFT(3) would contain 0.)

2. Use the subroutine written for the above problem to write a flowchart to read in a number N followed by a list of N data items and build an ordered binary tree structure. START, FREE, and LEFT[I] should be initialized on the assumption that there are 100 spaces in the arrays.

3. Write a pair of function subroutines to implement the actions "Put PTR on top of stack. PTR ← LEFT(PTR)" and "Remove top level of stack and put in PTR" used in Figure 7.36. Implement the stack by means of a list and rewrite the flowchart in Figure 7.36 to use the functions you program.

7.4 USE OF RECURSION

In this section we will look at the use of recursion in tree manipulation. First we note that we not only can use recursive procedures effectively, but also can use recursion as a technique for the definition of various structures. Consider, for example, the definition of a binary tree by the following:

A tree is either NULL or it is the ordered triplet

$$(tree, DATA, tree)$$

We see that a *tree* is defined by a *tree*. This is recursive. However, there is a way out because a tree can also be NULL. We can generate any finite tree by a finite number of applications of this rule. Thus we can say a tree is (tree1, DATA1, tree2), tree1 is (tree3, DATA2, tree4) so a tree is ((tree3, DATA2, tree4), DATA1, tree2). Similarly tree2 could be (tree5, DATA3, tree6), while trees 3 through 6 could be NULL. Thus a tree could be ((NULL, DATA2, NULL),DATA1,(NULL, DATA3, NULL)).

This can also be drawn as in Figure 7.42.

The advantages of recursive procedures are illustrated beautifully in some of the tree manipulation programs. Suppose, for example, we wish to print a sorted tree in order. The recursive procedure shown in Figure 7.43 accomplishes this. The triplets are assumed

296

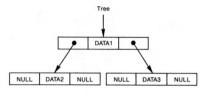

Fig. 7.42 Tree

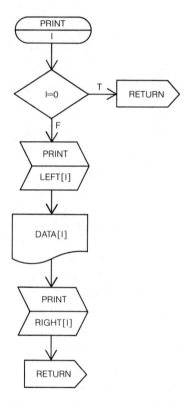

Fig. 7.43 Recursive method for printing sorted tree in order

to be LEFT, DATA, and RIGHT, indexed by the pointer variable I.
A null pointer is indicated by zero. This program is logically simpler
than the iterative program for the same task shown in Figure 7.36.
Similarly, we can define the search function LOOK, given as an iterative procedure in Figure 7.24, by the simpler recursive procedure
in Figure 7.44. It would be called by writing LOOK(NAME,START).

297

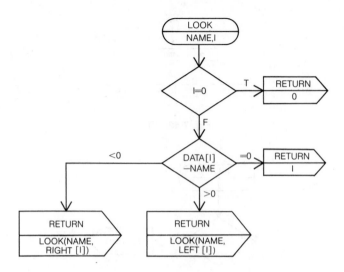

Fig. 7.44 Recursive procedure for searching ordered tree

Problems

*1. Assume that the data in the node of a binary tree is a floating-point number. Write a recursive function SUM(I) that forms the sum of the data in all nodes of the tree rooted at I.

2. The length of a path in a tree is the number of branches on a path connecting two nodes. The depth of a tree is one more than the length of the longest path from the root to any other node. Thus the depth of

is 2, while the depth of

is 4. Write a recursive function to compute the depth of a binary tree.

7.5 Graphs

We have discussed two basic forms of data structure—lists and trees—in earlier sections of this chapter. A list is a linear (that is, sequential) arrangement of nodes. It can be stored as a one-dimensional array, but such a method makes the task of editing the list tedious. The most flexible way of storing a list was seen to be as a chain of nodes with one node pointing to the next. Thus a list is characterized as containing one single path connecting all nodes shown in Figure 7.45. If each node in the list consists of one pointer and data, it is a *one-way list* as shown in Figure 7.45a.

In some applications it is desirable to be able to move through the list in both directions. This requires two pointers in each node, one pointing to the preceding node and one to the following node. This gives a *two-way list* as shown in Figure 7.45b. We also refer to a one-way list as a *directed list* and a two-way list as an *undirected list*. Which form of list we use depends on the application.

We found that for some applications a single path was inadequate, so we introduced tree structures. Whereas a list contains only a single path without branching, a tree structure can have several branches from a node. It is restricted, however, to containing one and only one path between any two nodes. (In our example earlier we used only binary trees, which can have no more than three branches at any node, one coming in from above and no more than two leaving to nodes below. We will discuss more general trees later in this section.) A list is a special case of a tree in which each node has only two branches, one entering and one leaving.

In this section we are going to discuss the most general type of structure that consists of nodes and branches. It is called a *graph* and is simply a collection of nodes and branches in which each branch links one node to another (including, possibly, to itself). An example of a graph is a road map. If each road junction is called a node, then each road is a branch. An *undirected graph* is a graph in which there is no particular direction associated with a branch. A *directed graph* (or *digraph* for short) is a graph in which there is a direction associated with a branch. Thus a road map in which every road is one-way would be a digraph. Some examples of graphs are

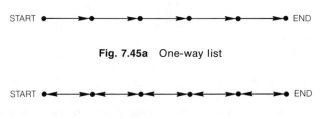

START ●————▸●———▸●———▸●———▸●———▸● END

Fig. 7.45a   One-way list

START ●◂———▸●◂———▸●◂———▸●◂———▸● END

Fig. 7.45b   Two-way list

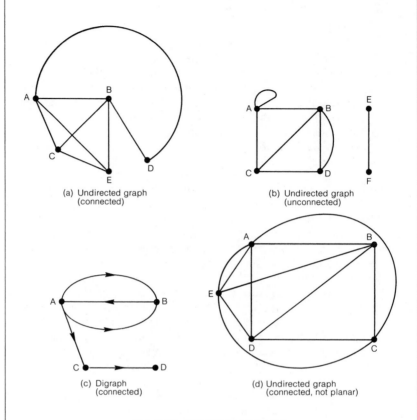

(a) Undirected graph
(connected)

(b) Undirected graph
(unconnected)

(c) Digraph
(connected)

(d) Undirected graph
(connected, not planar)

Fig. 7.46 Examples of graphs

shown in Figure 7.46. Several other features of graphs are shown in this figure. In Figure 7.46b we see that there can be more than one path between two points (between points B and D in this example) and that a point can be connected to itself (as point A is). Also we see that there need be no path between two points (point E cannot be reached from point B.) Such a graph is *unconnected*. Usually we will deal with *connected graphs*. In Figure 7.46c we see a directed graph that is connected, although there is no way to go from D to C following the direction of the graph. Again there can be several branches between two points in either direction. In Figures 7.46a and 7.46d we see branches crossing. There is no significance to the position of the nodes and the branches, as a graph displays only the connections between the nodes, that is, the *topology* of the system. We could redraw Figure 7.46a as shown in Figure 7.47. It is the same graph but now has no crossings. A graph that can be so drawn is called a *planar* graph because it can be drawn on a plane. (Before the advent of freeways with their overpasses, road maps

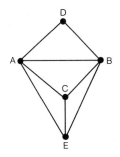

Fig. 7.47   Figure 7.46a redrawn

were all planar graphs.) Figure 7.46d is an example of a nonplanar graph. There is no way of drawing it on a plane without branches crossing.

We have introduced road maps as an example of graphs. We may have data associated with either the nodes or the branches, or both. For example, the name of the junction (town, if the only junctions are at towns), population, and elevation are all examples of data that could be associated with the nodes of a road map. Distance, average driving time, and vertical climb and fall are examples of data that could be associated with the branches of a graph.

There are a number of problems in which graph structures are of interest. We will investigate one problem in detail in this section.

Example 7.2—Finding the Best Route Between Two Nodes

A simple problem we can tackle is that of finding the best route between two cities. We must define "best" in some precise way— for example, as the path with the shortest length or as the path that passes through the minimum number of intermediate nodes. We will examine the minimum distance problem. The branches in a graph are labeled with numbers that represent the distance between the nodes.

One such graph is shown in Figure 7.48. Suppose we wish to find a path from node A to node Z whose length is no greater than any other path from A to Z.

One method of solution that should not be used in problems of this form is enumeration. We could generate all paths between A and Z and then select the shortest. However, there are many paths in a complex graph. If, for example, there are 12 cities and each city is connected to every other city by a road, there are about four million different paths. For 14 cities the number increases to about seven billion paths. This type of method is called *combinatorial* because each combination is examined.

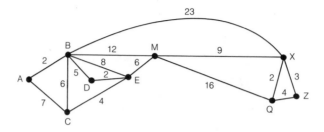

Fig. 7.48 Roads between cities as a graph

Fortunately, we can eliminate many combinations. Consider Figure 7.48. Two possible paths are ABEMXZ and ACEMXZ. These paths are common after city E. Consequently, if we find that the partial path ABE is shorter than ACE, there is no reason to continue the path starting ACE. In fact, any path that starts ACE will be improved by changing it to ABE. Therefore we will develop a method that constructs the shortest path to each intermediate city.

We can visualize a way of solving this problem as follows. Suppose we have as many people as we needed stationed at each city. We could send one down each road leaving A with instructions to go to the city at the end of the road and place a sign there saying how far it was from the starting point A. After each traveler has arrived at each of those cities, he could send another person down each road from that city to the next city with similar instructions. He should put up a sign that gives the distance from A as the sum of the distance just covered plus the distance of the city he just left. It should also say where he came from. However, when he gets to the next city, he might find that there was already a sign. If this sign shows a shorter distance, he should simply quit. For example, when the person sent from B to C gets to C, he will have computed a distance of eight miles (B is two miles from A, and he has just traveled six miles). However, a sign will already say seven miles for the path directly from A to C. Therefore, this person now knows that a better path exists than the one he knew about. In fact, the sign will say come from A directly. However, if the person coming in sees that he has a better path, he should replace the sign with his own. Thus, when the person going from B to E gets there, he will put up a sign saying "10 miles by coming from B." However, in a little while a person will arrive from D and find that he has a route that requires only nine miles. He must replace the sign. Unfortunately, the earlier arrival at E from B has already sent out people to more distant cities. Therefore, this new arrival must send out additional people with the new information. Eventually, all cities connected to A will be sign-posted and no people will be arriving with shorter routes. Then all activity will stop and at this time the shortest path from any city to

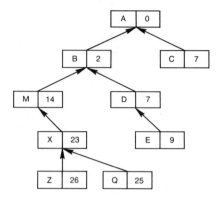

Fig. 7.49 Tree structure of best route

A can be found by starting from that city and going back as directed by each signpost.

Each city will have a pointer back to the next closest city on a best route, so the data forms a tree structure with pointers up towards the root city A, as shown in Figure 7.49. Each entry is a triplet, consisting of city name, distance from A, and pointer up the tree.

The tree can be constructed by a computer by simulating the behavior of our travelers. We start with the root city A and consider all roads leaving it. This enables the first part of the tree to be constructed as shown in Figure 7.50. Next, we must consider all branches from the nodes we have just added. Each node connected to nodes B or C must be added to the tree if it is not already present. If one of these nodes is already present, but the new path is shorter than the one in the tree, the node present must be removed and the new one entered. Suppose we start by considering branches from B. It is connected to A, X, M, E, D, and C. Since B is length 2 from the root, paths through B to these nodes will have lengths 4, 25, 14, 10, 7, and 8, respectively. Node A is the root and node C is already in the tree closer to the root than the new path; therefore, the present entries for A and C are not changed. However, X, M, E, and D are not present, so they must be added to the tree. The result is the tree shown in Figure 7.51.

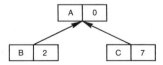

Fig. 7.50 First part of tree

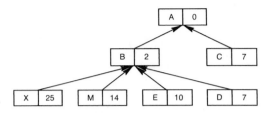

Fig. 7.51 Expanded tree

Next we must consider all branches from C. It is connected to A, B, and E in the graph. The paths are of lengths 14, 13, and 11, respectively. However, these paths are all longer than the existing paths in the tree, so the tree in Figure 7.51 is unchanged.

Four new nodes, X, M, E, and D, were added to the tree when branches from node B were considered. We must now consider branches from those new nodes. For a moment we must digress and consider the problem of how we can keep a record of those nodes that have been recently added to the tree, because their branches should be checked. A simple mechanism is to introduce yet another temporary data structure—namely, a list. Whenever a new node is added to the tree, it should be added to the end of a list of new nodes if it is not already in the list. Initially this list is empty. When the root node A is put in the tree, it is added to the list. Each node can be removed from the front of the list and all roads from that node considered. Since nodes are added to the list only when a shorter path has been found, no nodes are added after the shortest paths have been found. Therefore all nodes will eventually be removed from the list, at which time the tree will be complete. The state of the tree and list at the stage reached in Figure 7.51 is shown in Figure 7.52.

Returning to construction of the tree, node C is now removed

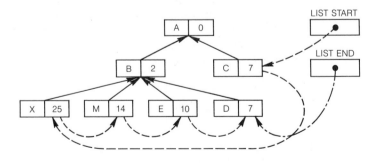

Fig. 7.52 Tree and list of nodes to be checked

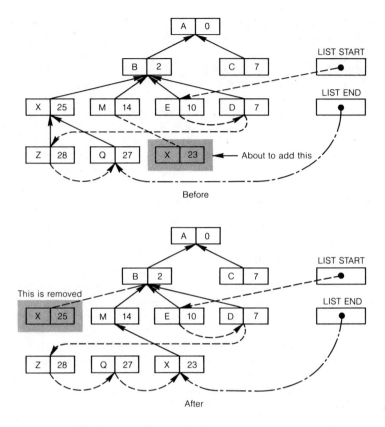

Fig. 7.53 Before and after adding a new node

from the list, but its branches do not cause any new nodes to be added to the tree, and hence no new nodes are added to the list. We next remove node X from the list. It has branches to nodes Z, Q, and M. Nodes Z and Q are added to the tree and the list at distances 28 and 27, respectively. Now we remove the next node, M, from the list. It has branches to nodes Q, X, B, and E. B, E, and Q are present in the tree with shorter path lengths, so are not changed. However, the new path to X has length 23, which is shorter than the present path. The existing node X in the tree is removed and a new node, X, is added on a branch from M. X must also be placed in the list. This action is shown in Figure 7.53.

The nodes Z and Q that were connected to node X are not now in the tree, so they must be discarded. This does not matter as we are going to reconsider branches from node X, since that node is in the list again. We also note that nodes Z and Q are still in the list. We could either remove them now or wait until we consider them later. At that time they can be ignored if they are not in the tree.

The process can be continued. Node E is removed from the list and causes no changes to the tree. Nodes Z and Q are removed and discarded because they are not in the tree. Finally, node D is removed and a shorter path of length 9 to node E is placed in the tree. E is then placed in the list again. Next, node X is removed from the list and paths to nodes Z and Q, of lengths 26 and 25, respectively, are added to the tree; nodes Z and Q are added to the list. Finally, nodes E, Z, and Q are removed from the list. No new paths of shorter lengths are found. The list is now empty, so the final tree is that shown in Figure 7.49. The shortest path from A to Z is via B, M, and X. It has length 26.

A high level flowchart solution to this problem is shown in Figure 7.54. DIST[NC] is assumed to contain the distance of city NC from A if it is in the tree.

The solution of this problem can be completed when we have decided how to store the input road map (that is, graph), tree, and list. General comments on storing graphs and trees will be delayed until later examples. For this problem we can use a straightforward approach. The road map can be represented in a two-dimensional array R[I,J]. If there is a road from city I to city J, then R[I,J] should contain its length, which is naturally a positive number. R[I,J] should contain a negative number as an indicator if there is no road. The set of linear arrays NAME, DIST, TREE, and LIST can contain the name, distance from the root, tree pointer, and list pointer, respectively. If the Ith city is not on the tree, TREE[I] can be negative. The same indicator can be used in the LIST array for cities not on the list.

One drawback of the solution proposed above is that a number of routes are investigated before an early part of them is discarded. For example, in Figure 7.53 we discard the first route found to X in favor of a shorter one found after the first route has been extended to Z and Q. In fact, in the high-level flowchart given in Figure 7.54, we even consider roads from Z and Q when they reach the top of the list, as we cannot determine easily from the data structure whether Z and Q are still in the tree. This represents wasted computation.

Let us return to our visualization of the solution. If we required the travelers to walk at the same speed, then the first traveler to arrive at a given city would automatically have the shortest path. We can simulate this by adding the nodes to the tree in order of distance, putting the ones closer to A in the tree first. This can be implemented by using the list to store those nodes that are about to be added to the tree, rather than those that have just been added. If this list is kept in numerical order with the closest to the root A at the beginning, nodes can be removed from the beginning and

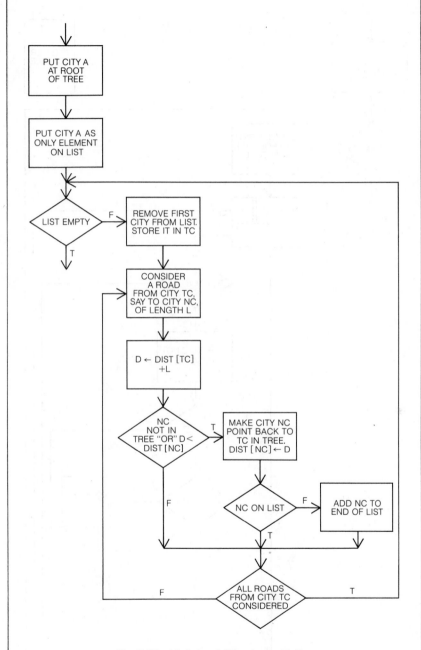

Fig. 7.54 High-level flowchart solution

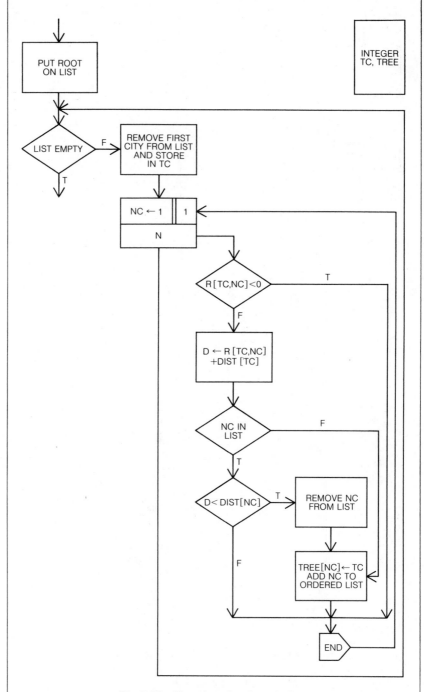

Fig. 7.55 Flowchart for the solution

added to the tree. At that time, all roads from the added node can be checked and the cities of the other ends added to the list unless they are already in the list with a shorter path. At the time an element is put on the list, the tree pointer can be inserted.

A flowchart for this solution is shown in Figure 7.55. It is similar to 7.54, but uses the technique for storing the road map and tree proposed above. The index of the root city is assumed to be in ROOT. There are assumed to be N cities in the map. Since elements may have to be removed from one position on the list and stored in another, it is helpful to have two-way lists, using two pointers. (Details are left for Problem 3.)

Problems

1. Can you draw a nonplanar graph with four nodes? Why?

*2. Prove that Figure 7.46d is nonplanar.

3. Using two pointers, LIST and LISTB, for forward and backward pointers in the list, complete the details of the flowchart in Figure 7.55.

7.6 Storage Management

In some problems, complex data structures are being built, edited, and (sometimes) deleted. In order to provide storage for these structures, we must develop a scheme for allocating storage as it is needed and "recovering" it when structures using it are deleted. By recovering it we mean that we must keep a record of its availability so that it can be reallocated. (We already touched on this subject when we introduced the free storage list.) The characteristics of a storage allocation and recovery scheme depend on the size of the storage we must allocate and the nature of the structure that will use it. If only large blocks of storage are allocated at a time, a table containing records of their use can easily be maintained. However, if very small sections of storage (two or three words, for example) are allocated at a time, it is necessary to use some other scheme, since a table would take up as much space as the storage being allocated. If storage is never freed during the course of a problem computation, a very simple scheme is possible. A block of storage can be set aside for use and the lowest available addresses in it can be allocated. It is necessary to remember only the address of the next available location.

The problem starts to get difficult when storage is also going to be released during the computation. Let us assume, first, that the storage is always used in the same size units, for example, always in two-word groups for list entries or three-word groups for tree entries. Then we can use a free list that contains all unused storage units on a chain. When storage is required, the desired number of units can be removed from the chain. When it is released, the free units can be returned to the chain. In some problems we will know when storage becomes free. For example, if we were to design the road map problem above for a situation in which we could add or delete routes or cities at any time, we would use a more flexible data structure than the arrays proposed in the last section. We could maintain a list of the cities on the map. Each entry on the list would have to contain the name of the city, its tree pointer, distance from the root of the tree, the list pointers, and a sublist of roads to other cities. In this particular case, we could conveniently work with triplets. The basic city entry could be

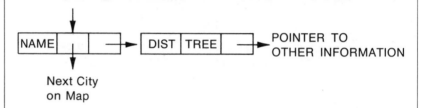

Next City
on Map

The list of cities about to be added to the tree with forward and backward pointers would also be a triplet, as would the road information. Thus storage would be allocated in triplets. When we were to remove an entry, we would know which storage triplets were now free.

On the other hand, there are problems in which we do not know when a datum is no longer in use. In such problems we will be left with pieces of storage containing data to which there are no pointers. This will result in memory slowly being filled up. When that happens, we must search through it to find unused locations. This can be done by going down each pointer chain and marking those locations that can be reached via the graphs, trees, or lists in use. (A mark can be made by setting a pointer negative, for example.) When this has been done, the storage area used for the data structures can be scanned sequentially and all of those units that are not connected to the data structures in use can be added back to the free storage list. This process is called *garbage collection*.

If the units of storage used are not of equal size, the storage recovery problem becomes very difficult. If there are only a few different sizes to deal with, then separate free storage lists can be kept for each size. If not, we will have to attempt to join the free pieces together to form as large units as possible. This may require that we move some of the data structures around in memory to "fill up holes" left when items are deleted, and hence to make the unused locations contiguous.

Problem

*1. Suppose that you have to design an online system for the AAA. It must store the road map of the United States. The data will be changed from time to time. The AAA wishes to have programs to add or delete roads and towns. It also wants a program that will print out the shortest distance and corresponding path between two towns. Design a method for storing the data.

Appendix

Answers to Selected Exercises,
Questions, and Problems

Answers to Selected Exercises, Questions, and Problems

Page 6
P1.

a. Student Records

A list of all students registered and a list of the courses they have taken and are taking, together with their grades, are kept in the computer.

b. Traffic Control

The computer has measuring devices attached that can determine the number of cars and their average speeds on roads in a city. It uses this information to figure out when to change traffic lights.

c. Design of Buildings

The user specifies the dimensions of various parts of a building; the computer computes how large the beams, columns, and so forth, must be and suggests standard parts that can be used.

P2.

a. The data structure is indicated above. The control structure is a set of rules that gives the requirements for staying in school, the degree requirements, and so forth, so that the computer can check the progress of each student.

b. The data structure would be some form of representation of the roads and intersections, together with their lengths, reasonable safe speeds, number of lanes, and so forth. (We will discuss the form of this type of data structure in Chapters 7 and 8.) The control structure will be a list of rules that gives ways to maximize the flow of cars along the roads, such as "Set light Y green 47 seconds after light X was set green if you do not want cars to stop."

c. The data structure is (for example) lists of available steel beams and lists of the plans of the building. The control structure is lists of building code rules and calculation methods for determining the minimum size of beam needed.

Page 16

P1. We must simply put the test for no more records at the start.

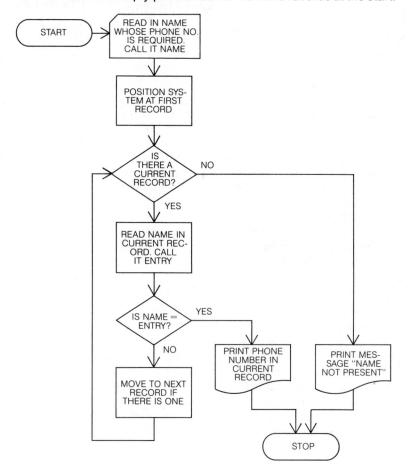

Page 22
P1.

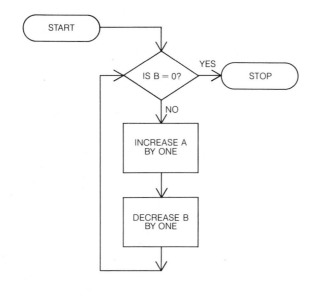

START

IS B = 0? — YES → STOP

NO

INCREASE A
BY ONE

DECREASE B
BY ONE

Page 23
P4.   If the boxes are numbered from left to right and top to bottom starting from 0, the following changes occur in the execution of each box:

Box No.	N	M	Result of Test	Output
1	17			
2		2		
3			No	
5			No	
8		3		
3			No	
5			No	
8		4		
3			No	
5			No	
8		5		
3			Yes	
4				Number is Prime

STOP

Page 42

E1a.   LOAD   C
           DIV   D
           MPY   E
           ADD   B
           STORE A

Note that the addition of B is done last because of the rules of arithmetic.

Page 42

E2a.   8 microseconds

Page 42

P3.   LOAD   A
       STORE T
       LOAD   B
       STORE A
       LOAD   C
       STORE B
       LOAD   T
       STORE C

Page 49

E1.   SKIPC
       READ T1
       READ T2
       PRINT T2
       PRINT T1
       SKIPL

Page 58

P1.   LOAD   C
       ADD   D
       SUB   A
       SUB   B
       BGE   T
       BRNCH X
    T . . . (next instruction)

Page 72

E1a.   15212521
E2a.   05245466

This would be stored as 05245465 if truncation were used.

E3a.   05225300
E4a.   14427300

Value is $-.273 \times 10^{-6}$

Page 73

Q1b.   09910000 and 09910000

(Product is $.1 \times 10^{97}$)

Page 56

E1.   200   00000
       210   00298
       210   01073
       000   00298
       010   01073
       020   01074
       230   01074
       220   00000

Page 57

E4.   LOAD   B
       SUB   A
       BGE   T
       LOAD   B
       ADD   C
       STORE A
    T LOAD   A
       SUB   B
       STORE D

Q1d.   09000000 and 09900000   (Integer sum is 18,900,000)

Page 73
P1.   No, the integer test for zero is adequate as normalized floating-point zero has the smallest possible exponent, namely, −50. The characteristic is −50 + 50 = 0, so it is stored as 00000000, which can be detected by the integer zero test.

Page 80
E1.   a is valid, b is invalid (it starts with a digit).
Q2.   Because it "puts together," i.e., assembles, the operation code and the operand address into a unit called an instruction, just as a manufacturer assembles pieces to get a finished product.

Page 90
E1a.	3FF	**E5a.**	40600000
E2a.	1010	**E5c.**	40555555
E3a.	0000007F		
	427F0000		

Page 91
P2.   1023

Page 105
E2b.	X ↑ (2 × Y)	**E4a.**	T1 ← B × C T2 ← D / E
E2c.	(A + B) × C		T2 ← D / E T1 ← B × C
E3a.	T1 ← R × S		A ← T1 + T2 A ← T1 + T2
	P ← Q + T1		

Page 113
E1a.	Floating Point	**E1f.**	Invalid
E1b.	Integer	**E1g.**	Character String

Page 113
E3a. $D = .33 \times 10^2$
E3b. $K = 0$
E3c. $E = .66670 \times 10^0$

(Note that I/J is −3.3333 because the operator / gives a five-digit floating-point result. On computers with greater precision, we would get a better approximation to 2/3 as the answer.)

Page 116
E1a.

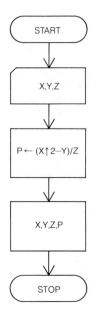

Page 126
E1a.

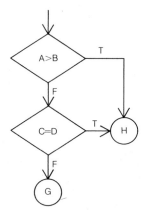

E1c.

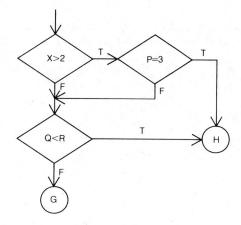

E2b. "NOT" C = 2 "OR" A = 3
(or C ≠ 2 "OR" A = 3)

Page 137
P1.

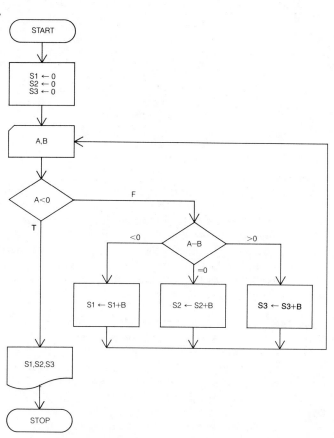

Page 146

Q2. Since A[3,3] is $1760 - 1756 = 4$ locations beyond A[2,3], the array must be stored by rows, so that the address of A[I,J] is $A + (I - 1) \times 4 + J - 1$. Therefore $A + (2 - 1) \times 4 + (3 - 1) = 1756$, so $A = 1750$. Hence A[4,4] is stored in $1750 + (4 - 1) \times 4 + (4 - 1) = 1765$.

P1. We assume that $N \geq 2$.

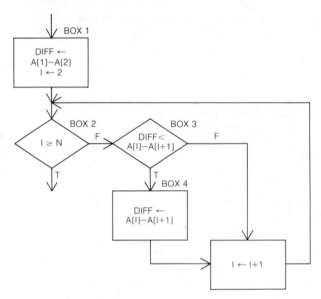

Page 169

Q2. If a user job could read directly from a card reader, that reader would have to be assigned to an individual user job for the whole time the job was in memory, even if it was not reading all the time. This would mean that the card reader would not be used efficiently. (Also, a card reader is slow, so the delays of the card reader would slow down the execution of the job, causing it to stay in memory longer, occupying valuable space.)

Page 186

Q1a. $L - J + 1$ (The loop is executed with $I = J, J + 1, \ldots, L$.)

Q1b. The loop is executed with $I = J, J + K, J + 2K, \ldots, J + N \times K$ where $J + N \times K \leq L$ and $J + (N + 1) \times K > L$. Hence, $N = (L - J) \div K$, so the loop is executed $(L - J) \div K + 1$ times, each time printing one number.

Q1c. If $K > 0$ and $L \geq J$, the answer is given in (b). If $K < 0$ and $L \leq J$, the answer is identical (as $(L - J) \div K$ is still a non-negative integer). If K > 0 and L < J or K < 0 and L > J, the loop is not executed, so no numbers are printed.

Page 187
P1.

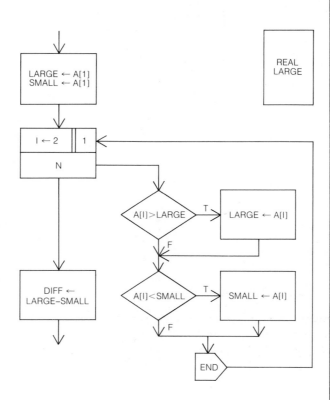

Appendix

Page 188
P3.

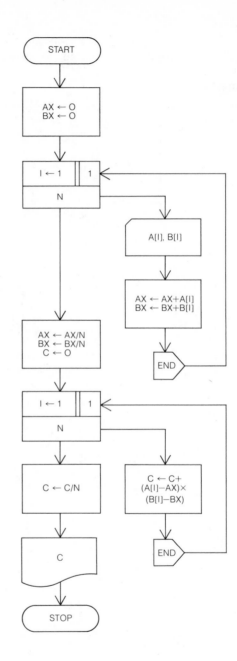

Page 192
P1.

Page 198
Q2a.   F(3) is 6 (= 1 + 2 + 3)

Page 199
P1.

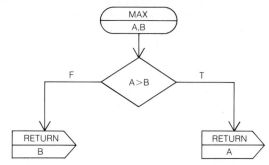

Page 199
P3.

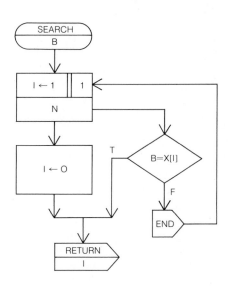

Page 210

Q1. The values put in a call box or used in a function when it is called. (They are also named *arguments*.) They provide the values substituted for the parameters (dummy arguments) used in the subroutine or function definition.

P1.

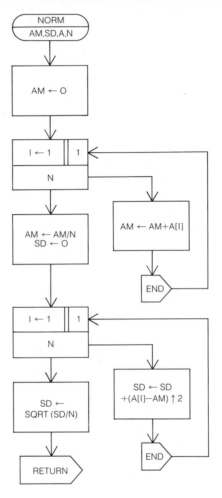

P4. One simple way is to put a special mark in one of the arrays, say N, in those elements N[I] that are not in use. In this case, N[I] is normally non-negative, so the unused entries in N[I] can be set to −1. Then, when a new customer's name is added, a search through N[I] for a negative entry can be made. The index of the first such entry can be used as the customer number for the new customer.

A better technique will be apparent when the section on lists in Chapter 7 is studied.

Page 220

P1.   Initially, J must be set to 1, and S and SS to zero. This is done with the second entry SGROUP.

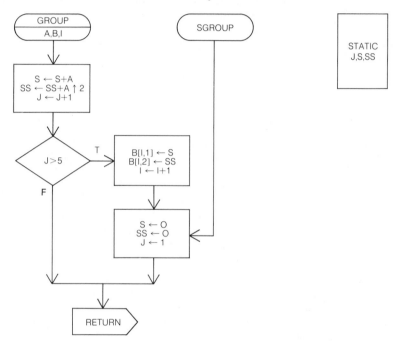

Page 221

Q1.   We do not need to know which variable names have been used for temporary variables inside a procedure.

Q3.   Separate storage space is not used for every procedure for its temporary variables.

Page 236

P1a.   On the first call with L = 1 and M = 10, J is set to 5 and X[5] is equal to CONS; hence one call is made.

Page 247

P1.   N is initialized to one and increased by one after each card with a non-negative number has been read. Hence N contains one more than required. The error can be corrected by initializing N to zero.

Page 255

Q1.   Rounding error is the error that occurs when a number is changed to another number that can be represented exactly in the computer.

Q3.   When two numbers that are nearly equal are subtracted, the number of significant digits in the answer is reduced, so the size of the rounding error is larger relative to the answer than it was relative to the original numbers.

Page 261

P1.   We will eliminate a from the first equation as follows: Divide the second equation by .826 to get

$$a + .499b = 1.03 \qquad (1)$$

Multiply this by .263 and add it to the first equation to get

$$(.527 + .263 \times .499)b = .392 + .263 \times 1.03$$
$$\text{or } .658b = .663$$

Hence

$$b = 1.01$$

From (1) $$a = 1.03 - .499 \times 1.01$$

$$\text{or } a = .526$$

Page 270

Q1.   In either of the forms shown in Figure 7.2. If an operation such as "search" is used, in which only a part of each string has to be used in many cases, the first form allows the most rapid processing.

Page 279

P1.   Subroutine APPEND adds an entry to the end of the list. Its parameters are D (the data) and X (an error return).

Subroutine REMOVE uses a parameter I, which is the index of the preceding item in the list, because the pointer in that item must be changed. If the item to be removed is first in the list, parameter I is zero.

Subroutine SEARCH has two parameters: D, the data to be located, and I, the result. I is set to the index of the item preceding the entry that matches D (if there is one), to zero if the matching item is first in the list, or to minus one if no match is found.

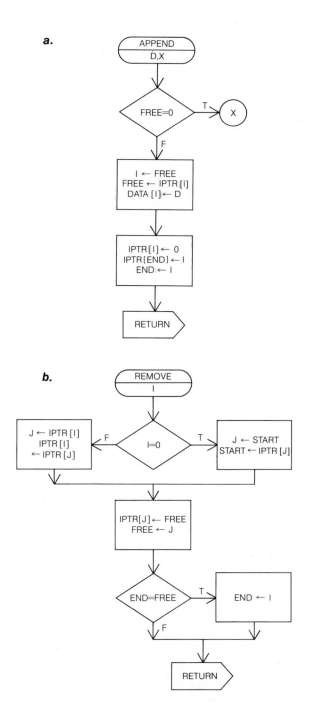

a.

APPEND
D,X

FREE=0 — T → X

F

I ← FREE
FREE ← IPTR [I]
DATA [I] ← D

IPTR[I] ← 0
IPTR[END] ← I
END ← I

RETURN

b.

REMOVE
I

J ← IPTR [I]
IPTR [I]
← IPTR [J]

F ← I=0 → T

J ← START
START ← IPTR [J]

IPTR[J] ← FREE
FREE ← J

END=FREE — T → END ← I

F

RETURN

c.

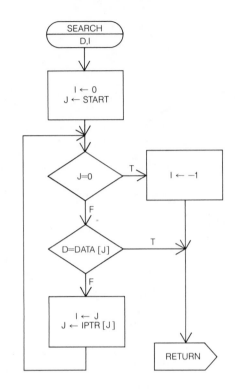

P1.   The parameter X is an error return used if the free storage
list is empty; the parameter Y is an error return used if A
is already in the tree.

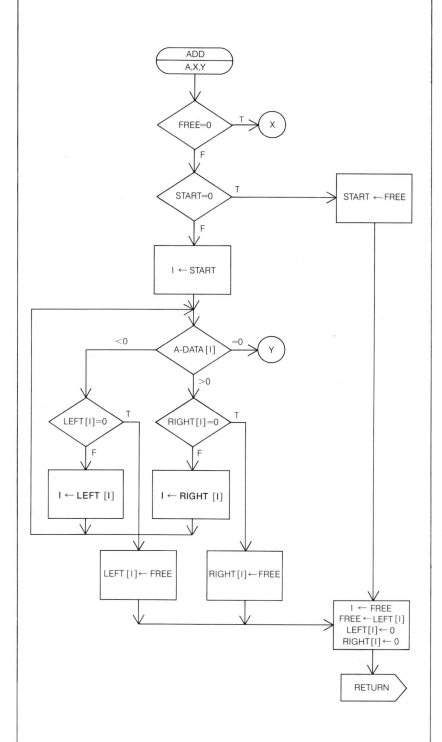

Page 298
P1.

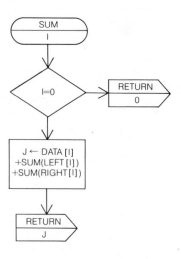

Page 309
P2. Apart from the fact that there are two branches connecting angles A and E, the graph in Figure 7.46d consists of five nodes, each node connected to every other node. It does not matter where we place the nodes, as we can distort the figure in any way we wish, so let us put them on a circle with each connected to its neighbor, as shown below.

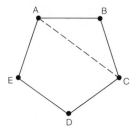

We now assume that the graph is planar and try to draw the other branches. At least one branch must go through the interior of this figure, say the branch AC. (If not, then branch AC is in the exterior, forcing the branch BD to be in the interior. We could rename the nodes so that this is branch AC.) If branch AD is in the exterior, it is impossible to connect E to B, as shown.

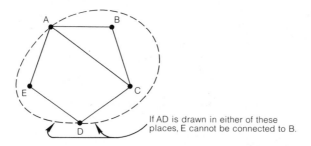

If AD is drawn in either of these places, E cannot be connected to B.

Hence branch AD is in the interior. This forces EC to be in the exterior, and in either position it prevents the branch DB from being drawn, as shown below.

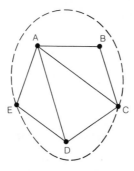

Page 311

P1.   Since the data is changed, all tables should be stored as lists, making deletion simple. To make a free storage list possible, equal-sized groups of words should be used in each list. In this case we will use three-word groups as indicated on the next page.

Town list element

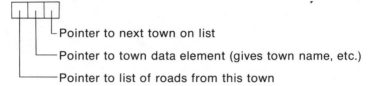

└ Pointer to next town on list

└── Pointer to town data element (gives town name, etc.)

└── Pointer to list of roads from this town

Road list element

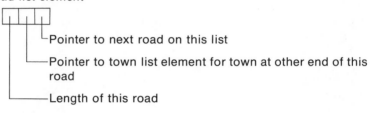

└ Pointer to next road on this list

└── Pointer to town list element for town at other end of this road

└── Length of this road

Town data element

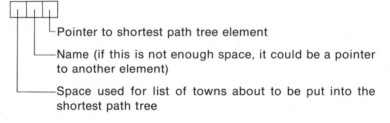

└ Pointer to shortest path tree element

└── Name (if this is not enough space, it could be a pointer to another element)

└── Space used for list of towns about to be put into the shortest path tree

Shortest path tree element

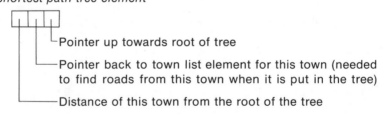

└ Pointer up towards root of tree

└── Pointer back to town list element for this town (needed to find roads from this town when it is put in the tree)

└── Distance of this town from the root of the tree

Index

335

The text of this book is nine-point Helvetica, a twentieth-century sans serif type face. Helvetica was designed to allow for greater white space around the letters than the earlier sans serif faces by use of simple straight and curved lines.

Heads are set in various sizes of Peignot, another modern face, designed by A. A. Cassandre. It is a sans serif face in which the lower-case letters, except the **b**, **d**, and **f**, are small capitals. Peignot was designed as an attempt to revive the original form of the Roman alphabet.

The text, set by the Linofilm process, and heads, set by PhotoTypositor, were composed by Applied Typographic Systems of Mountain View, California. Line drawings and technical illustrations were rendered by the House of Graphics of Palo Alto, California.

Project editor: Kay Nerode
Sponsoring editor: Stephen Mitchell
Book designer: Judith Olson
Cover design: Mike Rogondino